The Canadia

*Twelfth Revised Edition*

# THE CANADIAN
# WRITER'S MARKET

*Twelfth Revised Edition*

Jem Bates

with an Introduction
by Adrian Waller

M&S

CANADIAN CATALOGUING IN PUBLICATION DATA
The Canadian writer's market

ISBN 0-7710-8769-1 (12th rev. ed.)
ISSN 1193-3305

1. Authorship – Handbooks, manuals, etc.  2. Publishers and
publishing – Canada – Directories.  3. Canadian periodicals –
Directories.  4. Advertising agencies – Canada – Directories.
5. Journalism – Study and teaching – Canada – Directories.

PN4908.C3     070.5'2'02571     C92-032255-7


Printed and bound in Canada on acid-free paper
Typesetting by M&S, Toronto

McClelland & Stewart Inc.
*The Canadian Publishers*
481 University Avenue
Toronto, Ontario
M5G 2E9


1  2  3  4  5     00  99  98  97  96

# Contents

# INTRODUCTION

Back in the 1970s, when *The Canadian Writer's Market* was first published, the country sported a mere 100 consumer magazines, about 150 trade journals, two dozen or so farm publications that appeared somewhat sporadically, and 147 book publishers. As time went on, however, the industry was caught in an upswing and, five or six years later, there were 225 consumer magazines in Canada, most sold by subscription or delivered to selected households free of charge, and almost as many trade publications distributed in various corners of the workplace and business world. As well, there were 50-odd farm publications and 160 book publishers.

According to *Canadian Advertising Rates & Data* (*CARD*), published monthly by Maclean Hunter Ltd., as the 1990s dawned there were over 400 consumer magazines, and trade journals were keeping pace. By Statistics Canada figures, in 1990–91 (the most recent year for which reliable data are available) there were 1,500 periodicals in Canada. The number of national book publishers had almost doubled!

Publishing, however, has always been an extremely transient business. In today's Canada, magazines come and go faster than they ever did. Thus, keeping *The Canadian Writer's Market* up-to-date over the years has required much research and revision.

A number of publications are distributed free as corporate public relations vehicles. However, a large number of magazines are still sold by subscription, while many are kept in business almost entirely by either government grants or funds from specific organizations. Whatever their method of funding or distribution, most Canadian magazines that buy freelancers' work have been included in the twelfth edition of *The Canadian Writer's Market*, making it a useful tool for all who seek to sell their words.

As we all know only too well, the recession of the past few years has put great pressure on the publishing industry. Since the last edition of this book, a significant number of publications have folded because of this pressure, and a number of publishers have been forced to reduce their operations, or cut back on their lists. Many good writer's markets have disappeared as a result.

This edition again focuses on English-language publishers and publications. In earlier editions we carried many francophone magazines and trade publications. By 1991, however, we had become uncomfortably aware that to do full justice to Quebec's large and dynamic publishing industry we would need virtually to double the size of this book. Yet any halfway point seemed to us an unacceptable compromise. So, as with the last two editions, this is a guide to the English-language publishing world, though we have again retained many bilingual publishers. We would refer readers looking to work in Québécois to the *CARD* directory for French-language magazines, and to *Quill & Quire*'s biannual guide, *Canadian Publishers Directory*, for a full listing of French-language book publishers.

Again we have chosen in general not to list the specialist educational and professional publishing houses, which offer few opportunities for the unspecialized writer, while retaining those publishers that also have a trade operation, and not to carry the many very small publishers who produce on an ad hoc, occasional basis, perhaps no more than one or two volumes a year.

For some writers, particularly those just starting out who need to build a portfolio of published works to show editors on larger magazines later, money can be secondary. Publication in a respected literary journal with little or no remuneration can only benefit a serious writer in the long term, particularly one who seeks to turn one day to books.

Few could have imagined, when *The Canadian Writer's Market* first appeared, the technical aids from computerized libraries, word processors, and memory typewriters to telephone answering machines, facsimile machines, and electronic mail communications that would become available to writers. Now it is possible to transmit story ideas – even clearly typed manuscripts – through the telephone lines from one side of the world to the other. More and more editors, in fact, solicit faxed story proposals and manuscripts to save time. Increasingly, too, magazine publishers especially are linking up to the Internet. This edition introduces e-mail addresses where these are used as a communication medium.

Except where editors have asked us not to, we have also included regular telephone numbers with each listing. Writers are always advised, however, to try to sell their work by letter or fax. While it is often perfectly acceptable to phone a publication to ask for its contributor's guidelines (which usually say how much it pays for those articles needed for its various editorial departments), business with editors is nearly always more effectively accomplished with a carefully compiled story proposal. And this may be faxed, too.

We have again opted to arrange the magazines into logically appropriate groups. The three main classes remain Consumer Magazines; Literary & Scholarly; and Trade, Business, Farm, & Professional Publications. And to better facilitate a quick and easy reference for writers seeking a suitable market for a good idea, or for those wanting to recycle an article to other buyers, we have narrowed down these groups further, according to subject. Inevitably, however, these classifications are somewhat arbitrary at times and have a tendency to overlap. Even the distinction between consumer and trade publications is sometimes difficult to delineate. Some "trade" periodicals – the book industry's *Quill & Quire*, for instance – have such a general popularity that they are equated to consumer magazines. In this edition, we have introduced a section of prominent business journals in Chapter 1 in order to describe the market they offer in greater detail. Most comparable business publications retain a simplified listing in Chapter 3. Women's magazines have been reinstated as a sub-group in Chapter 1. These popular, high-circulation magazines are among the most successful areas in Canadian publishing and can offer freelancers some of the best markets.

Consumer magazines, therefore, appear in fourteen sub-groups: arts & cultural; business; city & entertainment; the environment; feminist; general interest; home & hobby; lifestyle; news, opinions, & issues; special interest; sports & outdoors; travel & tourism; women's; and youth & children's. Trade publications are divided into twenty sub-sections according to the professions or trades they serve. These groups range from advertising, business, and data processing to electronics, transportation, and travel.

To sharpen this reference book as a marketing tool, we provide thumbnail sketches for each consumer magazine to explain in the limited space available what kinds of articles it carries. This is useful because so many magazines have names that give little indication of what they really are, who reads them, and, consequently, the kinds of articles or stories they buy. No one would ever guess, for instance, that a monthly Vancouver magazine called *Kinesis* is a forum for feminists. Nor that, far from being a farm publication, as one might first suspect, *Grain* is a spunky little literary publication that has been produced quarterly in Regina since 1973.

We use the term publication often throughout this book because, strictly speaking, many of its listings are not really magazines as we have come to know them. Some may be tabloid newspapers, some simple, one-colour, staple-bound periodicals that feed the needs, sometimes sporadically, of a smallish group of loyal readers. Others, however, are magazines in the truest sense: glossy, highly professional consumer or trade journals that boast respectable circulations. The word publication, then, seems to safely cover all listings, both large and small.

Much more important to the writer is that all these publications provide opportunities both for established freelancers wanting to break fresh ground and for neophyte writers seeking to have their work published. Each magazine listed accepts outside contributions with varying frequency and for equally varying fees.

Some publications, particularly among the scholarly journals and the literary and arts magazines, do not pay their writers at all. Others pay fees that are among the highest in North America, and expect high standards of writing and reporting in return.

## Marketing

Too few novice writers understand that marketing is as vital an element of their craft as style and subject matter. Without a successful marketing strategy, their words and ideas may never see print.

The professional way to sell your writing is with a coherently written proposal. This eliminates the risks inherent in producing work on speculation. When an idea is accepted, the writer and the editor discuss fee, deadline – an *obsession* in the business, by the way – and the preferred writing style for the finished article.

Writers should always study the magazines for which they would like to write so they can immediately address the question, What does this particular editor want? Ultimately, though, they are aiming to satisfy not the editor but the editor's readers, and the only way to find out what *they* like is by reading the kind of material they have been purchasing in the past.

Another sure-fire way of becoming acquainted with a specific group of readers, and getting a feel for what they want, is to take careful note of the type and quality of the advertising within the magazine. In other words, you can only really know what to suggest to an editor after diligently studying his or her issues – and lots of them – as regularly as you can, in libraries, on the newsstands, or in doctors' offices.

Unquestionably, the hardest writing to sell is the novel. No matter how timely or ingenious a story may be, the effect a piece of fiction ultimately has on readers will depend almost entirely on how well it is constructed and written. Some of this, of course, also applies to non-fiction writing, particularly first-person experience pieces so much a part of the writer, and essays that must intelligently set out opinions and arguments. But, whereas the worthiness of most suggestions for magazine articles can be demonstrated aptly in a proposal, the power of a novel really cannot.

Some publishers are able to judge the merits of a piece of fiction from two or three sample chapters accompanied by a synopsis of the entire work. Ideally, this should explain the plot and show the very thing that holds fiction together – the theme. On the basis of this initial work, some publishers will give an experienced writer a contract and an advance against royalties to complete the book. Usually, though, they only commit themselves to novels submitted by an unknown author after seeing the completed text.

To help sell their work, fiction writers often seek out literary agents like those we have listed in Chapter 6. But don't expect agents to possess magic wands that they can wave to find a market for everything that crosses their desks. On the contrary, they must work extremely hard to sell whatever they can, and their best acquisitions, usually from experienced writers, are nearly always the first to find a buyer. So, to make their lives easier, reputable agents only ever handle a work they think will sell so well that it will be financially beneficial for both themselves and their clients.

In some large cities in the United States, agents also place magazine articles and essays, but only those written by frequently published authors who are exceptionally well known. In Canada, however, this is seldom the case. Virtually all articles are sold directly to magazines and publishing houses by authors themselves – with well-crafted proposals.

Not surprisingly, then, the query letter to an editor and the full, detailed proposal or outline that follows it may well be the most significant piece of work the beginning writer ever undertakes. It not only sells a suggestion, after all, but the writer with it. It should serve to demonstrate to an editor that, beyond any shadow of doubt, the person who conceived the idea and refined it really *is* the one best able to turn it into a strong, informative piece of writing for a lot of readers to enjoy.

## Copyright

Whatever you sell, and by whatever means you choose to do it, one of the most crucial legal elements of the writing craft is copyright. This is usually discussed the moment an editor responds favourably to a writer's suggestion.

Copyright is an *extremely* complex area of law, and writers are advised to read up on it all they can before negotiating the sales terms of their work, thus putting themselves in a stronger bargaining position. Put simply, copyright means the sole right to reproduce – or allow others to reproduce – a literary or artistic work. It begins upon creation rather than on publication, and exists until fifty years after the creator's death.

The *assignment* or *licensing* of copyright is what is negotiated in any deal between a publisher and a writer. Depending on the nature of the contract, the author can sell rights in many different ways.

Some publishers, often book publishers, will ask an author to assign copyright. This means that the publisher has control of all aspects of the copyright, including subsidiary rights such as translation rights, reprint rights, or even film rights, for the period of the agreement. The work is then published with copyright in the publisher's name. Such a contract will generally stipulate that once the publisher has allowed the book to go out of print, the rights revert to the author. The writer will likely find that it is preferable to *grant a licence* to a publisher, specifying the rights of the publisher with respect to territory and time. In this way, the publisher is given the right to use the work in different markets or at a later date, and will be able to negotiate separately for subsidiary rights.

Terms of a copyright agreement may vary greatly in nature or content – a contract, after all, can include whatever conditions one party feels pertinent – but not in principle. Canadian magazines with large circulations most often buy North American rights – the right to publish an article to be read by an audience scattered across the entire continent. Some large Canadian magazines are content simply to buy Canadian rights – the right to publish a work that will be read only within the country. Some acquire serial rights – the right to publish a work in a sister publication without having to pay extra for it.

Some smaller publications, however, simply buy one-time rights. Under this type of agreement, copyright ownership automatically reverts to the writer, either immediately upon publication or shortly afterwards, depending on the agreement. This leaves the writer legally free to sell the same article in the same words to what is called a secondary market. If that new market also buys only one-time rights, the same article may then be re-sold to a third magazine without the need for any alteration, then a fourth, and so on down the line.

Another variation of one-time rights, which is preferred by many of the larger magazines, is for *first-time* rights, giving the publisher the right to be the first to publish an article. In other words, they may indeed want one-time rights, but these must be first-time.

This usually leaves writers with two main options. They can either sell a story several times over to those magazines willing to buy one-time rights, not caring if these are first, second, or even third, or they can take what most experienced freelancers have come to regard as the more lucrative road. That is, they can write a piece for a top fee from a large magazine first, then try selling the same idea to smaller magazines later.

Be careful here, though. While ideas can't be copyrighted, the words used to express or explain them can, and are. This is why our copyright laws came into being: to prevent people from taking and using something – in this case, words, phrases, expressions, literary structures – that does not belong to them. So if you have sold North American, Canadian, or even world rights to a magazine, remember that before being offered elsewhere, your piece must be totally rewritten and restructured. As it passes from the original buyer to others wanting first-time rights, each text must avoid any of the original word combinations, structures, or echoes. If, on the other hand, you have sold one-time rights and the copyright has reverted to you, you may send off your article in its original, unaltered form as many times as you wish.

Some magazines – *Reader's Digest*, for example – buy what are known as reprint rights, yet another corner of the maze of copyright. Under this agreement, editors may pick up and re-publish articles that have appeared elsewhere so long as they pay the original publishers, and/or the writers, fees for their one-time use. This practice is always restricted to publishers and must *never* be confused with recycling. It is merely an arrangement made between two magazines, with the copyright laws in mind, which gives the writer a little extra money as a bonus for his or her initial efforts.

Here are some of the most frequently posed questions about copyright, with general answers:

*Is every piece of written work copyrighted?*

No. In Canada, copyright on a work lasts for the life of the author plus fifty years. After that, the work falls into the public domain and may be legally copied at will.

*How can I tell who the rightful owner of a copyright is?*

In the first few pages of a book or magazine there is a copyright notice. Typically, it will read: Copyright Josephine Blow, 1996; or Joseph P. Blow & Sons, Publishers, 1996. Beneath this will usually appear the publisher's address. Even if the copyright is held in the author's name, it is generally the publisher who has the right by contract to authorize reprints of excerpts. If, however, the author has retained these rights exclusively, which may sometimes be the case, he or she can be contacted through the publisher.

*How does copyright infringement occur?*

Usually through carelessness or ignorance. Few writers, after all, deliberately set out to steal something that doesn't belong to them. They either quote too much of someone else's work without first seeking permission to do so, or use previously written words without making a sufficiently concerted effort to rework them.

*What is too much of someone else's work?*

The answer to this isn't easy. It depends on several factors, principally the quantity and quality of the portion taken and whether its use will detract from the impact and/or the marketability of the original. No one loses sleep if a writer uses a line or two from a book and attributes its source; to reproduce three or four key paragraphs without permission, however – even *with* attribution – could lead to problems. The writer is always advised to contact the copyright holder, quoting the extract(s) he or she wants to use in full, giving a true indication of context, details of format (magazine article, script, or book), and size of audience, and ask for permission to reproduce it. A neophyte writer wanting to use 100 words for publication in a small magazine probably will not be charged what a name writer would be expected to pay for a similar-sized extract in an article for one of the big players. Many copyright holders, however, do not charge for so few words.

*How can I copyright my work?*

The moment you have written something it is automatically copyrighted. If, however, you feel there is a chance someone may one day say your manuscript is theirs, you may register it for a fee with the Federal Department of Communications' Copyright and Industrial Design Branch. If your work is registered in this way, should a dispute over copyright arise, you would be in a much stronger position if the case ever went to court. It would be up to the other party to prove that you are not the creator of your work. You can also mail a copy of your manuscript to yourself in a registered package. This would provide you with a dated receipt, which you would be able to produce when opening the package before a judge, should the manuscript's rightful ownership ever become a legal issue.

*If I work for a newspaper, who owns the copyright on my work?*

Usually, if you are employed by a company, it automatically owns the copyright of everything that is published by it in the course of your work. This cannot be reproduced or re-sold in any form without permission first being obtained. Often, newspapers generously allow articles, or portions of them, to be reprinted without charge.

*Can a magazine editor steal the idea contained in my story proposal and assign it to someone else to write?*

Yes, but the good ones won't. For this reason, it is not necessary to write copyright on your proposal. You would be wasting words anyway. Ideas like titles are in the public domain and cannot be protected by copyright laws unless they are part of an invention. And that is yet another branch of copyright law. If you intend to sell movie scripts in Hollywood (in which case you will definitely need an agent to negotiate rights on your behalf), have faith in the people you deal with. Good magazines and publishing houses stay in business because their editors are ethical.

*Should I copyright the book I have been contracted to write before sending it to the publisher?*

No. All publishers will copyright your work for you, under either their name or yours, depending on the terms of the contract you should already have signed. They will also register it for you, at the National Library in Ottawa, as an original Canadian work.

## Libel

Jonathan Swift, in *A Tale of a Tub*, complained loudly and logically that writers were no longer able to lash out at particular people for particular vices and had to content themselves with general satire on mankind. More than two hundred years later, we still must take heed. We must do our best not to make any direct, unfair, or inaccurate allusion to the living that might shed bad light upon their reputations.

Libel suits are notoriously complex – and the traps are wide. Many writers hold the mistaken belief that the use of fictitious names, or a statement saying that any resemblance between the characters in the book and living persons is purely coincidental, will automatically protect them from the possibility of a libel suit. This assumption is wrong. If the average reader associates a character described in a manuscript with an actual person, and the description reflects unfavourably on that person's reputation or integrity, there is always the danger of libel.

Fiction writers must always strive to ensure that the resemblance really *is* coincidence, and must certainly avoid the intention. Apparent *intention* to libel an actual person, even in fiction, could be interpreted by legal minds as a personal attack, and could possibly lead to an action.

All writers need to understand enough about Canadian libel laws to protect both themselves and their publishers against court action. This is absolutely necessary since nearly all publishers' contracts provide for indemnification by the author in cases where a person maligned in a manuscript resorts to a suit.

Libel in Canada is mostly covered by civil law and comes under provincial jurisdiction. Its principles are based on English common law for all provinces, except in Quebec, where the law stems directly from the French Civil Code. But the principles remain: libel is a printed statement or picture that exposes a person to hatred, ridicule, or contempt, and imputes to that person immorality, crime, or disorderly conduct, or tends to injure that person in the pursuit of a profession, office, or trade. In short, anything that might discredit a person may be construed as libellous. And under some circumstances, this can also apply to corporations or their individual members.

If such a statement or picture is printed, the publisher must be prepared to defend his publication on three fronts: truth of the statement; privilege; and fair comment on a matter of public interest. If the author's statements are accurate and true, there may be no basis for a civil action for libel, but any false or defamatory statement that tends to harm a person's reputation may constitute libel.

Privileged reports fall into two classifications: absolute privilege and qualified privilege. If published at the same time as they took place, a fair and accurate report without editorial comment on proceedings heard before a court of justice is absolutely privileged. Qualified or conditional privilege is enjoyed by reporters while covering proceedings in any government body, whether legislative or administrative, any commission of inquiry or organization whose members represent any public authority in Canada, or municipal council, school board, or board of health meetings.

The defence of qualified privilege extends to the findings or decisions of those Canadian organizations formed to promote the interests of any art, science, religion, or learning; any trade, business, industry, or profession; any game, sport, or pastime to which members of the public are invited as spectators or participants.

Fair and honest comment on matters of public interest, as long as it is true, is privileged. An author who comments on current affairs or writes a biography is permitted to express honest opinions or fair criticism of someone's works or accomplishments because this is usually in the public interest and serves to promote a useful purpose. Fair comment extends to criticism of books, magazines, articles, plays, and films.

Another defence often resorted to by newspapers and magazines is mitigation of damages based on a retraction of a statement that was made in error. While this action does not absolve the publication from libel, it nevertheless tends to show that any injury was purely accidental, and this may lessen the amount of the damages levied by the court.

## Simultaneous Submissions

There is absolutely nothing wrong with writers sending the same article, proposal, or book manuscript to more than one potential market at the same time. It is their work, after all, so they can do whatever they please with it. But unless they are sending off material simultaneously to those magazines that are happy to buy second, third, or fourth rights, they could run into problems.

The practice can sometimes be unethical. Busy magazines need about a month to assess an idea or a manuscript properly, sometimes more. During this time, several people may be assigned to the job of writing an informed critique explaining to both the writer and the senior editor how the manuscript or article is effective, how it isn't, and what revisions may be necessary.

In publishing houses, this work takes considerably longer and is correspondingly more expensive. Judging a promising book proposal or an intriguing manuscript of several thousand words usually means that an editor must set aside present work. If the editor is rushing to complete a book for the upcoming spring list, an outside reader might have to be hired to do this job instead. Readers are also hired for their specialized expertise, to judge whether a writer has covered a topic, fact or fiction, properly and accurately. If an idea or manuscript appears tempting, the publisher may recruit market researchers to assess its sales potential. By sending the same material to several houses, the writer may automatically involve them all in the expense of assessing something only one of them would eventually be able to acquire.

Indeed, to established writers, the idea of simultaneous submissions is distasteful. Knowing how busy editors can be, they give them reasonable time to respond – about six weeks on a magazine and as long as three months in a publishing house. If after that they have heard nothing, they fire off a reminder, then turn immediately to other productive work. The publishing business is notorious for its slowness and, unfortunately, this is something all writers have to learn to accept.

## Photocopies

Simultaneous submissions often means sending out photocopies of manuscripts, rather than the original. Editors on good magazines will sometimes refuse to read photocopies – they immediately suspect that they have been sent a copy because other copies are in the process of being offered elsewhere. And why should editors bother investing time in something they are not quite sure they will even have the chance to buy?

But there is also a strong argument for keeping originals safe to preclude their getting lost in the mail. It is usually wise to explain to an editor that you are sending a photocopy for precisely this purpose, and that the original *is* available if required. If you are using a computer, however, none of this needs to be considered, since you will always have a back-up on your disk. You can simply print out and send off "originals" as the need arises.

## Word Processing

Thanks to modern technology, more and more writers are crafting their poems, articles, and books on personal computers using a word processing program. Most publishers prefer authors to use computers, not because it saves them money, but because typesetting from disk speeds up the production process and helps prevent errors from creeping into the manuscript at a later stage.

The personal computer enables the writer to compose words and keep them in files – one file per story or article, perhaps, or one per chapter – then recall them. As long as a file has been properly stored, it can be retrieved at any time. Word processing enables writers to edit, cut, and paste limitlessly, without resorting to such traditional and perfectly respectable writers' tools as scissors, stapler, or glue. Thus they are spared the drudgery of seemingly endless retyping while striving to make their prose sparkle or their narrative flow in a smoother, clearer line. At the end of the day, with the final text saved on a disk, a clean copy can be printed out in a matter of minutes.

Many word processing programs contain a spell-check and a thesaurus. The spell-check, of course, helps eliminate poor spelling and typographical errors, and the thesaurus gives the writer instant access to a wide choice of synonyms and antonyms. With just another keystroke, any word can be selected from the thesaurus to replace one that is no longer wanted in the text.

In recent years, as personal computers have flooded the market, the consumer has become increasingly confused about what product to buy. Strange as it may seem, the least important part of word processing is the computer itself. This – the hardware – is really nothing more than an electronic box with switches, coils, and microchips. It is only as good as whatever program – the software – is inserted into a drive to make it perform in a specific way. Thus, software capabilities must always be foremost in the writer's mind, and he or she is far better off seeking out the most suitable word processing program first, then buying the right computer to accommodate it.

Your choice of program will ultimately determine the type of hardware you buy to run it. Powerful software packages need equally powerful computers to absorb them, make them run, and still have enough working memory, or RAM.

For books, by the way, a powerful computer and decent software is essential. When buying a computer you should choose one with a built-in hard-disk drive. This allows you plenty of storage memory in which to keep your programs and files, and means an end to relying on floppy disks for all your operations. Some writers do manage to write books on small home computers, but all too often their software restricts them, and the computer's capacity is such that they can only get one or two chapters on a single disk. If you find yourself with half of a chapter on one disk, and the other half on another, you can bank on awkward technical problems when the time comes for you to print out your work.

Power, memory, and software capability are one thing. Another aspect of word processing worthy of almost equal consideration is your working speed, which lies largely in using a good keyboard, one with which you feel comfortable.

It is also important to remember that just how quickly a manuscript can be produced does not necessarily depend on how good or expensive your printer is, but how suitable. Your printer should provide a clear, draft-quality text in an easy-to-read typeface. Script typefaces resembling italics or Old English should be avoided because they are harder to read. This rule applies to both a computer and a typewriter, electric or otherwise.

Another component of the home computer, and one more integral to comfort than any other, is the piece of equipment you must stare at for hours on end – the screen. Many efficient home computers are sold with colour screens. These are fine for games and, for some graphics, imperative. But for simple word processing, they are not only superfluous, but expensive. Conversely, other computers come with much cheaper screens that show bulky, disjointed lettering that is difficult and uninviting to read.

Ideally, the writer should aim somewhere between these two extremes. Best is what is called a high-resolution screen. This not only costs significantly less than a colour screen, but helps to reduce eyestrain. Suffice it to say that endlessly watching your work spring to life on a screen you are not comfortable with will make word processing a chore, and certainly not a pleasure.

Before buying a word processor, shop around, and talk to other writers to ascertain what computers and software packages *they* bought, and why. Judge your needs by theirs. And make certain that your sales clerk understands the amount of revising and polishing you will be doing, so that you obtain the type of software best suited to the writer's needs.

## Manuscripts

It goes without saying that manuscripts that have been poorly typed and are littered with spelling errors look amateurish. Editors don't necessarily expect word processed texts, but they should be well-prepared and double-spaced on white bond letter-size paper, with a covering page bearing a title. If your article is accepted, it is doubtful that the title you gave it will survive. It is likely to undergo several changes as editors put their heads together to dream up something that suits it better, according to the style of their magazine. When first submitting a piece, then, its title is of little consequence. Your job is to merely call your work *something* so it can be recorded as such when the editorial department receives it.

Much more of a priority is the other information you must put on the title page – your name, complete address, and telephone number.

Of course, editors are most interested in such ingredients as uniqueness or importance of subject, and whether it has been properly covered and deftly illustrated with anecdotes. They look, too, for good writing – this does not translate to clever or fancy as much as it does to clear and coherent. Editors do find, however, that a neat manuscript is infinitely more inviting to read than an untidy one.

When submitting a book manuscript, each new chapter should be denoted as such by starting partway down the page. All pages must be numbered, double-spaced, and have margins about an inch wide. The text will require a title page, too, and others devoted to a full, accurate listing of any permissions the author needed to acquire to be legally entitled to quote from copyrighted works. Do not bind or staple your manuscript.

While editors used to like to see an entire manuscript, this is usually no longer the case. Many publishing houses will not accept unsolicited manuscripts, and if you do manage to convince a busy editor to take a look at your work, two sample chapters plus a synopsis will be sufficient. You can always courier the balance of the manuscript if required.

When using a computer it is always wise to co-ordinate your efforts with those of the publisher so that your disks will not be useless. Many instructions are specific to the type of software used, but some are general: 1) each article or chapter should have its own file; 2) never fill your disks – always leave room, at least 40K "working space" on each, for the typesetter's format instructions; 3) always make back-up disks; 4) never centre or justify the text, which makes it difficult for the publisher to obtain an accurate word count and creates problems for the typesetter during formatting; 5) set your margins so that there are no more than sixty characters per line; 6) never hyphenate a word at the end of a line unless that word has a hyphen already; 7) make very clear your codes for accents, currency symbols, fractions, and footnote or endnote numbers, and don't overuse bold and italic typefaces.

## Style

By style, most book and magazine editors mean the conventions of spelling, punctuation, and capitalization. There is, of course, no universally accepted manual for style because it varies from periodical to periodical, publishing house to publishing house, not to mention from fiction to non-fiction, from genre to genre, and from discipline to discipline. Writers should remember, however, that style is an integral part of their craft and, by showing a blatant disregard for it, they can quite inadvertently prejudice an editor against their work.

Writers are expected to observe at least *some* of the basic house rules, and these should be obvious in what has already been published by those magazines and book publishing houses for which they aspire to write. If they are not, the writer is always wise to find out as much as possible about what these rules are, and what stylistic traits – as idiosyncratic as many may appear to be – are preferred.

Canadian newspapers generally follow *The Canadian Press Stylebook* (which also contains some good tips on reporting, by the way), and magazines tend to develop their own standards and preferences from one authoritative source, or a compilation of several.

Book publishers, however, usually adhere to well-known manuals. A selection of the best style and resource books is provided at the end of this book.

Very often, a publishing house has compiled its *own* guide to house style, and the aspiring writer should never be afraid to ask for a copy of this.

## The Word Count

The number of words a manuscript contains is another consideration for editors. A large part of their job is to ensure that stories will fit into an allotted space. When they order 2,000 words, the manuscript should not be appreciably longer, and preferably 100 words or so less.

For books, the word count is more crucial, because cutting, even merely trimming to a publishable size, is a lot more work than many writers realize. Doing it properly almost always means having to judiciously remove material – a sentence here or a couple of paragraphs there – throughout an entire text and not just from one part of it. The time involved explains why authors lament that they have had potentially good works either rejected out of hand, or returned swiftly to them for drastic shortening.

Always remember that the real skill in writing is being able to tell a story, fact or fiction, in the shortest number of necessary words. To achieve this, good writers develop keen powers of self-criticism. They are constantly scrutinizing their work for wordiness, clutter, unnecessarily long quotes, or characters that do nothing to enhance the subject of their story, or move the action along. The moment they come upon any of them, they ruthlessly pare away the superfluous material so as to make their text tighter.

They also check regularly to see how many words they are writing. A simple way to count them is to set the left-hand margin of the typewriter or word processor at twenty and the right at seventy-five so that each line of type will then contain an average of ten words. Twenty-five double-spaced lines on a standard-size page, therefore, will equal roughly 250 words.

## Postage

These days all publishers are under pressure to reduce costs wherever possible. Postage rates have soared in recent years and so, for any business that relies heavily on our mail system, they represent a bigger expense than ever. It should now be taken for granted that if you want your manuscript returned you must include a self-addressed, stamped envelope, so that it can be returned without cost. Increasingly, publishers will assume that you do not want your material back if an SASE is not included, and will simply throw it away. During the research for this edition, magazine and book editors stressed this point again and again, and writers ignore it at their peril. If submitting to U.S. publishers, enclose international postage coupons or keep a supply of American stamps. You can stock up on a visit, arrange for a friend visiting the States to bring some back for you, or buy them through a Canadian dealer (*Canadian Author* magazine often carries advertisements for these).

## Income Tax

In Canada, the Income Tax Act is good to writers, allowing them to deduct legitimate work expenses from their taxable incomes. In return, writers are trusted to show all their earnings, particularly fees that are unsupported by T4, T4A, or T5 slips from magazines and publishing houses that have printed their work.

Basically, writers come under three classifications:

- Salaried employees who supplement incomes by earning a little extra money as occasional freelance writers.
- Part-time writers whose major income comes from another job that will almost certainly be cast aside the moment writing becomes more profitable.
- Totally self-employed, full-time writers not on any payroll, who are expected to file honest returns mindful that no income taxes have been deducted at source.

Writers with other jobs need only attach to their income tax returns a statement summarizing writing income and expenses, and to show whether this extra work resulted in a profit or a loss. Any profit must be added to that taxable income earned from the other job. Losses, however, may be used to reduce it.

Writers living entirely from their craft must keep many more details – a list of all income and its sources, and receipts and vouchers to support expenses. Maintaining proper financial records not only serves as a reminder of cash that has flowed both in and out, but also helps to reduce problems that might be encountered should a tax return be audited.

All writers may reasonably deduct the cost of all stationery, including letterhead, envelopes, typewriter ribbons, computer paper and ink cartridges, pencils, pens, and paper clips. Telephone costs, particularly long-distance calls, are also deductible, as are postage, membership dues in writers' organizations, union dues, accountants' fees, secretarial help, research assistance, subscriptions to newspapers and magazines, reference books, copyright costs, and photocopying charges.

Many writers find that their biggest annual deduction is for their work space. Those who work in an outside office may claim its rent as an expense. If, however, they work at home, they may write off a reasonable portion of their living space. A writer using one room as an office in a six-room apartment, for example, may claim one-sixth of the rent plus one-sixth of such other expenses as municipal taxes, heating, lighting, minor repairs, and ordinary maintenance. However, work space related costs can only be deducted from your *net income from writing* after you have deducted all your other costs.

An area of tax deduction often overlooked is the depreciation of office furniture and equipment. Both may be written off according to a fixed percentage determined by the income tax regulations. A typewriter or word processor can be depreciated by 20 per cent of the total cost each year for five years. The same tax saving may be applied to printers, cameras, tape recorders, filing cabinets, desks, chairs, and telephone answering machines.

Travel is also an allowable expense, whether it is to visit a publisher or gather research for an article. Here the non-fiction writer is at a distinct advantage, because in most cases, interviewing people in a different town is absolutely necessary. This could conceivably mean a bus trip from downtown Vancouver to nearby Burnaby, on the one hand, or a flight from Halifax to Istanbul, on the other.

The simple rule is that to be tax deductible, travel *must* relate to work. For the novelist who cannot secure an advance commitment from a publisher, a legitimate business trip may be extremely hard to prove. All is not lost, however. If a visit to Turkey is necessary to gather material that cannot be found elsewhere, it can either be claimed as an expense when the work is published, or written off against royalties.

Car travel, hotels, meals, and entertainment – the drinks you may want to buy a useful contact, the dinner you host for a person who is figuring prominently in your story, or the editor on your latest book – are also legitimate writers' expenses. Remember, though, that you cannot claim on your income tax form any expenses that a magazine or publishing house may already have refunded to you. Apart from being illegal, it is dishonest.

## American Markets

The English-speaking Canadian who has begun to sell with some consistency enjoys a unique geographical advantage over colleague writers overseas. Canada has a southerly neighbour with a population of some 260 million people, most of whom speak English and are thus potential readers of English writing.

The most recent edition of *Writer's Market* (see Chapter 10, Book Resources) lists more than 4,000 paying markets in the United States for novels, short stories, fillers, plays, gags, verses, even photographs the freelancer may take during travels. This book also gives the names and addresses of editors, and sets out their requirements – what they expect from a manuscript in content and length, and how long it takes them to report back to a writer with a decision on whether or not to publish.

Two U.S. monthly magazines are also indispensable to Canadian writers seeking new markets south of the border – *Writer's Digest* itself, the publisher of the annual *Writer's Market*, produced in Cincinnati for practical-minded freelancers, and *The Writer*, published in Boston for those with more literary tastes. These journals not only keep readers informed about markets and trends, but provide both a stimulus and a constant flow of fresh ideas. Writer's Digest Books, by the way, publishes an astonishing range of practical books for writers – from guides to writing genre fiction to manuals on magazine article writing.

The much-repeated rule about studying markets, as you must when writing for Canadian magazines, applies more than ever in the United States, because the array of American publications is awesome, and those that may at first appear similar most certainly are not on closer examination. Nearly all magazines have their own special character and narrow, specific needs to go with it.

The enormous selection of American magazines, however, in no way diffuses the difficulty in breaking into the huge market they have come to constitute, particularly with a Canadian story. The first point to ask yourself here is, "Why would an American magazine be interested in Canada?" A quick answer to the question is that most really aren't unless they can be *made* to be interested in Canada, or unless the story has a broad appeal to both nations.

Some Canadian stories, of course, will have an obvious and natural tie-in with American events. A perceptive article on NAFTA from a Canadian perspective might attract the interest of a U.S. business magazine. As a Canadian writer you will have to work hard to penetrate the American market, especially with ideas for the consumer magazines.

Most Canadians who have consistently sold their writing in the United States can thank those opportunities provided by the vast collection of American trade publications. If Canada is related to the United States at all, it is through sharing common trade channels, and having similar concerns about world politics and business. The moment American equipment and/or expertise is brought to bear on a Canadian building site, for example, there could legitimately be the makings of a story for an American trade or professional magazine. Sometimes, there may also be a story in how Canada sees, or deals with, problems specific to both countries.

But there is yet another hurdle to cross. Many American trade magazines are staff-written. This means that a staff writer will travel to Canada to cover an American story rooted here, so a manuscript from a Canadian freelancer must be exceptionally strong to win a place.

The odds can be beaten, though. After accepting a few manuscripts from a Canadian contributor, the editor of an American trade magazine might be willing to publish a monthly feature written by a Canadian on the Canadian viewpoint: what his or her country thinks about mutual problems and issues, and what solutions it can offer.

It is well worth trying to secure a foothold in the American market, for purely economic reasons. It is still difficult, after all, for Canadians to make a satisfactory living by writing exclusively for magazines and publishing houses in their own country, which helps explain why most combine crafting poetry, novels, magazine articles, and non-fiction with other work. The situation may change though. Writing opportunities for Canada's writers have certainly increased since this book first appeared; with more settled economic times they are almost certain to continue to do so. And when they do, *The Canadian Writer's Market* will be there with a richer list than ever.

*Adrian Waller*

# 1

# CONSUMER MAGAZINES

"Magazines constitute the only national press we possess in Canada. . . . Magazines, in a different way from any other medium, can help foster in Canadians a sense of themselves."
– *Report of the Special Senate Committee on Mass Media*, 1970

At the time of this report, 70 per cent of all magazines sold in Canada originated in the United States. Since then, protective federal legislation has helped to foster the growth of a vigorous local industry: twenty years on, Canadian magazines had captured 40 per cent of the local market, and had done so despite the fact that a mere 6 per cent of Canadian magazines ever reached our American-dominated newsstands. Today, almost half Canadian magazines reach readers through the mail as paid subscriptions, with a further 35 per cent delivered as free, controlled-circulation copies, yet in recent years this remarkable success story has faced threats from all sides. The first was to the postal subsidy.

Canada's enlightened federal postal subsidy program was established more than a century ago to help compensate for the isolation of many Canadian communities. The guiding principle was that all Canadians, wherever they lived, should have equal access to their nation's magazines. Over the years, the preferential postal rates for subscriber magazines have played a vital role in fostering the growth of the local industry by subsidizing distribution costs for magazines heavily reliant on subscription sales. The Canadian Magazine Publishers Association and other industry advocates had long warned that removing or reducing the subsidy would threaten many fragile publishing operations. Nevertheless, in December 1989, a cash-strapped federal government announced the incremental phasing out of the program. By 1995 it had been cut by two-thirds, and soon it will likely be removed altogether.

Magazines struggling with extra postal costs have also faced strong consumer resistance to price hikes in the wake of the 7 per cent increase imposed by GST. Coinciding with the recession, the introduction of the GST in January 1990 was a body blow to the industry. According to a report by the CMPA, the first year of GST brought a devastating 62.5 per cent decrease in magazine profits. On top of the direct impact on subscription and advertising sales, Canadian magazines stood at an extra 7 per cent competitive disadvantage in relation to their U.S. competitors, as more than 50 million copies of U.S. magazines enter Canada each year without being taxed.

The stealthy introduction of split runs from across the border presented another threat to the industry. Split runs are special editions of magazines imported into Canada with U.S. editorial content but discounted Canadian advertising. They siphon off advertising that would otherwise go to Canadian magazines, eroding their market share. Consumer magazines simply cannot survive without a reliable level of advertising, their main source of revenue. This threat, at least, appears finally to have been heeded by the federal government, who in June 1995 tabled long-delayed legislation empowering them to collect an 80 per cent excise tax on advertising revenue of split-run editions.

As a result of these combined assaults, Canadian magazines have suffered heavy losses in revenue during the 1990s. The number of full- and part-time magazine employees decreased by more than 30 per cent between 1990 and 1993, while the number of unpaid voluntary staff increased by some 60 per cent. To underscore just how fragile the magazine publishing industry is, 47 per cent of the periodicals surveyed by Statistics Canada in 1984 ran at a loss, while only 41 per cent reported after-tax profits. In 1990–91, according to StatsCan, average pre-tax profit was 2 per cent, but a breakdown of this figure reveals how unequally this "profit" was spread: while the market leaders averaged a 4 per cent profit, a larger number of magazines – those with modest annual revenues below $100,000 – were averaging pre-tax losses of 22 per cent. The big players will sometimes use the profits from their successful, high-circulation publications to support a smaller one not making a profit – an option not available to solo magazines. As the recession eases, however, magazines are showing an extraordinary resilience. In 1993, according to figures from the industry magazine *Masthead*, 120 new magazines were launched while 89 ceased operations; the following year saw a similar number of launches (115), while only 40 were forced to close down.

It is perhaps a cause for wonder that the industry survives at all, let alone as the dynamic profusion of voices that it is. It is also a tribute to those who make it happen – to loyal Canadian readers, who continue to support their national press through their subscriptions; to the freelance writers who are its creative backbone; and to the publishers, editors, designers, and production staff who dream up and sustain the magazines. So when you're feeling especially frustrated about how poorly paid you were for that last article, spare a thought for your "tight-fisted" employer. During the research for this book, it was striking how many publishing ventures (smaller arts magazines stood out especially) are kept alive – indeed, in creative terms, are flourishing – through the enthusiasm, hard work, and sheer willpower of a few committed, stubborn, underpaid (often unpaid) individuals.

Most consumer magazines continue to rely heavily on freelancers in these difficult economic times, and the range of opportunity for the skilled and imaginative writer remains broad. Large-circulation consumer magazines that are heavily supported by advertising can usually afford to pay most for a writer's work – fifty cents to a dollar a word at the top of the scale. Standouts here are high-calibre general interest magazines like *Equinox*, *Canadian Geographic*, and *Saturday Night*, glossy inflight magazines like *Canadian* and *enRoute*, top women's magazines like *Chatelaine*, and leading business journals like *Profit* and the *Globe*'s *Report on Business*.

Many other magazines pay fees that can amount to between $1,000 and $1,500 for a professionally written feature article. Magazines with smaller circulations, which include the majority of those listed in the following pages, for obvious reasons tend to pay less –

anything from $100 to $800 for an article of up to 3,000 words – though there is often some room for negotiation over the fee, depending on the writer's experience and the amount of research needed.

A last class comprises those magazines and journals that either generate much of their own editorial copy, or rely almost entirely on the voluntary contributions of professional colleagues or qualified readers. They may pay only occasionally for freelance contributions, sometimes in the form of free magazines. The committed freelance writer should consider contributing to these too, recognizing the long-term benefits in terms of experience and professional development. It is a reflection of the times that more entries than ever before fall into this class in the present edition of *CWM*. More positively, however, it also reflects the large number of exciting and stimulating small magazines that are determinedly holding their own despite hostile market conditions. They should be supported.

Today, more than ever, writing for publication is an intensely competitive business, and to succeed requires the right approach, good research, and plenty of hard work. The first, golden rule is to familiarize yourself thoroughly with the magazine's agenda and style before you approach the editor with a proposal. Find out whether they have an editorial calendar or run special or theme issues (the *CARD* directory sometimes lists these – see Chapter 10, Book Resources). You will often have time to prepare your submission ahead of schedule. Seasonal stories may need to be submitted up to six months in advance.

Copyright is a complex, thorny issue (for more discussion on this subject, see Adrian Waller's introduction). In general, however, it is in the writer's interest to limit the transfer of rights. Be wary of selling all rights to your work, since you may be giving up several opportunities for milking further payment from your efforts. Most magazines seek first Canadian serial rights – that is, first-time publication in a Canadian periodical. Once your piece has appeared in print you are free to recycle it elsewhere if you can. With bilingual publications, restrict your agreement to English-language rights so that you are paid again if your piece is translated for the French edition. Maclean Hunter, for instance, will pay you up to 40 per cent of your original fee for articles translated for their French-language sister publications. Before signing a contract, check out PWAC's Standard Agreement (see below). You'll also want to know what "kill fee" is offered – that is, what percentage of the agreed fee you will be paid if the magazine for some reason doesn't publish your assigned piece. Again, PWAC can offer advice in this area.

The successful freelancer keeps abreast of the changes and developments in the industry. One excellent conduit for this information is the Periodical Writers Association of Canada. PWAC membership entitles you to a subscription to their informative bimonthly newsletter, *PWAContact*; a comprehensive listing in their annual directory, sent to editors and publishers nationwide; a free subscription to *Sources*, a biannual directory of contacts for journalists and other writers; and, not least, the opportunity to exchange market information and make important contacts with other writers. The monthly *Canadian Author* magazine carries a useful section on new magazine markets for writers, and you'll also learn about new magazine launches in the pages of *Masthead*.

The most financially secure freelancers are those who are most versatile. They may feed feature articles steadily to a handful of consumer magazines, develop a working relationship with the editors of a couple of specialist trade publications, and write a regular column for a weekly newspaper. Or perhaps they have approached the director of communications of a government department or corporation and now have irregular (but often startlingly lucrative) commissions to write reports, newsletters, or information packages. As professionals, they are ready to practise their craft in unexpected – even initially unappealing – contexts as well as in their chosen areas of interest.

Target your articles, but remember that other publications might also be interested in the fruits of your research. Always look for research follow-on ideas. Research for a feature on city gardens for a general interest consumer magazine might also turn up useful background material for an article on the gardening centre phenomenon for a business journal or a more technical piece for a trade publication.

Note the magazines that interest you in the following pages and send for sample copies, or search them out in a good bookstore or your public library. Generally, it is not a good idea to send unsolicited work without an initial written inquiry. Always request contributor's guidelines where these are available (enclosing an SASE with your request). They may be a few short, practical remarks or several pages of background and detailed instructions, but close attention to these guidelines will often make the difference between your submission being taken seriously or not. Be sure to check what form your submission should take. Many magazine editors now prefer to receive them on disk. Ensure that you provide it in the appropriate program, or in a readily convertible, text-only form. Provide hard copy back-up, too, in case the disk presents problems or the editor chooses to do an initial edit on paper.

Nothing will endear you less to a hard-pressed editor than to present him or her with an unintelligible disk or a poorly presented article. A submission full of spelling and punctuation errors, and a manifest ignorance of basic grammar, will not impress. On the other hand, clean copy, delivered on time, may win you an important friend. Your first submission to a periodical should always include a story outline along with a brief summary of your professional experience and cuttings of previously published stories (tearsheets). Mention any experience that qualifies you to write on the topic. For most editors, evidence of previous experience is initially the single most attractive feature in a submission. Always be businesslike in your dealings with editors – respond immediately to letters or phone calls, and be friendly and co-operative. And always include an SASE with *every* inquiry or submission that requires a response.

## Arts & Cultural

**Aboriginal Voices**
116 Spadina Avenue, Suite 201, Toronto, Ont. M5V 2K6
Phone: (416) 703-4577  Fax: (416) 703-4579
E-mail: eric_gabriel@tvo.org
Contact: Millie Knapp, editor
Circulation: 8,000
Published quarterly
   A new magazine whose purpose is to reclaim aboriginal writings, images, sounds, dance, and arts, and to inspire the reclamation of First Nations culture. Received the Native American Journalists

Association's 1995 award for excellence. Articles 1,500 to 2,000 words. Cannot pay but welcomes submission inquiries.

## Applied Arts Magazine

885 Don Mills Road, Suite 324, Don Mills, Ont. M3C 1V9
Phone: (416) 510-0909  Fax: (416) 510-0913
E-mail: elink@interlog.com
Contact: Joanna Pachner, editor
Circulation: 15,000
Published 5 times a year

Targeting the communication arts market, *AAQ* spotlights the work of graphic design, advertising, photography, and illustration professionals, featuring outstanding examples of their work. Carries profiles and interviews. Pays 60¢/word on acceptance for articles of 1,000 to 2,500 words. Fees vary and in some cases are negotiated.

## Artfocus Magazine

P.O. Box 1063, Station F, Toronto, Ont. M4Y 2J7
Phone: (416) 925-5564  Fax: (416) 925-5564
Contact: Pat Fleisher, publisher/editor
Circulation: 6,000
Published quarterly

Features art gallery and museum reviews and previews, profiles of contemporary artists, dealers, and collectors, and articles on media and technique by prominent artists. Also comments on controversial issues in the arts. Carries short articles of 500 to 600 words, features of 1,500 to 2,000 words. Fees range from $50 to $150, paid after publication. Query first with samples of written work.

## Art Impressions Magazine

344 Edgeley Boulevard, Unit 16-17, Concord, Ont. L4K 4B7
Phone: (905) 738-2310  Fax: (905) 738-4994
Contact: Michael J. Knell, editor
Circulation: 18,500
Published bimonthly

For collectors of Canadian art, especially realistic, impressionist, and wildlife. Carries articles on Canadian art, art history, artists, and art-related issues. Preferred length 2,500 to 3,500 words. Pays on publication at negotiated rates. Written proposals welcome.

## ArtsAtlantic

145 Richmond Street, Charlottetown, P.E.I. C1A 1J1
Phone: (902) 628-6138  Fax: (902) 566-4648
Contact: Joseph Sherman, editor
Circulation: 2,700
Published 3 times a year

Award-winning arts review carrying features, reviews, and reports on Atlantic Canada's fine arts, cinema, video, artisanship, performance, literature, and topics with national resonance. Reviews are 600 to 800 words, feature articles 1,200 to 3,000 words. Pays a flat rate of $75 per review, 15¢/word for features – up to a maximum of $400 – on publication. Welcomes approaches by mail, phone, or fax.

## Azure

2 Silver Avenue, Toronto, Ont. M6R 3A2
Phone: (416) 588-2588  Fax: (416) 588-2357
Contact: Nelda Rodger, editor
Circulation: 12,000
Published bimonthly

A design review, covering developments in graphic, interior, and industrial design and art in Canada and abroad; directed toward designers, architects, and the visually aware. Pays on publication. Guidelines available.

## Blackflash

12 – 23rd Street E., Saskatoon, Sask. S7K 0H5
Phone: (306) 244-8018  Fax: (306) 665-6568
Contact: Wallace Polsom, editor
Circulation: 1,300
Published quarterly

The only magazine in Canada that focuses on critical writing about photography. Pays $100 to $250 for pieces from 1,500 to 2,500 words. Accepts proposed outlines only; no unrequested submissions. Guidelines available.

## Border Crossings

393 Portage Avenue, Suite Y300, Winnipeg, Man. R3B 3H6
Phone: (204) 942-5778  Fax: (204) 949-0793
Contact: Meeka Walsh, editor

Circulation: 4,000
Published quarterly

An interdisciplinary arts review featuring articles, book reviews, artist profiles, and interviews covering the full range of the contemporary arts in Canada and internationally. Subjects include architecture, dance, fiction, film, painting, photography, poetry, politics, and theatre. Pays a negotiated fee on publication. Use the magazine as your guide when formulating submissions.

## C Magazine
P.O. Box 5, Station B, Toronto, Ont. M5T 2T2
Phone: (416) 539-9495  Fax: (416) 539-9903
Contact: Joyce Mason, editor/publisher
Circulation: 4,500
Published quarterly

A leading review of Canadian and international contemporary visual art and criticism. Features should be 500 to 2,500 words, reviews 500 words maximum. Feature rates vary; $100 paid per review. Pays on publication. Guidelines available.

## Canadian Art
70 The Esplanade, 2nd Floor, Toronto, Ont. M5E 1R2
Phone: (416) 368-8854  Fax: (416) 594-3375
Contact: Betty Ann Jordan, managing editor
Circulation: 18,000
Published quarterly

Covers visual arts in Canada in a lively and opinionated way. Includes articles on painting, sculpture, film, photography, architecture, design, video, and television, with critical profiles of new artists and assessments of established art-world figures. Articles 150 to 2,000 words. Pays $100 for 150 words, up to $1,000 for 3,000 words, on publication. Inquire first. No unsolicited submissions.

## Canadian Musician
23 Hannover Drive, Unit 7, St. Catharines, Ont. L2W 1A3
Phone: (905) 641-3471  Fax: (905) 641-1648
Contact: Shauna Kennedy, editor
Published bimonthly

A magazine for professional and amateur musicians, as well as serious music enthusiasts and industry personnel. Accepts articles of 2,000 to 3,000 words. Most articles are assigned and fees are negotiable. Pays on acceptance. All writers are required to be technically and musically literate. Guidelines available.

## Canadian Theatre Review

Department of Drama, Queen's University, Kingston,
    Ont. K7L 3N6
Phone: (613) 545-2104
Contact: Natalie Rewa, editor
Circulation: 1,200
Published quarterly

Publishes playscripts, essays of interest to theatre professionals, and interviews with playwrights, actors, directors, and designers. Issues are thematic. Preferred article length 1,500 to 3,000 words. Pay scale and guidelines available on request. Hard copy must be included with IBM WordPerfect diskette.

## Chart Magazine

P.O. Box 332, Willowdale, Station A, North York, Ont. M2N 5S9
Phone: (416) 363-3101  Fax: (416) 363-3109
E-mail: chart@chartnet.com
Contact: Nada Laskovski, editor/publisher
Circulation: 20,000
Published monthly

Established 1990. Covers new music for a high school/university audience. Canadian bands, independent/alternative music, campus radio, pop culture. Reviews and articles. "Although we pay for most articles, it is only a token amount." Guidelines available.

## CineACTION!

40 Alexander Street, Apartment 705, Toronto, Ont. M4Y 1B5
Phone: (416) 964-3534
Contact: editorial collective
Circulation: 2,000
Published 3 times a year

A film magazine that explores neglected and unconventional

cinema, both mainstream and independent productions, from a feminist and socialist perspective. Submission inquiries welcome. It is the magazine's policy to pay for contributions, but limited funds mean payment is sometimes delayed.

## Classical Music Magazine

P.O. Box 45045, Mississauga, Ont. L5G 4S7
Phone: (905) 271-0339  Fax: (905) 271-9748
Contact: Anthony Copperthwaite, publisher
Circulation: 7,000
Published quarterly

Featuring classical music in all its aspects, including news stories, photo features, historical articles, personality profiles, and interviews. Pays on publication for articles of 2,500 to 3,000 words. Appropriate short news items (100 to 200 words) earn $50; longer articles up to $300. Send $5 for writer's guidelines.

## Coda Magazine

P.O. Box 1002, Station O, Toronto, Ont. M4A 2N4
Phone: (416) 593-7230  Fax: (416) 593-7230
Contact: Bill Smith, editor
Circulation: 3,000
Published bimonthly

The Canadian jazz and improvised music magazine with an international reputation, published since 1958, with articles, essays, personality profiles, and reviews. "*Coda* is a specialized periodical and only publishes work by experts in this field, so all is negotiable."

## Dance Connection

815 – 1st Street S.W., Suite 603, Calgary, Alta. T2P 1N3
Phone: (403) 263-3232  Fax: (403) 237-7327
Contact: Heather Elton, editor
Circulation: 5,000
Published 5 times a year

Reflects a commitment to a broad view of dance. Through feature articles, critical essays, profiles, and literature, it examines contemporary issues relating to dance. Pays 10¢/word on publication for articles of 800 to 2,500 words. Guidelines available.

## Dance International

Roedde House, 1415 Barclay Street, Vancouver, B.C. V6G 1J6
Phone: (604) 681-1525 Fax: (604) 681-7732
Contact: Maureen Riches, editor
Circulation: 3,000
Published quarterly

Formerly *Vandance International*. Provides a forum for lively and critical commentary on the best in national and international dance, including features, reviews, reports, and commentaries. Preferred length 1,000 to 2,000 words. Pays on publication $100 to $150 for features, $65 to $80 for commentaries, $40 to $60 for reviews, $60 to $75 for notebook. Full guidelines available.

## Diva

364 Coxwell Avenue, Toronto, Ont. M4L 3B7
Phone: (416) 461-2744 Fax: (416) 461-3315
Contact: Fauzia Rafiq, editor
Circulation: 1,500
Published quarterly

An arts magazine targeting women of South Asian origin and women of colour, and featuring the development of women's art and literature. Articles of 1,500 to 3,000 words receive $50; poetry $25; fiction $75; art work $150 for colour, $30 for b&w. Query first.

## FUSE Magazine

401 Richmond Street W., Suite 454, Toronto, Ont. M5V 3A8
Phone: (416) 340-8026 Fax: (416) 340-8458
Contact: Tom Folland, editorial collective member
Circulation: 5,000
Published 5 times a year

Addresses all aspects of contemporary culture. Special emphasis on issues relating to different cultural communities, including feminist issues, gay and lesbian culture and politics, minority and labour struggles, and economic and policy analysis. Also reviews visual arts, from independent production to mass media, including video, film, television, music, performance art, theatre, and books. Articles from 5,000 to 7,000 words. Pays 10¢/word on publication for reviews, and a flat rate of $700 for full-length features. "Please request guidelines before submitting unsolicited copy."

**Inuit Art Quarterly**
2081 Merivale Road, Nepean, Ont. K2G 1G9
Phone: (613) 224-8189  Fax: (613) 224-2907
Contact: Marybelle Mitchell, editor
Circulation: 4,000
   Devoted exclusively to Inuit art, and directed toward art specialists, artists, historians, teachers, and all interested readers with the purpose of giving Inuit artists a voice. Carries feature articles, profiles, interviews, news and reviews, and reader commentary. Pays a variable fee on publication. Query editor first.

**Matriart**
80 Spadina Avenue, Suite 506, Toronto, Ont. M5V 2J3
Phone: (416) 703-0074  Fax: (416) 703-0441
E-mail: warc@intacc.web.net
Contact: Linda Abrahams, editor
Circulation: 2,000
Published quarterly
   Established 1990. Journal of contemporary women's art for a general audience as well as academic and feminist communities. Committed to cultural diversity. Issues are thematic. Reviews 750 to 1,000 words; feature articles 2,000 words. Pays 5¢/word. Guidelines available.

**Mix: The Magazine of Artist-Run Culture**
401 Richmond Street W., Suite 446, Toronto, Ont. M5V 3A8
Phone: (416) 506-1012  Fax: (416) 340-8458
Contact: Margaret Christakos or Amy Gotlieb, co-editors
Circulation: 4,000
Published quarterly
   Formerly *Parallélogram*, a national magazine that traces developments in contemporary art, including painting, sculpture, installations, video, new music, dance, and performance. Articles 2,000 to 2,500 words. Contact editor for guidelines and pay rates.

**MUSICWORKS: The Journal of Sound Exploration**
179 Richmond Street W., Toronto, Ont. M5V 1V3
Phone: (416) 977-3546  Fax: (416) 208-1084
Contact: Gayle Young, editor

Circulation: 2,500
Published 3 times a year

Distributed with audio component – cassettes or CDs – to illustrate articles and interviews covering a broad range of contemporary classical and experimental music. Also ethnic music and sound related to dance and visual art. Features are 1,000 to 3,500 words. Fees depend on length, complexity, and other factors. Pays on publication. Welcomes inquiries. Guidelines available.

## Opera Canada

366 Adelaide Street E., Suite 434, Toronto, Ont. M5A 3X9
Phone: (416) 363-0395  Fax: (416) 363-0396
Contact: Jocelyn Laurence, editor
Circulation: 5,000
Published quarterly

Devoted for more than 30 years to Canadian opera. Reviews international performances, interviews Canada's best singers, and addresses opera-related cultural issues. Reviews up to 300 words; features 1,200 to 1,500 words. Accepts submissions and submission inquiries. Pays $300 on publication for 1,500 words.

## Parachute

4060 St. Laurent Boulevard, Suite 501, Montreal, Que. H2W 1Y9
Phone: (514) 842-9805
Contact: Chantal Pontbriand, editor
Circulation: 3,000
Published quarterly

A bilingual review offering readers in-depth articles on the theory and practice of art today – interviews with artists, and articles on music, cinema, photography, theatre, dance, and video. Pays about $100 for reviews and issues column (to a maximum of 1,000 words), up to $500 for articles and interviews (3,000 to 5,000 words), on publication. Guidelines available.

## Performing Arts & Entertainment in Canada

104 Glenrose Avenue, Toronto, Ont. M4T 1K8
Phone: (416) 484-4534  Fax: (416) 484-6214
Contact: Karen Bell, editor
Circulation: 44,000

Published quarterly

Explores the issues and trends affecting performing arts in Canada – primarily theatre, dance, opera, ballet, and film. Also carries profiles on individual performers, companies, and troupes. Prefers articles of 600 to 1,500 words, which earn $95 to $180, paid on publication. Query first.

## Proscenium

189 Laurier Avenue E., Ottawa, Ont. KIN 6PI
Phone: (613) 238-3561  Fax: (613) 238-4849
Contact: editorial department
Circulation: 2,500
Published quarterly

A bilingual arts and culture news magazine presenting innovative cultural ideas. Follows political, cultural, and educational developments, at national and provincial level, of concern to artists and arts administrators. Preferred length 750 to 1,000 words. Pays $200 for columns, $350 (maximum) for features.

## Shift Magazine

174 Spadina Avenue, Suite 407, Toronto, Ont. M5T 2C2
Phone: (416) 504-1887  Fax: (416) 504-1889
Contact: Andrew Heintzman, publisher
Circulation: 30,000
Published bimonthly

A broad cultural magazine with a vigorous and youthful editorial agenda. Focuses on entertainment media and technology, featuring the people shaping the media, as well as travel writing. Articles 800 to 2,000 words. Pays up to $800 for a feature with photos. Welcomes submissions, which should include author bio.

## Stage

15 Curly Vineway, North York, Ont. M2J 4J9
Phone: (416) 493-5740  Fax: (416) 493-5740
E-mail: 75709.3331@compuserve.com
Contact: Katherine Goodes, publisher
Circulation: 3,800
Published 5 times a year

Formerly *Theatrum*. Directed toward both patrons and practitioners of the theatre as a forum for the working professional to discuss his/her craft. Provides a place for discussion and exposure, in "an art form that is becoming increasingly exciting and complex." Includes feature articles, artist profiles, production and book reviews, festival reports, and a national calendar of events. Welcomes unsolicited manuscripts. Pays an honorarium of from $50 (reviews) to $300 (articles) after publication. Guidelines available.

**Studio Magazine**
124 Galaxy Boulevard, Toronto, Ont. M9W 4Y6
Phone: (416) 675-1999  Fax: (416) 675-6093
Contact: Barbara Murray, executive editor
Circulation: 12,000
Published 7 times a year

A large-format, full-colour design magazine. Buys factual articles with appeal to professional designers, illustrators, and photographers. Pays on publication. Mail inquiries only, enclosing published samples and references. Length and fee discussed case by case.

**VOX Magazine**
Room 127, MacEwan Hall, 2500 University Drive, Calgary,
    Alta. T2M 0X1
Phone: (403) 220-5165  Fax: (403) 289-8212
Contact: Ian Chiclo, editor
Circulation: 15,000
Published monthly

An alternative arts and entertainment magazine with a strong focus on local artists. Stories should be 1,500 to 2,000 words. *VOX* is run entirely by volunteers. Submission inquiries are welcomed, but contributors are unpaid.

## Business

**AgriFamily Business Magazine**
93 Lombard Avenue, Suite 108, Winnipeg, Man. R3B 3B1
Phone: (204) 942-2214  Fax: (204) 943-8991
Contact: Stuart Slayen, editor

Circulation: 30,000
Published bimonthly
Aims to empower Canadian agricultural producers with the information they need to make effective business decisions. Provides news, features, and columns. Most feature stories run at 1,300 to 1,800 words. Fees vary according to story length and research needed. Guidelines available.

### Atlantic Business Report/Brunswick Business Journal
599 Main Street, Suite 203, Moncton, N.B. EIC IC8
Phone: (506) 857-9696  Fax: (506) 859-7395
E-mail: abjpubl@nbnet.nb.ca
Contact: Susanne MacDonald-Boyce, editor
Circulation: 35,000
Published monthly
Two regional business magazines that aim to foster economic development in Atlantic Canada by publishing stories about economic trends and issues and featuring successful businesses and business people. Preferred length 750 to 1,000 words. Pays around 15¢/word on publication. Guidelines available.

### Atlantic Lifestyle Business Magazine
197 Water Street, P.O. Box 2356, St. John's, Nfld. AIC 6E7
Phone: (709) 726-9300  Fax: (709) 726-3013
Contact: Edwina Hutton, managing editor
Circulation: 25,000
Published bimonthly
Examines culture, lifestyle, and business in Atlantic Canada. Pays 15¢/word on publication for articles of 2,000 to 2,500 words, a fixed rate for cover stories. Story ideas are welcomed. Guidelines available.

### B.C. Business
4180 Lougheed Highway, Suite 401, Burnaby, B.C. V5C 6A7
Phone: (604) 299-7311  Fax: (604) 299-9188
Contact: Bonnie Irving, editor
Circulation: 26,000
Published monthly

Directed toward business owners, managers, entrepreneurs, and professionals, its aim to inform readers of the trends, people, and companies shaping the business environment in British Columbia. Pays 35¢/word on acceptance for articles of 1,000 to 2,500 words. "Tell us something we don't know." Guidelines available.

## Business Quarterly

Western Business School, University of Western Ontario, London, Ont. N6A 3K7
Phone: (519) 661-3309  Fax: (519) 661-3838
E-mail: asmith@novell.business.uwo.ca
Contact: Angela Smith, publisher/editor
Circulation: 9,000

A long-established business journal directed toward senior executives with the purpose of improving the practice of management. Most articles are between 2,000 and 3,000 words. Contributors are unpaid, but submission inquiries welcome. Guidelines available.

## Canadian Business

777 Bay Street, 5th Floor, Toronto, Ont. M5W 1A7
Phone: (416) 596-5151  Fax: (416) 596-5155
Contact: Arthur Johnson, editor
Circulation: 90,000
Published monthly

Canada's premier national business journal, carrying incisive and thoughtful commentary and advice on business issues and profiles of successful business people. Articles 800 to 4,000 words. Pays $500 to $3,000 on acceptance, depending on assignment and experience. Prefers initial inquiries by mail.

## Canadian Business Life

1 St. John's Road, Suite 501, Toronto, Ont. M6P 4C7
Phone: (416) 766-5744  Fax: (416) 766-1970
Contact: Darryl Simmons, associate publisher
Circulation: 50,000
Published quarterly

Focuses on the concerns of small business. Preferred length 1,000 to 2,000 words. Pays on publication. Welcomes inquiries.

## Canadian Money Saver

P.O. Box 370, Bath, Ont. KOH 1GO
Phone: (613) 352-7448
Contact: Dale Ennis, publisher
Circulation: 30,100
Published 11 times a year

A national consumer finance magazine offering articles (750 to 1,500 words) on such current topics as personal finance, tax, investment techniques, retirement planning, consumer purchases, small business practice, and discount service. Cannot pay but welcomes submission inquiries. "Writers contribute for the benefits of national exposure. Conference and seminar participation available. Other writing projects possible." Guidelines available.

## The Financial Post Magazine

333 King Street E., 3rd Floor, Toronto, Ont. M5A 4N2
Phone: (416) 350-6172  Fax: (416) 350-6171
Contact: Peter Carter, senior editor
Circulation: 200,000
Published 11 times a year plus *FP 500* annual

An executive lifestyle magazine featuring political, business, and general interest articles and personal finance columns, mostly written by experts or seasoned journalists. Articles 1,500 to 3,000 words. Pays top rates (approx. $1/word) on acceptance.

## The Home Business Report

2949 Ash Street, Abbotsford, B.C. V2S 4G5
Phone: (604) 857-1788  Fax: (604) 854-3087
Contact: Barbara Mowat, publisher
Circulation: 50,000
Published quarterly

A magazine to link home-based businesses across the country, providing a network for sharing experiences, including advice for launching new businesses and support for those that are struggling. Articles 600 to 1,200 words. Pay rates depend on assignment – from 10¢/word to $250 to $400 for a 1,200-word feature – paid on publication. Very interested in successful rural and small-town home-based businesses offering an unusual product or service. Guidelines available.

**Money Issues**
3 Church Street, Suite 505, Toronto, Ont. M5E 1M2
Phone: (416) 947-0747  Fax: (416) 947-1651
E-mail: waysmag@hookup.net
Contact: Kelvin Browne, editor
Circulation: 125,000
Published bimonthly
  Established 1995. Provides advice on personal financial planning for upscale Canadian investors. Pays 60¢ to $1/word 30 days after publication.

**Nova Scotia Business Journal**
6029 Cunard Street, Halifax, N.S. B3K 1E5
Phone: (902) 420-0437  Fax: (902) 423-8212
Contact: Ken Partridge, editor
Circulation: 14,100
Published monthly
  Informs and educates Nova Scotia's business community on issues, people, and activities of interest to them. Articles of 500 to 1,000 words preferred. Pays 10¢/word on publication. Send query letter. Deadline is 15th of month preceding publication.

**Ontario Business Journal**
100 Main Street E., 40th Floor, Hamilton, Ont. L8N 3W6
Phone: (905) 526-8600  Fax: (905) 526-0086
Contact: Mark Higgins, assistant editor
Published monthly
  Provides comprehensive regional news coverage and advisory editorial for small and medium-sized businesses in Ontario. Articles 750 to 1,500 words. Pay rates vary, depending on project. Guidelines available.

**PROFIT: The Magazine for Canadian Entrepreneurs**
777 Bay Street, 5th Floor, Toronto, Ont. M5W 1A7
Phone: (416) 596-5999  Fax: (416) 596-5111
E-mail: profit@cbmedia.ca
Contact: Rick Spence, editor
Circulation: 100,000
Published bimonthly

Features regular columns and departments along with articles on management topics and issues of interest to owner/managers of small to medium-sized businesses. Offers insights and practical advice in the areas of marketing, technology, finance, innovators and trends, and personnel management. Pays 60¢ to 75¢/word on acceptance for features of 1,500 to 2,500 words and shorter items. "You must know something about business and be prepared to rewrite." Guidelines available.

### Report on Business Magazine
444 Front Street W., Toronto, Ont. M5V 2S9
Phone: (416) 585-5499  Fax: (416) 585-5705
Contact: David Olive, editor
Circulation: 300,000
Published monthly

A news magazine covering the national business scene and international developments affecting Canada. Carries profiles of prominent business and political personalities, book reviews, and regular columns on personal finance and national opinion. Pays about $1/word. Full-length feature fee varies from $1,500 to $4,000, depending on length, complexity of topic, and writer's style and experience. Pays on acceptance.

### Small Business Week Magazine
c/o The  Bowering Group, P.O. Box 116, Winnipeg, Man. R3C 2G1
Phone: (204) 958-7540  Fax: (204) 958-7547
Contact: Lorna Wenger, editor
Circulation: 30,000
Published annually

Provides a range of helpful material for Manitoba-based small business owners, managers, and staff. Articles 700 to 2,000 words. Pays $150 for 1,500 words, on publication. Rates are negotiable, depending on the story. Writers are encouraged to phone the editor to discuss story ideas before submitting. Guidelines available.

### Trade & Commerce
P.O. Box 6900, 1700 Church Avenue, Winnipeg, Man. R3C 3B1
Phone: (204) 632-2606  Fax: (204) 694-3040
Contact: Laura Jean Stewart, editor

Circulation: 10,000
Published 5 times a year
　Profiles companies and communities with an emphasis on their contribution to the economy or economic development activity. Pays 20¢ to 30¢/word on publication for 1,500 to 2,500 words. Works with freelance writers all over Canada and the United States. Guidelines available.

**Victoria's Business Report**
1609 Blanshard Street, Victoria, B.C. v8w 2j5
Phone: (604) 382-7777  Fax: (604) 381-2662
Contact: Gery Lemon, editor
Circulation: 14,000
Published monthly
　Focuses on the concerns of south Vancouver Island business. Articles 500 to 1,000 preferred. Rates range from $50 to $400, paid on publication.

**Ways**
3 Church Street, Suite 505, Toronto, Ont. m5e 1m2
Phone: (416) 947-0747  Fax: (416) 947-1651
E-mail: waysmag@hookup.net
Contact: Merv Walker, editor
Circulation: 35,000
Published bimonthly
　Established 1994. Provides ideas, methods, solutions, and case studies of how organizations are managing strategic change in order to remain competitive in a global economy. Length 250 to 3,000 words. Pays 60¢ to $1/word 30 days after publication.

## City & Entertainment

**Avenue**
200 – 625 14th Street N.W., Calgary, Alta. t2n 2a1
Phone: (403) 283-8260  Fax: (403) 288-6026
Contact: Valerie Fortney, editor
Circulation: 40,000
Published 10 times a year

Devoted to celebrating all aspects of Calgary life for those interested in a wide variety of activities, events, and issues of the city. A strong emphasis on local arts and entertainment. Pays 25¢/word on acceptance for 300 to 2,000 words, although rates can vary for features. Guidelines available.

## Cityscope

1324 11th Avenue S.W., Suite 304, Calgary, Alta. T3C 0M6
Phone: (403) 228-7020  Fax: (403) 228-7193
E-mail: cityscope@lexicom.ab.ca
Contacts: Larry B. Jones, Gary M. Pirart, publishers
Circulation: 60,000
Published bimonthly

A city magazine focusing on arts and entertainment, sports and recreation, in and around Calgary. Articles 250 to 3,500 words. Pays 30¢/word on publication plus expenses. Guidelines available.

## eye Weekly

57 Spadina Avenue, Suite 207, Toronto, Ont. M5V 2J2
Phone: (416) 971-8421  Fax: (416) 971-7786
E-mail: eye@interlog.com
Contact: Bill Reynolds, managing editor
Circulation: 100,000

A weekly Toronto arts journal of commentary, humour, information, and opinion, with some political/social writing. Preferred length 500 to 1,000 words. Pay rates vary, paid on publication. Query first.

## Georgia Straight

1235 West Pender Street, 2nd Floor, Vancouver, B.C. V6E 2V6
Phone: (604) 681-7000  Fax: (604) 681-0272
Contact: Charles Campbell, managing editor
Circulation: 93,000
Published weekly

Event-oriented yet thoughtful articles on the arts, music, movies, style, food, sports, and outdoor recreation, anchored by a general interest news feature. Articles 200 to 4,000 words. First send an inquiry with writing samples. Pays 15¢ to 30¢/word on publication. Guidelines available.

## Hamilton This Month
875 Main Street W., Hamilton, Ont. L8S 4R1
Phone: (416) 522-6117  Fax: (416) 529-2242
Contact: Wayne Narciso, editor/publisher
Circulation: 40,000
Published 8 times a year

A news and general interest magazine for Hamilton and its suburbs, focusing on public issues, events, and concerns – and the personalities behind them. Also covers fashion, interior decorating, electronics, cars, and restaurants. Feature length 2,000 to 4,000 words. Phone with ideas. Fees negotiable.

## London Magazine
231 Dundas Street, Suite 203, London, Ont. N6A 1H1
Phone: (519) 679-4901  Fax: (519) 434-7842
Contact: Jackie Skender, editor
Circulation: 35,000
Published 7–11 times a year

Covers lifestyles, fashion, city issues, art, food, history, business, sports, and entertainment for Londoners and residents of southwestern Ontario. Features regular columns by local writers. Articles 200 to 2,000 words. Fees negotiable, paid on acceptance. Guidelines available.

## Marquee Entertainment Magazine
77 Mowat Avenue, Suite 621, Toronto, Ont. M6K 3E3
Phone: (416) 538-1000  Fax: (416) 538-0201
Contact: Ron Base, editor
Circulation: 700,000
Published 9 times a year

Now distributed in newspapers across Canada, *Marquee* continues to carry short feature stories, previews, and profiles of upcoming movies and personalities while expanding its coverage of video, music, and fashion. Given the magazine's advanced deadline, writers need access to on-set and on-location interview opportunities. Articles 300 to 1,500 words. Pays on publication. Fees vary.

## Montreal Mirror
400 McGill Street, 2nd Floor, Montreal, Que. H2Y 2G1

Phone: (514) 393-1010  Fax: (514) 393-3173
E-mail: peter_scowen@babylon.gc.ca
Contact: Peter Scowen, managing editor
Circulation: 80,000
Published weekly

An alternative tabloid featuring articles on major issues written from a local perspective. Also reviews and previews music releases and concerts, films, art shows, books, and theatre. Features are 2,000 to 3,000 words. Fees are negotiated, and paid on publication. Guidelines available.

**Network**
287 MacPherson Avenue, Toronto, Ont. M4V 1A4
Phone: (416) 928-2909  Fax: (416) 928-1357
Contact: Stephen Hubbard, managing editor
Circulation: 150,000
Published bimonthly

A national entertainment magazine featuring predominantly pop/rock music interviews and reviews, with some movie and video coverage. Pays on publication $40 to $300 for short pieces between 150 and 700 words. Three-month lead time. Query letter advisable.

**The Newfoundland Herald**
P.O. Box 2015, Logy Bay Road, St John's, Nfld. A1C 5R7
Phone: (709) 726-7060  Fax: (709) 726-8227
Contact: Greg Stirling, editor-in-chief
Circulation: 50,000
Published weekly

A family entertainment and local interest magazine focusing on people. Articles 1,000 to 5,000 words. Pays 10¢/word on publication. "Read at least three recent issues before deciding on story angles, then contact the editor by phone or mail with ideas."

**NOW**
150 Danforth Avenue, Toronto, Ont. M4K 1N1
Phone: (416) 461-0871  Fax: (416) 461-2886
Contact: Michael Hollett, editor/publisher
Circulation: 100,000
Published weekly

A news, entertainment, and listings magazine for Toronto's young adults. Covers film, music, theatre, art galleries, books, fashion, personalities, and current events. Most work assigned. Uses very few out-of-town writers. No freelance entertainment submissions. Toronto region news submissions with alternative perspective have best chance. All fees negotiable. Inquiries welcome.

**Ottawa Magazine**
1312 Bank Street, 2nd Floor, Ottawa, Ont. KIS 3Y4
Phone: (613) 731-9194  Fax: (613) 731-9884
Contact: Mark Sutcliffe, editor
Circulation: 40,000
Published bimonthly
A city magazine exploring the news, social issues, cultural and consumer interests, and personalities of the capital. Pays 30¢ to 50¢/word on acceptance for articles between 1,000 and 2,500 words. Inquire by mail or fax. Guidelines available.

**Starweek Magazine**
1 Yonge Street, Toronto, Ont. M5E 1E6
Phone: (416) 869-4901  Fax: (416) 865-3635
Contact: Jim Atkins, editor
Circulation: 806,000
Published weekly
Carries profiles of top entertainers plus articles on sports, music, videos, and cooking, to complement Toronto-area weekly television listings. Pays on publication for articles of 800 to 1,100 words. Mail or fax queries. Fees negotiated for new freelancers.

**Toronto Life**
59 Front Street E., 3rd Floor, Toronto, Ont. M5E 1B3
Phone: (416) 364-3333  Fax: (416) 861-1169
Contact: John Macfarlane, editor
Circulation: 100,000
Published monthly
Established 1962. A classy city magazine that tells readers how Toronto works, lives, and plays. Examines city politics, society, business, entertainment, sports, food and restaurants, and shopping in a unique mix of hard-nosed reporting and rigorous service

journalism. Also publishes supplements. Draws on a stable of experienced writers and rarely accepts outside submissions. Pays on acceptance between $1,000 and $4,500 for 400 to 6,000 words, depending on assignment. Guidelines available.

**TV Guide**
25 Sheppard Avenue W., North York, Ont. M2N 6S7
Phone: (416) 733-7600  Fax: (416) 733-3568
E-mail: tvguide@telemedia.org
Contact: Bill Anderson, features editor
Circulation: 850,000
Published weekly
Carries television listings and articles on the entertainment industry, children's programming, sports, food, and showbiz personalities. Pays competitive, always negotiable rates on acceptance for articles of 800 to 1,200 words. "Read the magazine. Be prepared to submit a single-page proposal with suggested contacts. This magazine is not for neophyte writers."

**Vancouver Magazine**
555 West 12th Avenue, Suite 300, S.E. Tower, Vancouver,
    B.C. V5Z 4L4
Phone: (604) 877-7732  Fax: (604) 877-4849
Contact: Jim Sutherland, editor
Circulation: 70,000
Published 9 times a year
A glossy city magazine focusing on current affairs and entertainment. Articles must be Vancouver specific. Pays on acceptance. Guidelines available.

## The Environment

**Common Ground**
P.O. Box 34090, Station D, Vancouver, B.C. V6J 4M1
Phone: (604) 733-2215  Fax: (604) 733-4415
Contact: Joseph Roberts, editor/publisher
Circulation: 85,000

Published 10 times a year

Aims to inform and inspire readers in the areas of personal growth, ecology, and healthy living. Pays 10¢/word on publication for articles from 500 to 1,800 words. "Make your first sentence and first paragraph great, or the article won't even get read."

## Green Teacher

95 Robert Street, Toronto, Ont. M5S 2K5
Phone: (416) 960-1244  Fax: (416) 925-3474
Contact: Tim Grant, co-editor
Circulation: 5,500
Published 5 times a year

A magazine by and for educators that aims to provide ideas, inspiration, and classroom-ready materials to help all educators (including parents) promote environmental and global awareness amongst young people, pre-school to college, in school and in the community. Articles 500 to 3,000 words. All writers are volunteers. Submissions welcome.

## Harrowsmith Country Life

25 Sheppard Avenue W., Suite 100, North York, Ont. M2N 6S7
Phone: (416) 733-7600  Fax: (416) 733-7981
Contact: Arlene Stacey, editor
Circulation: 150,000
Published bimonthly

A magazine for a thoughtful, critical audience interested in self-reliance and country living. Subject areas most frequently covered include country life, food gardening, solar and wind energy, folk arts, ecology, and owner-builder architecture. Pays around 75¢/word on acceptance for 1,200 to 2,500 words; rate varies according to complexity and writer's experience. Guidelines available.

## Natural Life

R.R.1, St. George, Ont. N0E 1N0
Phone: (519) 448-4001  Fax: (519) 448-4001
Contact: Wendy Priesnitz, editor
Circulation: 20,000
Published bimonthly

An environmental magazine focusing on ways to live a self-reliant, environmentally friendly, and sustainable lifestyle. Pays 10¢/word ($100 maximum) on publication for articles of 800-plus words. Query first with outline, after you have read the magazine. Guidelines available.

## Nature Canada

1 Nicholas Street, Suite 520, Ottawa, Ont. KIN 7B7
Phone: (613) 562-3447  Fax: (613) 562-3371
Contact: Barbara Stevenson, editor
Circulation: 17,000
Published quarterly

Published by the Canadian Nature Federation. Began in 1939 as *Canadian Nature*. Focuses on Canadian natural history and environmental issues. Designed to educate, entertain, and increase readers' awareness and understanding of nature. Features 2,000 to 3,000 words. Pays $750 on publication. Guidelines available.

## Seasons

355 Lesmill Road, Don Mills, Ont. M3B 2W8
Phone: (416) 652-6556  Fax: (416) 444-9866
Contact: Gail Muir, editor
Circulation: 16,000
Published quarterly

A nature and outdoors magazine published by the Federation of Ontario Naturalists and designed to enhance knowledge about natural history and the environment in Ontario. Features Ontario wildlife, wilderness, parks, and conservation issues. Preferred length 1,500 to 3,000 words. Pays up to $700 on publication. "Be familiar with the magazine before querying. We accept phone inquiries." Guidelines available.

## Watershed Sentinel

P.O. Box 25, Whaletown, B.C. VOP 1Z0
Phone: (604) 935-6992  Fax: (604) 935-6992
Contact: Delores Broten, editor
Circulation: 3,000
Published bimonthly

Environmental news for Georgia Strait with a provincial,

national, and international perspective. Articles are 450 to 1,500 words. Pays in copies. Guidelines available.

## Wildflower

90 Wolfrey Avenue, Toronto, Ont. M4K 1K8
Phone: (416) 466-6428
Contact: James Hodgins, editor
Circulation: 5,000
Published quarterly

Devoted to the conservation, cultivation, and study of North American wildflowers and other flora. Contains essays, book reviews, notices of coming events, and plant sources. Articles 1,500 to 5,000 words. Published by the Canadian Wildflower Society, for gardeners, naturalists, field botanists, and teachers. Cannot pay but welcomes submissions. Guidelines available.

## Feminist

## Fireweed: A Feminist Quarterly

P.O. Box 279, Station B, Toronto, Ont. M5T 2W2
Phone: (416) 504-1339
Contact: Sandra Haar, co-ordinating editor
Circulation: 2,000
Published quarterly

Established 1978. A journal of politics and the creative arts, featuring a wide range of cultural expression, including fiction, poetry, critical texts, interviews, reviews, visual art. Aims to provide a forum for a lively mix of voices, engaging issues of race, class, and sexuality. "A vital, nervy feminist statement" – Judy MacDonald (author). Length up to 5,000 words. Pays on publication, $30 first page and $10 thereafter. Guidelines available.

## Herizons

P.O. Box 128, Winnipeg, Man. R3C 2G1
Phone: (204) 774-6225
Contact: Penni Mitchell, editorial co-ordinator
Circulation: 5,000
Published quarterly

A feminist periodical focusing on women's issues and the women's movement. Articles 500 to 3,000 words. Pays 10¢/word. Send query and sample of previous published work written from a feminist perspective. Guidelines available.

## Kinesis

1720 Grant Street, Suite 301, Vancouver, B.C. V5L 2Y6
Phone: (604) 255-5499  Fax: (604) 255-5511
Contact: Agnes Huang, editor
Circulation: 3,000
Published 10 times a year

A nationwide feminist newspaper for all women. Articles of 800 to 1,600 words cover the struggles of women activists in Canada and abroad. Issues of interest include health politics, poverty, violence against women, and aboriginal women's news. Also discusses music, dance, literature, film, and the visual arts from a feminist perspective. Contributors are unpaid. Guidelines available.

## Northern Woman Journal

P.O. Box 144, Thunder Bay, Ont. P7C 4V5
Phone: (807) 346-8809
Contact: Jane Saunders, editor
Circulation: 200
Published quarterly

Feminist news and views, poetry, and analysis of issues affecting women, with a particular focus on northern women. Cannot pay but welcomes submission inquiries. Guidelines available.

## The Womanist

41 York Street, 3rd Floor, Ottawa, Ont. KIN 5S7
Phone: (613) 562-4081  Fax: (613) 562-4033
Contact: Joan Riggs, editor
Circulation: 20,000
Published quarterly

A national newspaper featuring feminist commentary and in-depth analysis on a range of subjects, from legislation on Parliament Hill to women's movement issues. Articles are from 750 to 2,000 words. Cannot pay but welcomes inquiries.

**Women & Environments**
736 Bathurst Street, Toronto, Ont. M5S 2R4
Phone: (416)516-2600  Fax: (416)531-6214
E-mail: weed@web.apc.org
Contact: Lisa Dale, co-ordinator
Circulation: 1,200
Published quarterly
   A forum for discussion, review, and research on women's built, natural, social, and political environments for feminists, academics, and a broad base of grassroots groups. Articles 400 to 1,500 words. Contributors are not paid, but submission inquiries welcome. "Clear English, no jargon, simple sentence construction: all these contribute to a well-written, well-thought-out, lively argument." Guidelines available.

**Women's Education des femmes**
47 Main Street, Toronto, Ont. M4E 2V6
Phone: (416) 699-1909  Fax: (416) 699-2145
Contact: Christina Starr, editor
Published quarterly
   A bilingual journal directed toward adult educators, teachers, students, education administrators, literacy workers, and other women. A feminist connection to the world of learning and education. Feature articles cover such diverse issues as antiracist education, violence as a barrier to education, women-positive learning and literacy, and feminist pedagogy. Articles 1,500 to 3,000 words. All contributions voluntary. Welcomes submission inquiries, and approaches from less experienced writers willing to contribute significant editorial support. Guidelines available.

# General Interest

**The Beaver: Exploring Canada's History**
167 Lombard Avenue, Suite 478, Winnipeg, Man. R3B 0T6
Phone: (204) 988-9300  Fax: (204) 988-9309
Contact: Christopher Dafoe, editor
Circulation: 45,000

Published bimonthly

A market since 1920 for lively, well-researched, informative articles on Canadian history. Articles based on unpublished journals or letters are of particular interest. Pays honoraria of $500 to $600 on publication for articles of 3,000 to 4,000 words. Guidelines available.

## Canadian Geographic

39 McArthur Avenue, Ottawa, Ont. KIL 8L7
Phone: (613) 745-4629  Fax: (613) 744-0974
E-mail: cangeo@achilles.net
Contact: Eric Harris, managing editor
Circulation: 245,000
Published bimonthly

Published by the Royal Canadian Geographical Society. Describes and illuminates, with fine colour photography, all aspects of Canada: its people, places, natural resources, and wildlife. Concerned with geography in its broadest sense, looking at the way our landscape was formed and human impact on it, and also reporting on discoveries in the sciences, from archaeology to zoology. The magazine is widely used as a high school and undergraduate teaching resource. Pays $1/word on acceptance for articles of 2,000 to 3,500 words. A large paid circulation helps make it one of the most lucrative freelance opportunities. Written queries preferred. Guidelines available.

## Equinox

25 Sheppard Avenue W., North York, Ont. M2N 6S7
Phone: (416) 733-7600  Fax: (416) 218-3633
Contact: Jim Cormier, editor
Circulation: 140,000
Published bimonthly

Canada's award-winning magazine of discovery is dedicated to exploring the human community, the natural world, and the wonders of science and technology – who we are, where we live, and why things happen – in a lively, engaging, and thoughtful way. Features of 1,200 to 5,000 words earn $2,000 to $5,500 on acceptance – more paid for photos; Nexus pieces earn $250. Always query in writing rather than by phone. Guidelines available.

## Imperial Oil Review

111 St. Clair Avenue W., Toronto, Ont. M5W 1K3
Phone: (416) 968-4883  Fax: (416) 968-4272
Contact: Sarah Lawley, editor
Circulation: 50,000
Published quarterly

This high-quality current affairs magazine, published by Imperial Oil since 1917, carries articles on important facets of Canadian living, profiles on our celebrated institutions, people, places, and culture, nostalgia, and in-depth pieces on travel and oil exploration. Preferred length about 2,500 words. Fees vary but are generally better than average. Pays on acceptance.

## Reader's Digest

215 Redfern Avenue, Westmount, Que. H3Z 2V9
Phone: (514) 934-0751
Contact: editorial department
Circulation: 1,226,000
Published monthly

This mass-interest magazine is among the freelancer's most lucrative potential markets. Carries articles on everything from nature, science, and politics to drama, self-improvement, and people, prominent or otherwise. All pieces contain advice, an experience, or a philosophical message of value to the magazine's more than 2 million readers. No fiction or poetry. Commissions original articles and adaptations of Canadian subjects of between 3,500 and 5,000 words, which earn $2,700. Also buys material previously published in books, magazines, or newspapers. Buys all rights and pays on acceptance for original articles, one-time rights for previously published "pickups." No unsolicited manuscripts. Send letter of inquiry with a two-page outline. Guidelines available.

## Saturday Night

184 Front Street E., Suite 400, Toronto, Ont. M5A 4N3
Phone: (416) 368-7237  Fax: (416) 368-5112
Contact: Kenneth Whyte, editor
Circulation: 410,000
Published 10 times a year

A sophisticated, award-winning magazine first published in 1887. Features profiles of the men, women, and institutions that shape and run Canadian society. Its insightful reporting goes far beyond explanations of events to focus on why things happen, who makes them happen, and how they may affect our future. Also publishes high-quality fiction. Boasts a list of contributing editors that reads like a *Who's Who* of Canadian literature. Pays about $1/word: $500 for one-page stories, $2,000 to $4,000 for features.

## This Country Canada

P.O. Box 39, 1 Mill Street, Pakenham, Ont. K0A 2X0
Phone: (613) 624-5000  Fax: (613) 624-5952
Contact: Judith Haines, editor
Circulation: 25,000
Published quarterly

A glossy, large-format magazine celebrating the people of Canada, carrying a mix of modern and historical features. Preferred length 1,500 to 2,000 words. Pays on publication. First send a one-page outline. Guidelines available.

## Up Here: Life in Canada's North

P.O. Box 1350, Yellowknife, N.W.T. X1A 2N9
Phone: (403) 920-4652  Fax: (403) 873-2844
Contact: Rosemary Allerston, editor
Circulation: 40,000
Published bimonthly

A lively, informative magazine about Northern travel, wildlife, arts, culture, lifestyles, and especially the people who live in the region and cope with the harsh winters there. Articles 750 to 3,000 words. Pays 20¢ to 25¢/word on publication for articles and features, with a standard fee for columns and photos. Complete manuscripts with photos welcome. "We're looking for solid reporting and research, and top-notch photos. Always tell your story through the people involved." Written queries only. Guidelines available.

## Western People

P.O. Box 2500, Saskatoon, Sask. S7K 2C4
Phone: (306) 665-9611  Fax: (306) 934-2401
E-mail: people@producer.com

Contact: Karen Morrison or Wendy Roy, features editors
Circulation: 100,000
Published weekly

A general interest, rural-oriented magazine featuring histories, memories, poetry, fiction, and contemporary profiles of western Canadians. Especially interested in well-researched features, profiles, and Western history. Preferred length 700 to 2,000 words. Pays $100 to $300 on acceptance for articles, depending on length, less for poetry. "Eastern Canadian and U.S. writers have a hard time catching the flavour of this magazine. People profiles are seldom of big names, almost never politicians. We require photos for most articles." Guidelines available.

## Home & Hobby

### Antiques!

55 Charles Street W., Suite 2402, Toronto, Ont. M5S 2W9
Phone: (416) 944-3880  Fax: (416) 944-3872
E-mail: dylmaa@dylcorp.dylex.com
Contact: Marni Andrews, publisher/editor
Circulation: 4,000
Published bimonthly

A magazine to inform collectors (beginning to intermediate level) on topics and trends in the antiques/quality collectibles market. Articles 1,500 to 2,000 words. Pays 5¢/word on publication. Guidelines available.

### B.C. Home

4180 Lougheed Highway, Suite 401, Burnaby, B.C. V5C 6A7
Phone: (604) 299-7311  Fax: (604) 299-9188
Contact: Ann Collette, editor
Circulation: 100,000
Published bimonthly

Targeting affluent homeowners, a regional home and garden magazine that features home profiles, a wide range of renovation-related information and tips, and ideas on decor and trends. Articles 500 to 1,000 words. Pays 30¢/word on publication, $300 to $350 for 1,000 words.

## Camera Canada

1140 South Dyke Road, New Westminster, B.C. V3M 5A2
Phone: (604) 524-5039  Fax: (604) 524-5039
Contact: Marilyn McEwen, editor
Circulation: 6,000
Published twice a year

Established 1968. Articles on basic camera handling techniques for new photographers, reports on new processes, personal experiences, etc. Also showcases the work of up-and-coming photographers through their portfolios, method, philosophy. Articles from 2,000 to 6,000 words. Cannot pay, but inquiries welcomed.

## Canadian Coin News

103 Lakeshore Road, Suite 202, St. Catharines, Ont. L2N 2T6
Phone: (416) 646-7744  Fax: (416) 646-0995
Contact: Bret Evans, editor
Circulation: 13,000
Published semi-monthly

A tabloid magazine for Canadian collectors of coins and paper money. Pays a month after publication. Fees negotiable. Prefers phone or fax queries.

## Canadian Gardening

130 Spy Court, Markham, Ont. L3R 0W5
Phone: (905) 475-8440  Fax: (905) 475-9560
Contact: Liz Primeau, editor
Circulation: 130,000
Published 7 times a year

A magazine geared toward the avid home gardener. Carries people-oriented feature articles on home gardens, garden design, and tips and techniques on gardening in the Canadian climate. Pays on acceptance for pieces of 1,000 to 2,500 words – $400 to $700, depending on length and research required. "We prefer outlines suggesting story ideas to unsolicited finished stories." Guidelines available.

## Canadian House & Home

511 King Street W., Suite 120, Toronto, Ont. M5V 2Z4

Phone: (416) 593-0204  Fax: (416) 591-1630
Contact: Cobi Ladner, editor
Circulation: 130,000
Published 8 times a year

Focuses on creative home decoration and design. Inspires and teaches through pictorial essays and how-to articles, featuring Canadian artisans, designers, and architects. Articles between 300 and 1,000 words. Always include colour photos with written submissions as visual confirmation of descriptions. Pays on publication. Fees vary according to project.

### Canadian Stamp News

202 – 103 Lakeshore Road, St. Catharines, Ont. L2N 2T6
Phone: (416) 646-7744  Fax: (416) 646-0995
Contact: Ellen Rodger, editor
Circulation: 9,500
Published semi-monthly

A tabloid magazine serving Canadian philatelists and enthusiasts around the world who collect Canadian stamps. Pays a month after publication. Fees negotiable. Query first. Guidelines available.

### Canadian Workshop

130 Spy Court, Markham, Ont. L3R 5H6
Phone: (905) 475-8440  Fax: (905) 475-9560
Contact: Hugh McBride, editor
Circulation: 113,000
Published monthly

Elucidates a variety of home projects for the avid do-it-yourselfer and woodworker – from laying floors and cleaning furnaces to renovating basements and making kitchen cabinets. Rates negotiable. Pays $800 on acceptance for features of 800 to 2,000 words; $300 for 800-word articles. "We are keen to hear from competent freelance writers with middle to advanced level skills in home renovation and repairs." Guidelines available.

### CenturyHome

12 Mill Street South, Port Hope, Ont. L1A 2S5
Phone: (905) 885-2449  Fax: (905) 885-5355

Contact: Joan Rumgay, publisher
Circulation: 40,000
Published 8 times a year

A magazine for lovers of vintage homes. Carries articles (1,000 to 1,500 words) about decorating, furnishings, art, crafts, architecture, restoration, renovation, gardens, and country fare. Fees vary according to project and are paid on publication. "Please know the magazine before submitting."

## Collectibles Canada

103 Lakeshore Road, Suite 202, St. Catharines, Ont. L2N 2T6
Phone: (416) 646-7744  Fax: (416) 646-0995
Contact: Bret Evans, editor
Circulation: 12,000
Published 7 times a year

A magazine about art collecting, containing information on collector plates, figurines, limited edition lithographs, new products, and interviews with Canadian artists. Also publishes *Canadian Collectibles Retailer*. Pays a month after publication for articles of 750 to 1,500 words. Fees negotiable. Phone or fax inquiries preferred.

## Crafts Plus Magazine

130 Spy Court, Markham, Ont. L3R 5H6
Phone: (905) 475-8440  Fax: (905) 475-9560
Contact: Erina Kelly, editor
Circulation: 90,000
Published 8 times a year

A practical magazine featuring instructional, project-based articles on sewing, knitting, floral arranging, folk art, and a range of other handicrafts. Pays on acceptance. Fees negotiable. Guidelines available.

## Homes & Cottages

6557 Mississauga Road, Unit D, Mississauga, Ont. L5N 1A6
Phone: (905) 567-1440  Fax: (905) 567-1442
Contact: Janice Naisby, editor
Circulation: 54,000
Published 8 times a year

For consumers as well as builders, lumber retailers, and architects. Provides thought-provoking and innovative ideas and technical information to help Canadians build or renovate their homes and cottages. Articles 1,500 to 2,000 words. Fees vary according to complexity but average $600. All articles are assigned. Pays on acceptance.

## Ontario Craft
Chalmers Building, 35 McCaul Street, Toronto, Ont. M5T 1V7
Phone: (416) 977-3551  Fax: (416) 977-3552
Contact: Anne McPherson, editor
Circulation: 4,500
Published quarterly
Represents the contemporary craft movement. Profiles interesting craftspeople and reviews their work. Articles 750 to 2,000 words. Pays on publication. Fees vary. "Familiarize yourself with *Ontario Craft* by looking through back issues." Guidelines available.

## Photo Life
130 Spy Court, Markham, Ont. L3R 0W5
Phone: (905) 475-8440  Fax: (905) 475-9560
Contact: Jerry Kobalenko, editor
Circulation: 40,000
Published 8 times a year
Established 1976. Articles provide serious information to advanced photographers in a readable way. Articles 1,500 to 3,000 words. Pays $500 on acceptance for feature articles, $75 for shorter items. "Our contributors are professional photographers who can write, or writers familiar with photography." Guidelines available.

## Plant & Garden
1, rue Pacifique, Ste.-Anne-de-Bellevue, Que. H9X 1C5
Phone: (514) 457-2744  Fax: (514) 457-6255
Contact: Michael Spillane, editor
Circulation: 35,000
Published quarterly
Established 1988. An informative, practical national magazine for Canadian gardeners. Articles 1,200 to 2,500 words. Pays 17¢/word on publication. Query with story outline first. "We publish informative, well-researched features relating to gardening, horticulture,

organic growing, nature, and the environment. Department articles (Environment, Junior Gardener, Step-by-Step, and Down to Earth) are about 500 to 750 words." Guidelines available.

### Renovation
178 Main Street, Unionville, Ont. L3R 2G9
Phone: (905) 479-4663  Fax: (905) 479-4482
Contact: Rïse Levy, editor
Published twice a year

Serving the Greater Toronto area, features home renovation projects performed by professionals. Subjects include advice on hiring professionals and profiles of completed projects. Most freelance projects assigned. Articles 500 to 1,500 words. Pays 30 days after publication.

## Lifestyle

### Alive: The Canadian Journal of Health and Nutrition
7436 Fraser Park Drive, Burnaby, B.C. V5J 5B9
Phone: (604) 435-1919  Fax: (604) 435-4888
Contact: Rhody Lake, managing editor
Published 11 times a year

A national magazine for health-conscious Canadians featuring articles of 600 to 800 words by health professionals and personalities. Also carries short book reviews. Pays 15¢/word on publication.

### Area Magazine
615 Mt. Pleasant Road, Suite 205, Toronto, Ont. M4S 3C5
Phone: (416) 368-9401  Fax: (416) 359-0755
E-mail: area.mag@canrem.com
Contact: Jason Patton, editor
Circulation: 50,000
Published 5 times a year

A lifestyle magazine, directed toward the upscale/affluent Toronto market, that seeks to entertain while offering insights into what makes Toronto vibrant and unique. Freelance fees, which are paid on publication, vary depending on project.

## Calgary This Season

2007 – 2nd Street S.W., Calgary, Alta. T2S 1S4
Phone: (403) 228-0605  Fax: (403) 228-0627
Contact: Heather Ellwood-Wright, editor
Circulation: 55,000
Published quarterly

A glossy quarterly lifestyle magazine, each edition reflecting the relevant season. Its broad coverage encompasses home and leisure, family life, entertainment, city life, and getaways and escapes. Articles mostly 1,000 to 2,000 words. Query all ideas by phone or letter before submitting. Pays a variable rate according to project.

## Campus Canada

287 MacPherson Avenue, Toronto, Ont. M4V 1A4
Phone: (416) 928-2909  Fax: (416) 928-1357
Contact: Sarah Moore, managing editor
Circulation: 125,000
Published 4 times during school year

A student lifestyle magazine featuring sports, entertainment, issues on campus, travel, and other topics of interest to university and college students. Short articles of 500 to 1,200 words preferred. Pays an average of $100 for 800 words on acceptance. Query first with story idea, by mail or fax.

## City Parent

467 Speers Road, Oakville, Ont. L6K 3S4
Phone: (905) 815-0017  Fax: (905) 815-0511
Contact: Jane Muller, editor-in-chief
Circulation: 160,000
Published monthly

A magazine to inform parents of news related to children and families. Also carries arts and entertainment news. Articles 500 to 750 words. Pays about 10¢/word, depending on research and quality. Welcomes submission inquiries.

## Cottage Life

111 Queen Street E., Suite 408, Toronto, Ont. M5C 1S2
Phone: (416) 360-6880  Fax: (416) 360-6814

Contact: Ann Vanderhoof, editor
Published bimonthly

An award-winning magazine directed toward those who own and spend time at cottages on Ontario's lakes. Examines and celebrates the history, personalities, and issues of cottaging. Also provides lots of practical advice to help readers keep their cottages, docks, and boats in working order. Pays on acceptance for articles of 150 to 3,000 words. Query all ideas before submission. Guidelines available with SASE.

### The Cottage Magazine

4611 William Head Road, Victoria, B.C. V9B 5T7
Phone: (604) 478-9209  Fax: (604) 478-1184
E-mail: chet@islandnet.com
Contact: Peter Chettleburgh, editor/publisher
Circulation: 10,000
Published 5 times a year

Established 1992. For cottage owners in Western Canada (B.C. and Alberta). Feature articles of 1,000 to 2,500 words include entertaining profiles on individuals and companies and analysis of political issues that affect cottage owners. Regular columns and departments on small boats, solar power, and other practical topics. Pays on publication $200 to $500 for features, $150 to $200 for columns; news items up to 400 words are paid at 20¢/word. Query the editor by phone or with a brief written proposal. Guidelines available.

### The Country Connection

P.O. Box 100, Boulter, Ont. K0L 1G0
Phone: (613) 332-3651  Fax: (613) 332-5183
Contact: Gus Zylstra
Circulation: 15,000
Published twice a year

A country magazine publishing informative, how-to, and historical pieces with rural themes and/or relating to central and eastern Ontario. Also humorous or light short fiction. Prefers articles and stories around 1,000 to 2,000 words. Submit article *ideas* and short fiction. Pays 10¢/word on disk or cleanly typewritten, 7¢/word handwritten, on publication. Guidelines available.

**Fifty-Five Plus**
P.O. Box 47, Battersea, Ont. KOH IHO
Phone: (613) 353-2060  Fax: (613) 353-7681
Contact: Sharon Freeman, editor
Circulation: 40,000
Published bimonthly
    Informs active retirees in eastern Ontario of options and opportunities for a successful retirement. Pays $60 to $350, depending on project and length, on publication for 800 to 2,500 words. Fees for features may be negotiated. This is a small operation, and writers should be prepared to wait up to six months for a response. Guidelines available.

**Good Times**
5148 St. Laurent Boulevard, Montreal, Que. H2T IR8
Phone: (514) 273-9773  Fax: (514) 273-3408
Contact: Denise Crawford, editor-in-chief
Published 10 times a year
    Addresses the concerns of retired Canadians and those planning retirement. Topics include financial planning, health and fitness, personal rights, interpersonal relationships, profiles of celebrities, and leisure activities. Articles are assigned. Welcomes inquiries, noting areas of expertise and suggestions, with writing samples. Pays 40¢/word on publication. "No phone or fax queries; material must be supplied on IBM-compatible disk."

**Great Expectations**
269 Richmond Street W., Toronto, Ont. M5V IXI
Phone: (416) 596-8680  Fax: (416) 596-1991
Contact: Holly Bennett, editor
Circulation: 200,000
Published 3 times a year
    Articles directed toward expectant and new parents, promoting healthy pregnancy and an active role in the birth and early care of the child. Encourages informed consumer choice, breastfeeding, and gentle parenting. Fees around $550 for departments, $450 to $1,000 for features, depending on level of research, medical complexity, and length, which should fall between 900 and 2,500 words. Pays 30 days after acceptance. "Most editorial is provided by our

regular freelancers. We are especially interested in writers with background in childbirth issues." Guidelines available.

## Highgrader Magazine

P.O. Box 714, Cobalt, Ont. POJ ICO
Phone: (705) 679-5533
Contact: Brit Griffin, publisher
Circulation: 3,000
Published bimonthly

A new magazine for readers interested in the unique culture of northern rural Canada, especially northern Ontario. Articles 500 to 2,000 words. Pays between $30 and $75; investigative/in-depth pieces $50 to $75. "We are interested in articulating self-reliance, with some how-to's and historical pieces. Nothing too folksy. Please read magazine before submitting." Guidelines available.

## Hi-Rise Magazine

95 Leeward Glenway, Unit 121, Don Mills, Ont. M3C 2Z6
Phone: (416) 424-1393  Fax: (416) 467-8262
Contact: Valerie Dunn, editor
Circulation: 30,000
Published 11 times a year

A magazine mirroring the concerns of high-rise dwellers. Carries self-help articles about tenants' rights and legal issues, issues of interest to condominium owners, plus regular features on food, travel, sports, hobbies, and business. Articles 400 to 600 words. Pays $25 for articles, $15 for short pieces. Guidelines available.

## Leisure World

1253 Ouellette Avenue, Windsor, Ont. N8X 1J3
Phone: (519) 971-3208  Fax: (519) 977-1197
Contact: Doug O'Neil, editor
Circulation: 342,000
Published bimonthly

Circulated to CAA members, this lifestyle magazine features travel, leisure, and automotive stories and articles. Seeks dramatic narratives of real-life experiences involving compelling characters. Articles 1,200 to 1,600 words. Pays $300 to $500 for first-run feature; $200 to $300 for second serial rights. "We purchase second rights only when article hasn't appeared in same geographic market. Travel features accompanied by slides stand a greater chance of publication. Completed manuscripts should be sent to the attention of the Editor-in-Chief." Guidelines and editorial calendar available.

## MENZ

130 Boulevard de Mortagne, Suite 201, Boucherville,
 Que. J4B 5M7
Phone: (514) 449-0722  Fax: (514) 449-1177
Contact: Bhaskar Patel, publisher, or Vanessa Berkling, associate
 editor
Circulation: 55,000
Published bimonthly
 Established 1994. This glossy magazine "finds itself in the enviable position of being the only male-targeted publication in the country." Encompasses features on health, finance, fashion, cinema, sports, etc. Articles 500 to 2,500 words. Pays $200/page for original, exclusive material, around $150 for used text. Welcomes all ideas and submission inquiries.

## Okanagan Life Magazine

P.O. Box 1479, Station A, Kelowna, B.C. V1Y 7V8
Phone: (604) 861-5399  Fax: (604) 868-3040
Contact: Holly McNeil, editor
Circulation: 18,000
Published bimonthly
 A lifestyle and personality-oriented magazine directed toward middle- and high-income families. Strictly local issues and people. Preferred length 1,000 to 1,500 words. Pays 15¢/word for articles, 10¢/word for fiction, on publication. Guidelines available.

## The Rural Voice

P.O. Box 429, Blyth, Ont. N0M 1H0
Phone: (519) 523-4311  Fax: (519) 523-9140
Contact: Keith Roulston, editor/publisher
Circulation: 15,000
Published monthly
 Established 1975. A regional periodical featuring agricultural

news, profiles, and politics, with regular sections on marketing, the law, finances, and home life. Aimed at the agricultural heartland of Ontario. Pays 12¢/word on publication for articles of 1,000 to 2,000 words. Guidelines available.

## The Senior Times

4077 Decarie Boulevard, Montreal, Que. H4A 3J8
Phone: (514) 484-5033  Fax: (514) 484-8254
Contact: Barbara Moser, editor/publisher
Circulation: 30,000
Published monthly

An informative news source targeting the English-speaking 50-plus community of Montreal and surrounding areas. Pays a variable amount on publication for pieces of 400 to 600 words.

## Today's Parent

269 Richmond Street W., Toronto, Ont. M5V 1X1
Phone: (416) 596-8680  Fax: (416) 596-1991
Contact: Fran Fearnley, editor-in-chief
Circulation: 160,000
Published 9 times a year

A parenting magazine for parents of children up to the age of 12. Carries articles about child development, education, health, and family life. Preferred length 1,200 to 2,500 words. Pays $700 to $1,500 for features, $650 for departments, 30 days after acceptance. "Always query first and include samples of published work. Do not send manuscripts." Guidelines available.

## Wedding Bells

120 Front Street E., Suite 200, Toronto, Ont. M5A 4L9
Phone: (416) 862-8479  Fax: (416) 862-2184
Contact: Crys Stewart, editor
Circulation: 110,000
Published twice a year

A fat, glossy magazine with editions in Atlantic Canada, Saskatchewan, Calgary, Edmonton, Hamilton, London, Ottawa, Montreal, Toronto, Vancouver, and Winnipeg, and a national edition. Directed toward brides and grooms and their families, offering information about every aspect of wedding planning. Pays on acceptance for articles of 1,000 to 2,000 words. Inquire by mail, but first read a couple of issues. Fees negotiable.

**Weddings & Honeymoons**
65 Helena Avenue, Toronto, Ont. M6G 2H3
Phone: (416) 653-4986  Fax: (416) 653-2291
E-mail: wed.hon.@watch.tor250.org
Contact: Joyce Barslow, editor
Circulation: 50,000
Published twice a year
A glossy magazine featuring information for brides-to-be and tips, trends, and how-to pieces on second marriages, honeymoons, and travel. Stories range between 50 and 1,250 words. Pays a negotiated rate of $50 to $150. Include SASE for return of material.

**Westcoast Reflections**
2604 Quadra Street, Victoria, B.C. V8T 4N5
Phone: (604) 383-1149  Fax: (604) 388-4479
Contact: Jane Kezar, associate editor
Circulation: 15,000
Published 10 times a year
A magazine for people 50 and older, carrying pieces on things to do, places to go; personalized travel stories; and positive, well-researched stories on health, hobbies, finance, the home, and activities with interviews. Pays 10¢/word on publication, 15¢/word for feature articles of 1,000 to 2,000 words. Good colour photos must be submitted with articles. Guidelines available.

**Western Living**
555 West 12th Avenue, Suite 300, East Tower, Vancouver,
    B.C. V5Z 4L4
Phone: (604) 877-7732  Fax: (604) 877-4849
E-mail: western.living@cyberstore.ca
Contact: Carolann Rule, editor
Circulation: 265,000
Published 10 times a year
A general interest and lifestyle magazine with a special emphasis on the home. The largest regional magazine in Canada. Regular features address social issues, trends, personalities, travel, fashion,

recreation, and cuisine. All stories should have Western Canadian focus. Articles 1,500 to 3,000 words. Pays 50¢/word on acceptance for pieces from 200 to 3,000 words. Guidelines available.

### Your Baby

269 Richmond Street W., Toronto, Ont. M5V 1X1
Phone: (416) 596-8680  Fax: (416) 596-1991
Contact: Holly Bennett, editor
Circulation: 250,000
Published 3 times a year

For parents of babies up to 24 months. Supportive articles focusing on baby care, health, fun and games, practical tips, and the experience of parenting. Emphasis on developmental issues. Distributed with *Chatelaine* magazine. Also published in French as *Mon Enfant*. Pays $300 to $1,000 on acceptance, depending on length and research required. Inquire in advance with samples of published work. Guidelines available.

## News, Opinions, & Issues

### Adbusters Quarterly

1243 West 7th Avenue, Vancouver, B.C. V6H 1B7
Phone: (604) 736-9401  Fax: (604) 737-6021
E-mail: adbuster@wimsey.com
Contact: Kalle Lasn, editor; Dan Deresh, managing editor
Circulation: 22,000
Published quarterly

Established 1989. A combative, uncompromising commentator on the politics of media control and environmental strategy. Produced by the Media Foundation. Pays on publication for pieces of 100 to 1,500 words. Rates vary. Contact editors first if planning a lengthy submission. Guidelines available.

### Alberta Sweetgrass

15001 – 112th Avenue N.W., Edmonton, Alta. T5M 2V6
Phone: (403) 455-2945  Fax: (403) 455-7639
Contact: R. John Hayes, editor
Circulation: 7,500

Published monthly

A community newspaper featuring news (300 to 500 words), sports, arts and entertainment, reviews, and features (500 to 1,000 words) about and by First Nations people. Stories should be of provincial interest or have a more local focus, with prominence given to people. Pays $3.00 to $3.60/column inch. "Query first. Sometimes we can talk a near-miss into a good story idea." Guidelines available.

## Alternatives Journal: Environmental Thought, Policy & Action

Faculty of Environmental Studies, University of Waterloo,
    Waterloo, Ont. N2L 3GI
Phone: (519) 888-4545  Fax: (519) 746-0292
E-mail: alternat@watservi.uwaterloo.ca
Contact: Susanna Reid, managing editor
Circulation: 4,000
Published quarterly

Informed analysis of Canadian and international environmental issues. Thought-provoking feature articles, reports of environmental happenings, provocative opinion pieces, and book reviews. Welcomes features (3,000 to 4,000 words), short news reports (500 to 1,000 words), humour, book reviews (750 to 1,000 words), and essays (2,500 to 3,000 words). "*Alternatives* is . . . reflective, topical and Canadian; it plays a uniquely important role in the field of environmental journalism" – Susan Holtz, vice-chair, National Round Table on Environment and Economy. Contributors are unpaid. Guidelines available.

## Anglican Journal

600 Jarvis Street, Room 224, Toronto, Ont. M4Y 2J6
Phone: (416) 924-9199, ext. 304  Fax: (416) 921-4452
E-mail: anglican_journal@ecunet.org
Contact: Bill Glisky, editor
Circulation: 265,000
Published 10 times a year

National publication of the Anglican Church of Canada, established in 1875. Contains news and features from across Canada and abroad. Subjects include news of all denominations and faiths, and articles on a range of social and ethical issues. Stories should be of interest to a national audience. Length 600 to 1,000 words maximum. Major articles earn $200 to $500; lesser features and news stories, $75 to $200; book reviews, $35 (plus the book). Initial inquiry recommended. Guidelines available.

## Annals of Saint Anne de Beaupré
P.O. Box 1000, St.-Anne-de-Beaupré, Que. GOA 3CO
Phone: (418) 827-4538  Fax: (418) 827-4530
Contact: Father Roch Achard, editor
Circulation: 50,000
Published 11 times a year

A general interest religious magazine, established in 1878. Buys fiction and articles with a Catholic dimension. Pays 3¢ to 4¢/word on acceptance for "educational, inspirational, objective, and uplifting" articles up to 1,500 words. Seeks analysis rather than reporting. No poetry. Guidelines available.

## bout de papier
45 Rideau Street, Suite 600, Ottawa, Ont. KIN 5W8
Phone: (613) 241-1391  Fax: (613) 241-5911
Contact: Debra Hulley, managing editor
Circulation: 2,500
Published quarterly

A must-read for all those interested in the world of diplomacy, this bilingual journal examines all aspects of Canadian foreign policy and life in the foreign service. Discusses international politics and global economic and security matters. Each issue includes guest columns, interviews, book reviews, media coverage, and reports on major issues. Contributors are not paid. Welcomes submission inquiries from qualified writers.

## Briarpatch
2138 McIntyre Street, Regina, Sask. S4P 2R7
Phone: (306) 525-2949  Fax: (306) 565-3430
Contact: George Martin Manz, managing editor
Circulation: 2,000
Published 10 times a year

An award-winning regional magazine providing alternative views on issues concerning Saskatchewan and Canada. Carries short critical articles of 600 to 1,100 words on politics, the environment, agriculture, aboriginal and women's rights, and labour. Specializes in investigative, activist journalism, its purpose "to publish articles that would not be published in the mainstream media." No poetry. Contributors are paid in free copies only, but submission inquiries are welcomed. Send short bio.

## British Columbia Report
535 Thurlow Street, Suite 600, Vancouver, B.C. V6E 3L2
Phone: (604) 682-8202  Fax: (604) 682-0964
Contact: Steve Leguire, executive editor
Circulation: 29,000
Published weekly
   This weekly news magazine gives analysis and news of B.C. from a conservative perspective. Preferred length 700 to 1,200 words. Unsolicited freelance material should be "hard news" from B.C.'s regions. Pays a variable rate on publication.

## Canadian Dimension
228 Notre Dame Avenue, Room 401, Winnipeg, Man. R3B 1N7
Phone: (204) 957-1519  Fax: (204) 943-4617
E-mail: info@canadiandimension.mb.ca
Contact: Michelle Torres, office manager
Circulation: 3,000
Published bimonthly
   Fact and analysis that bring Canada and the world into focus. Carries alternative information on issues concerning women, the labour movement, peace politics, Native peoples, the environment, economics, and popular culture. "*CD* is a magazine for people who want to change the world. We debate issues, share ideas, recount our victories, and evaluate our strategies for social change." Articles 600 to 2,000 words. Can occasionally pay those whose sole income comes from writing. Guidelines available.

## Canadian Forum
804 – 251 Laurier Avenue W., Ottawa, Ont. K1P 5J6
Phone: (613) 230-3078  Fax: (613) 233-1458
Contact: Duncan Cameron, editor

Circulation: 10,000
Published 10 times a year

Tackles a wide range of subjects, including politics, national and international affairs, the arts in Canada, economics, travel, civil liberties, the environment, film, and literature. Carries some high-quality fiction. Publishing for 75 years. Articles 2,500 to 3,000 words. Pays an honorarium of $100 per article and $50 per review on publication. Guidelines available.

## Canadian Public Policy

c/o C.M. Beach, School of Policy Studies, Queen's University,
    Kingston, Ont. K7L 3N6
Phone: (613) 545-6644  Fax: (613) 545-6606
E-mail: beach@qucdn.queensu.ca
Contact: Charles M. Beach, editor
Circulation: 1,600
Published quarterly

A bilingual, refereed journal providing a forum for information about economic and social policy developments affecting all Canadians. Reviews books, articles, and government reports. Accepts submissions up to 5,000 words. Submission inquiries welcomed, but no payment is made and a per-page printing fee is charged.

## Companion Magazine

P.O. Box 535, Station F, Toronto, Ont. M4Y 2L8
Phone: (416) 690-5611  Fax: (416) 690-3320
Contact: Friar Richard Riccioli, editor
Circulation: 4,800
Published monthly

A Catholic inspirational magazine whose purpose is to "build community, foster renewal, and provide hope for our readers." Prefers strong human-interest feature articles that are "positive, upbeat, brief, and from a first-hand point of view." Pays 6¢/word on publication for 600 to 1,200 words. Guidelines available.

## Compass: A Jesuit Journal

50 Charles Street E., P.O. Box 400, Station F, Toronto,
    Ont. M4Y 2L8
Phone: (416) 921-0653  Fax: (416) 921-1864

E-mail: 74163.2472@compuserve.com
Contact: Robert Chodos, editor
Circulation: 3,200
Published bimonthly

A review for Catholic and informed general readers, publishing articles on contemporary social and religious issues with an ethical and ecumenical perspective. Judged best Catholic magazine in North America by the Catholic Press Assoc. Articles 750 to 2,000 words. Pays $150 for 750 words, $250 for 1,000 to 1,500 words, $300 to $500 for 2,000 words, on publication. Guidelines available.

## Connexions

P.O. Box 158, Station D, Toronto, Ont. M6T 3J8
Phone: (416) 537-3949
Contact: Ulli Diemer, editor
Circulation: 2,000
Published quarterly

A digest containing reprints from other sources as well as original pieces addressing social and environmental issues from a grassroots perspective. Carries analytical articles on social change and justice, projects, and organizations, and reviews of books, films, and new resources and teaching materials. Pays honoraria when possible. Phone or mail inquiries with ideas welcome.

## Education Forum

60 Mobile Drive, Toronto, Ont. M4A 2P3
Phone: (416) 751-8300  Fax: (416) 751-3394
Contact: Neil Walker, editor
Circulation: 43,000
Published 3 times a year

A magazine of news, views, and personal experience. Published by the Ontario Secondary School Teachers' Federation and distributed to Ontario education workers. Buys articles of 2,000 to 3,000 words. Fees vary. Inquiries welcome. Guidelines available.

## Emergency Librarian

P.O. Box 284, 810 West Broadway, Vancouver, B.C. V5Z 4C9
Phone: (604) 925-0266  Fax: (604) 925-0566
E-mail: rockland@mindlink.bc.ca

Contact: Ken Haycock, editor
Circulation: 26,000
Published 5 times a year

Canada's independent library journal. Lively, provocative articles (1,000 to 4,000 words) address all aspects of library services for children and young adults. Designed for school and public librarians. Pays a small honorarium on publication. Guidelines available.

### Humanist in Canada

P.O. Box 3769, Station C, Ottawa, Ont. KIY 4J8
Phone: (613) 749-8929
Contact: J.E. Piercy, president, Canadian Humanist Publications
Circulation: 1,500
Published quarterly

For non-believers with an interest in social issues, its aim "to print literature with a humanist content, reflecting the principle that human problems can best be solved by people relying on their own capabilities, without belief in the supernatural." Articles 1,000 to 2,500 words. Cannot pay but welcomes submission inquiries. Guidelines available.

### Legion Magazine

359 Kent Street, Suite 407, Ottawa, Ont. K2P OR6
Phone: (613) 235-8741  Fax: (613) 233-7159
Contact: Dan Black, managing editor
Circulation: 475,000
Published 10 times a year

Established 1926. A magazine for Canada's war veterans, RCMP members, forces personnel and their families, and the wider public. Carries news, views, and opinions, and serious articles on issues of interest to veterans, seniors, and others. Subjects include defence, veterans affairs, health, and pensions. Also buys memoirs and nostalgia. Articles 600 to 2,200 words. Pays $150 to $1,200 on acceptance (fee determined after final edit). Query first. Sample copies available on request. Average assessment time is 6 months.

### Maclean's

777 Bay Street, Toronto, Ont. M5W IA7
Phone: (416) 596-5386  Fax: (416) 596-7730

Contact: Robert Lewis, editor
Circulation: 540,000
Published weekly

Canada's most widely read news magazine, with about 2.6 million readers. Examines news events, trends, and issues from a Canadian perspective. Has a broad network of bureaus, with correspondents in 5 Canadian cities and 35 other countries. Staff writers and freelancers contribute to weekly sections on politics, business, entertainment, sports, leisure, science, medicine, and technology. Pays a variable but competitive fee on acceptance.

## McGill News

3605 Mountain Street, Montreal, Que. H3G 2M1
Phone: (514) 398-3552  Fax: (514) 398-7338
E-mail: janicep@martlet1.ian.mcgill.ca
Contact: Janice Paskey, editor
Circulation: 120,000
Published quarterly

For McGill University graduates. Features articles about current affairs, entertainment, the humanities, medicine, and science with a McGill connection, and profiles of graduates. Pays a variable rate on acceptance for features of 1,000 to 2,000 words ($350 to $500 for 2,000 words). Also buys news stories of 200 to 600 words. Prospective contributors may write for a sample copy.

## New Internationalist

1011 Bloor Street W., Toronto, Ont. M6H 1M1
Phone: (416) 588-6478  Fax: (416) 537-6435
Contact: Richard Swift, co-editor
Circulation: 8,000 in Canada; 70,000 worldwide
Published monthly

An uncompromising international periodical providing information and analysis on the major issues concerning international development. Exposes the politics of aid, militarism, and national and multinational exploitation of the developing countries, and discusses racial, gender, and social politics in the developed and developing worlds. Issues are thematic. Articles 500 to 1,800 words. Pays $400 on publication for full-length article. Guidelines available.

## New Maritimes

P.O. Box 31269, Halifax, N.S. B3K 5Y5
Phone: (902) 425-6622
Contact: Scott Milsom, editor
Circulation: 2,300
Published bimonthly

A radical regional commentary carrying some of Canada's best journalism. Highlights areas of interest to Maritimers, addressing issues such as politics, labour, culture, history, social justice, environmentalism, feminism, and minority and welfare rights from an alternative viewpoint. Reviews books relating to the Maritimes. Regularly includes fiction and poetry. Can rarely pay contributors. Guidelines available.

## NeWest Review

P.O. Box 394, R.P.O. University, Saskatoon, Sask. S7N 4J8
Phone: (306) 934-1444  Fax: (306) 242-5004
Contact: D. Larson, manager
Circulation: 1,000
Published bimonthly

Carries news and opinion on western Canadian cultural, social, and political issues. Reviews books and theatre, and carries some fiction and poetry. Articles/stories 1,500 to 2,500 words. Pays $100 for 2,000 words; $25 for reviews; $60 for gazette items (800 words). Pays on publication. Prefers initial proposals. Guidelines available.

## Our Family

P.O. Box 249, Battleford, Sask. S0M 0E0
Phone: (306) 937-7771  Fax: (306) 937-7644
Contact: Nestor Gregoire, editor
Circulation: 10,000
Published monthly

A Christian general interest magazine. Buys photo stories on personalities, events, and issues mostly with religious themes. Pays 7¢ to 11¢/word on acceptance for pieces from 1,000 to 3,000 words. Guidelines available.

## Our Times

390 Dufferin Street, Toronto, Ont. M6K 2A3

Phone: (416) 531-5762  Fax: (416) 533-2397
Contact: Lorraine Endicott, editor
Circulation: 4,000
Published bimonthly
   Produced by a unionized, worker-owned co-operative to focus on current issues vital to today's labour movement. Most contributions written by labour activists to be used as educational tools. Pays small honoraria ($25 for book reviews; $75 to $200 for features of 1,500 to 2,500 words) on acceptance. Guidelines available.

**Peace Magazine**
736 Bathurst Street, Toronto, Ont. M5S 2R4
Phone: (416) 533-7581  Fax: (416) 531-6214
Contact: Metta Spencer, editor
Circulation: 2,000
Published bimonthly
   A magazine providing interviews, commentary, and topical features relating to multilateral disarmament and non-violent conflict resolution. Covers domestic and world issues. Articles 1,000 to 3,000 words. Cannot pay but welcomes submission inquiries. "We prefer clearly focused, thoroughly researched material on topics the mainstream media ignore."

**Perception**
441 MacLaren, 4th Floor, Ottawa, Ont. K2P 2H3
Phone: (613) 236-8977  Fax: (613) 236-2750
Contact: Nancy Perkins, communications co-ordinator
Circulation: 3,500
Published quarterly
   Provides information and analysis on issues of social development, including income security, employment, health and social services, and aboriginal and women's issues. Articles 700 to 1,500 words. Cannot pay but welcomes submission inquiries. Guidelines available.

**Policy Options**
1470, rue Peel, Bureau 200, Montreal, Que. H3A 1T1
Phone: (514) 985-2461  Fax: (514) 985-2559
Contact: Alfred LeBlanc, editor

Circulation: 3,000
Published 10 times a year

Published by the Institute for Research on Public Policy, a national, independent, not-for-profit think-tank. Carries analyses of public policy so as to encourage wide debate of major policy issues. Articles from 2,500 words. Contributors are unpaid, but submission inquiries by qualified writers welcome. Guidelines available.

**The Social Worker**
383 Parkdale Avenue, Suite 402, Ottawa, Ont. KIY 4R4
Phone: (613) 729-6668  Fax: (613) 729-9608
Contact: Penny Sipkes, co-ordinator
Circulation: 13,500
Published quarterly

A bilingual forum in which social workers and others share their knowledge, skills, research, and information with each other and with the general public. Articles around 2,500 words. Cannot pay but welcomes submission inquiries. Guidelines available.

**Teaching Today Magazine**
12644 – 126th Street, Edmonton, Alta. T5L 0X7
Phone: (403) 455-1718  Fax: (403) 451-4786
E-mail: 71023.2150@compuserve.com
Contact: Michael Staley, publisher/editor
Circulation: 10,000
Published 6 times a year

Established 1982. A resource for classroom teachers and administrators providing current information on educational issues and practical new ideas for classroom use. Preferred length 250 to 1,200 words. Cannot pay but welcomes submission inquiries. "Articles that provide solutions to teaching problems and creative ideas based on experience are most welcome." Guidelines available.

**This Magazine**
401 Richmond Street W., Suite 396, Toronto, Ont. M5V 3A8
Phone: (416) 979-8400  Fax: (416) 979-1143
E-mail: this_magazine@intacc.web.net.
Contact: Clive Thompson, editor

Circulation: 7,000

Published 8 times a year

A radical alternative news and opinion magazine carrying investigative features and researched commentary on culture, politics, labour, and other issues. Features of 1,500 to 3,000 words are paid a negotiated fee of between $200 and $400 on publication; $250 to $500 for a cover story. "We prefer clearly focused, thoroughly researched, and sharply written material on topics the mainstream media ignore." Send a query letter. Guidelines available.

### The United Church Observer

478 Huron Street, Toronto, Ont. M5R 2R3

Phone: (416) 960-8500  Fax: (416) 960-8477

Contact: Fran Oliver, editorial assistant

Circulation: 140,000

Published monthly

The national magazine of the United Church of Canada. Provides news of the church, the nation, and the world, while maintaining an independent editorial policy. Prints serious articles on issues such as human rights, social justice, and Christian faith in action, and stories of personal courage – all with a Christian perspective. Also covers the religious dimension of art, literature, and theatre. Articles 850 to 1,000 words. Uses freelancers infrequently. Fees negotiable, paid on publication. Personal stories are paid at lower rates. Guidelines available.

### University of Toronto Magazine

21 King's College Circle, Toronto, Ont. M5S 1A1

Phone: (416) 978-2988  Fax: (416) 978-7430

E-mail: georgec@dur.utoronto.ca

Contact: George Cook, editor

Circulation: 190,000

Published quarterly

Promotes the University of Toronto to its graduates by publishing articles on research, issues, university news, profiles, and more. U. of T. angle must be strong. Pays 25¢ to 60¢/word for articles from 500 to 3,500 words. Guidelines are not available, but editor responds to all inquiries.

## Windspeaker

15001 – 112th Avenue, Edmonton, Alta. T5M 2V6
Phone: (403) 455-2700  Fax: (403) 455-7639
Contact: Linda Caldwell, editor
Circulation: 15,000
Published monthly

A national First Nations newspaper with a regional section focusing on local issues. Includes sports and entertainment, columns, and features of 300 to 800 words. Welcomes stories and profiles on issues of concern to Native peoples and those who work with them. Pays $3.00 to $3.60 per published column inch on publication for multi-source stories and profiles. Guidelines available.

# Special Interest

## Abilities: Canada's Lifestyle Magazine for People with Disabilities

Access Place Canada, College Park, 444 Yonge Street, Toronto,
    Ont. M5B 2H4
Phone: (416) 977-5185  Fax: (416) 977-5098
E-mail: rdc@interlog.com
Contact: Lisa Bendall, editorial co-ordinator
Circulation: 50,000
Published quarterly

A source of information and inspiration for people with disabilities. Articles/stories 1,000 to 2,500 words. Fees, paid on publication, vary and may be negotiated. Guidelines available.

## The Atlantic Co-operator

P.O. Box 1386, Antigonish, N.S. B2G 2L7
Phone: (902) 863-2776  Fax: (902) 863-8077
E-mail: atlcoop@fox.nstn.c2
Contact: Brenda MacKinnon, editor
Circulation: 60,000
Published bi-monthly

Established 1939. An educational resource for co-ops and credit unions throughout Atlantic Canada. Pays about 20¢/word on publication for pieces between 600 and 800 words. Guidelines available.

## Boudoir Noir

P.O. Box 5, Station F, Toronto, Ont. M4Y 2L4
Phone: (416) 591-2387  Fax: (416) 591-1572
E-mail: boudoir@the_wire.com
Contact: Robert Dante, editor
Circulation: 5,000
Published bimonthly

A forthright erotic magazine for people interested in the leather/fetish/consensual SM scene. Aims to "integrate psychosexuality into the larger context of the world as it is, bringing the kink out of the closet into the warm light of day. Query first. Editors will help with resources, contacts. We tend to use the same writers regularly. We are *very* approachable." Pays $25 to $100 on acceptance for 500 to 1,500 words.

## Cannabis Canada

21 Water Street, Vancouver, B.C. V6B 1A1
Phone: (604) 669-9069  Fax: (604) 669-9038
E-mail: muggles@hemppbc.com
Contact: Dana Larsen, editor
Circulation: 8,000
Published monthly

For cannabis consumers and those interested in drugs and drug policy. "We exist to bring an end to prohibition and censorship in Canada and everywhere else. We are printed entirely on tree-free cannabis hemp paper. Read us to see what we print." Articles 700 to 2,500 words. Pays 3 to 4¢/word on publication, depending on quality and content.

## Detective Files Group

1350 Sherbrooke Street W., Suite 600, Montreal, Que. H3G 2T4
Phone: (514) 849-7733  Fax: (514) 849-8330
Contact: Dominick Merle, editor-in-chief
Circulation: 100,000/month
Published bimonthly

A stable of six bimonthly true crime magazines. Stories from 3,000 to 6,000 words. Pays on acceptance $250 to $350 per article including photos. "Over 90 per cent of our readership is in the United States, but we welcome queries on Canadian cases as well." No phone queries. Guidelines available.

## Disability Today
627 Lyons Lane, Suite 203, Oakville, Ont. L6J 5Z7
Phone: (905) 338-6894  Fax: (905) 338-1836
Contact: Jeff Tiessen, editor
Circulation: 45,000
Published quarterly

An access and awareness magazine aimed at better informing readers about physical disabilities and opportunities that exist for this population. Directed particularly toward educators, employers, and advocates. Articles are 1,000 to 3,000 words. Pays about $300 on publication. Guidelines available.

## Dogs in Canada
89 Skymark Avenue, Suite 200, Etobicoke, Ont. M9W 6R4
Phone: (416) 798-9778  Fax: (416) 798-9671
Contact: Allan Reznik, editor
Circulation: 30,000
Published monthly

Geared toward the dog breeder and exhibitor, and the serious purebred dog enthusiast. (A separate annual issue is broadened to appeal to new and prospective dog owners, with complete information on selecting, caring for, and training a pet.) Articles 1,000 to 3,000 words. Pays $150 and up for 1,000 + words, on acceptance. "The monthly is quite specialized while the annual appeals to a broader readership. Query in detail before submitting. Written queries should include outlines and tearsheets for new contributors." Guidelines available.

## Food & Drink
55 Lakeshore Boulevard E., Toronto, Ont. M5E 1A4
Phone: (416) 864-6630  Fax: (416) 365-5935
Contact: Jody Dunn, co-ordinator
Circulation: 300,000

Published quarterly

Established 1988. Published by the Liquor Control Board of Ontario. Pays up to $1/word on publication. Guidelines available.

## Hecate's Loom
P.O. Box 5206, Station B, Victoria, B.C. v8R 6N4
Phone: (604) 388-7370  Fax: (604) 721-1029
E-mail: un837@freenet.victoria.bc.ca
Contact: Yvonne Owens, senior editor
Circulation: 1,500
Published quarterly

Established 1986. Publishes articles on the traditions of paganism, witchcraft, and goddess-worship, past and present, Gaia consciousness, shamanism, history, culture, magic, and herbology. Short fiction, poetry, reviews of pagan books, art, and performance. Cannot pay but welcomes inquiries. Guidelines available.

## Pets Magazine
10 Gateway Boulevard, Suite 490, North York, Ont. M3C 3T4
Phone: (416) 696-5488  Fax: (416) 696-7395
Contact: Edward Zapletal, editor
Circulation: 51,000
Published bimonthly

Offers advice and guidance to Canadian pet owners, including general pet care, human interest (working dogs), obedience and training, grooming, and breeding. Preferred length 500 to 1,500 words. No fiction or poetry. First send one-page outline. No U.S. postage on SASES – only international postage coupons. Pays 12¢ to 15¢/word on publication. Guidelines available.

## Sound & Vision
99 Atlantic Avenue, Suite 302, Toronto, Ont. M6K 3J8
Phone: (416) 535-7611  Fax: (416) 535-6325
Contact: Alan Lofft, editor
Circulation: 30,000
Published bimonthly

An entertaining, informative, and technically literate magazine that explores new audio and video technology, tests new products, and looks at trends in home entertainment. Pays $500 to $900 on acceptance for features of 2,000 to 4,000 words, $250 to $450 for columns (1,000 words). "Writers must combine technical knowledge with a lively, entertaining prose style."

## Stitches: The Journal of Medical Humour

16787 Warden Avenue, R.R.3, Newmarket, Ont. L3Y 4WI
Phone: (905) 853-1884  Fax: (905) 853-6565
E-mail: 74710.2737@compuserve.com
Contact: Simon Hally, editor
Circulation: 42,000
Published 10 times a year

Formerly the *Punch Digest for Canadian Doctors*, a magazine of humour for practising physicians. Pays 30¢ to 35¢/word on publication for 20 to 2,000 words. "Aspiring contributors are encouraged to request a free sample copy of the magazine. We are eager to hear from genuinely funny writers."

## Toronto Computes!

99 Atlantic Avenue, Suite 408, Toronto, Ont. M4V 1M7
Phone: (416) 588-6818  Fax: (416) 588-4110
E-mail: paull@tcpon.com
Contact: Paul Lima, editor
Circulation: 100,000
Published monthly

Runs articles and features about the full spectrum of personal computers and related technologies, with regular software and hardware reviews and an emphasis on local events. Pays 30 days after publication for articles of 100 to 5,000 words. Fees negotiable. Inquiries first, please. Guidelines available.

## Vancouver Computes!

3661 West 4th Avenue, Suite 8, Vancouver, B.C. V6R 1P2
Phone: (604) 733-5596  Fax: (604) 732-4280
E-mail: scribe@mindlink.bc.ca
Contact: Linda Richards, editor
Circulation: 40,000
Published monthly

Topical news and information for today's computer user. Articles 200 to 1,000 words. Pays 10 to 15¢/word on publication. "We are especially in need of stories with a strong regional focus. B.C. is our beat, and there's room for contributors here."

## Winetidings

5165 Sherbrooke Street W., Suite 414, Montreal, Que. H4A 1T6
Phone: (514) 481-5892  Fax: (514) 481-9699
Contact: Tony Aspler, editor
Circulation: 16,000
Published 8 times a year

A magazine for discerning wine lovers. Reports on price trends and vintages, offers recipes, and profiles well-known wine cellars. Also compares wines and grape types, and reviews developments in the Canadian wine industry. Article length varies from 500 to 1,500 words, the longer paying $200. Pays on publication. "Advanced knowledge of wine and wine tasting is a prerequisite."

## World of Wheels

1200 Markham Road, Suite 220, Scarborough, Ont. M1H 3C3
Phone: (416) 438-7777  Fax: (416) 438-5333
Contact: Joe Duarte, editor
Circulation: 127,000
Published bimonthly

A magazine for auto enthusiasts, and for those interested in developments in the auto industry and their impact on Canada. Evaluates and compares the latest in cars, light pickup trucks, vans, and sport-utility vehicles. Pays 30¢/word on publication for articles of between 400 and 2,500 words.

## Sports & Outdoors

## The Atlantic Salmon Journal

P.O. Box 429, St. Andrews, N.B. E0G 2X0
Phone: (506) 529-4581  Fax: (506) 529-4985
Contact: Harry Bruce, editor
Circulation: 13,000
Published quarterly

A glossy, full-colour magazine for serious anglers who fly fish and Atlantic salmon conservationists. Carries articles on researching salmon and where to catch them, and focuses on angling adventures and conservation. Knowledgeable, lucid, and lively prose as well as superior photography and art. Pays $300 to $500 on publication for articles of 1,500 to 2,500 words, $50 to $100 for short items, including book reviews. "We normally expect writers to provide photos for their stories." Guidelines available.

### B.C. Outdoors

1132 Hamilton Street, Suite 202, Vancouver, B.C. v6b 2s2
Phone: (604) 687-1581  Fax: (604) 687-1925
Contact: Karl Bruin, editor
Circulation: 40,000
Published 8 times a year

Carries articles up to 2,000 words on outdoor recreation and conservation – wildlife, camping, hunting, sports shooting, and saltwater and freshwater fishing. Pays 27¢/word on publication for articles accompanied by photos. Guidelines available.

### Camping Canada

2585 Skymark Avenue, Suite 306, Mississauga, Ont. l4w 4l5
Phone: (905) 624-8218  Fax: (905) 624-6764
Contact: Diane Batten, editor
Circulation: 50,000
Published 7 times a year

Focuses on recreational vehicle lifestyle articles featuring travel routes, destinations, and technical information on motor homes, wide-body vans, trailers, and trailer homes. Accepts articles of 1,500 to 3,000 words on rv camping in Canada. Destinations stories should have photos/slides with credits. Fees negotiable, paid on publication. Guidelines available.

### Canadian Biker

P.O. Box 4122, Victoria, B.C. v8x 3x4
Phone: (604) 384-0333  Fax: (604) 384-1832
E-mail: canbike@islandnet.com
Contact: Len Creed, publisher/editor
Circulation: 25,000
Published 8 times a year

A family-oriented motorcycle magazine carrying a variety of

articles and columns for sport and touring enthusiasts. Subjects include new products, events, racing, vintage, and custom motorcycling. Preferred length 500 to 1,500 words. "Articles paid according to quality rather than quantity. Preference given to work sent on 3½ in. disk with hard copy and a minimum of two photos (captioned)." Pays a variable rate on publication. Guidelines available.

## Canadian Horseman

225 Industrial Parkway S., P.O. Box 670, Aurora, Ont. L4G 4J9
Phone: (905) 727-0107  Fax: (905) 841-1530
Contact: Lee Benson, managing editor
Circulation: 10,000
Published bimonthly

Profiles the Western rider, discussing everything from training and horse care to farm management. Interesting reading for horse enthusiasts of all disciplines, competitive and non-competitive. Preferred length 500 to 1,500 words. Pays a negotiated rate on publication. Guidelines available.

## Canadian Rodeo News

2116 – 27th Avenue N.E., Suite 223, Calgary, Alta. T2E 7A6
Phone: (403) 250-7292  Fax: (403) 250-6926
Contact: Kirby Meston, editor
Circulation: 48,000
Published monthly

A tabloid of news, views, and opinions from the Canadian and U.S. rodeo circuit. Also accepts articles related to the West or to Canada's Western heritage. Pays $50 on publication for stories of 1,000 to 1,200 words, $25 for 500 to 600 words, $10 for photos. Phone editor with ideas before submitting. Guidelines available.

## Canadian Sportfishing Magazine

937 Centre Road, Dept. 2020, Waterdown, Ont. LOR 2H0
Phone: (905) 689-1112  Fax: (905) 689-2065
E-mail: 70713.300.compuserve.com
Contact: Kerry Knudsen, editor
Circulation: 45,000
Published 6 times a year

Aimed at active readers engaged in a range of sportfishing

techniques and issues in Canada. Accepts articles of 250 to 2,500 words. Pays 15 to 25¢/word on publication. Guidelines available.

## The Canadian Sportsman
P.O. Box 129, 25 Old Plank Road, Straffordville, Ont. NOJ 1YO
Phone: (519) 866-5558  Fax: (519) 866-5596
Contact: Gary Foerster, editor
Circulation: 5,500
Published biweekly

"The voice of harness racing since 1870." Carries features and news mostly about harness racing in Canada. Mail, phone, or fax inquiries welcome. Fees negotiable.

## Canadian Thoroughbred
225 Industrial Parkway S., P.O. Box 670, Aurora, Ont. L4G 4J9
Phone: (905) 727-0107  Fax: (905) 841-1530
Contact: Susan Jane Anstey, publisher
Circulation: 5,000
Published bimonthly

Canada's national journal on thoroughbred racing features news and information on horses and their owners – pedigrees and stable product updates. Fees negotiable. A very specialist market, so always inquire first. Guidelines available.

## Canadian Yachting
395 Matheson Boulevard E., Mississauga, Ont. L4Z 2H2
Phone: (905) 890-1846  Fax: (905) 890-5769
Contact: Graham Jones, editor
Circulation: 15,000
Published bimonthly

Written for sailboat enthusiasts across Canada. Includes adventure, regattas, profiles, maintenance, boat reviews, news and gossip for cruisers, racers, keelboat and dinghy sailors. Features of 2,000 to 3,000 words earn $400 to $600; shorter pieces for departments (1,200 to 2,000 words) earn $200 to $250. Pays 60 days after publication. Send initial letter of inquiry.

## Cycle Canada
86 Parliament Street, Suite 3B, Toronto, Ont. M5A 2Y6

Phone: (416) 362-7966  Fax: (416) 362-3950
Contact: Bruce Reeve, editor
Circulation: 31,000
Published 10 times a year

A magazine written for Canadian motorcycle enthusiasts, with product tests and evaluations, technical information, and how-to maintenance articles, plus profiles in the world of biking. Pays on acceptance $50 for brief news items of approx. 100 words, $500 for a top feature up to 4,000 words plus photos.

### Diver Magazine

10991 Shellbridge Way, Suite 295, Richmond, B.C. v6x 3c6
Phone: (604) 273-4333  Fax: (604) 273-0813
Contact: Stephanie Bold, editor
Circulation: 15,000
Published 9 times a year

For North American sport divers. Carries regular articles on travel destinations and snorkelling, and scuba and deep-water diving. Also covers marine life and underwater photography. Articles 500 to 1,000 words. Pays $3/column inch after publication. Check guidelines before submitting material.

### Explore: Canada's Outdoor Adventure Magazine

301 – 14th Street N.W., Suite 420, Calgary, Alta. T2N 2AI
Phone: (403) 270-8890  Fax: (403) 270-7922
Contact: Marion Harrison, editor
Circulation: 30,000
Published bimonthly

For people who enjoy self-propelled outdoor recreational activities such as backpacking, cycling, paddling, and backcountry skiing. Articles of 1,500 to 2,500 words cover adventure, outdoor equipment evaluations, new products, and environmental issues. Pays $500 for 2,000 words on publication. Payment includes use of photos. Fees may in some cases be negotiated. "Published writers query first. Unpublished writers should send ms. and photos on spec." Guidelines available.

### Gam On Yachting

250 The Esplanade, Suite 202, Toronto, Ont. M5A 1J2

Phone: (416) 368-1559  Fax: (416) 368-2831
Contact: Karin Larson, publisher/editor
Circulation: 17,000
Published 8 times a year

A magazine for the racing and cruising sailor, with how-to articles, upcoming events, harbour profiles, book reviews, safety information, and humour. Special issues coincide with Canadian boat shows. "Exists as a medium of communication between Canadian sailors, and as such cannot pay for contributions."

**Horse Sport Magazine**
225 Industrial Parkway S., P.O. Box 670, Aurora, Ont. L4G 4J9
Phone: (905) 727-0107  Fax: (905) 841-1530
Contact: Susan Stafford, managing editor
Circulation: 10,000
Published monthly

An authoritative equestrian periodical featuring articles on horse care, riding and training techniques, breeding, animal health, and the industry at large. Provides coverage of equestrian sporting events in Canada and abroad, profiles of top riders, and how-to articles. Preferred length 1,000 to 2,000 words. Pays 10¢ to 15¢/word on publication. Contact editor before submitting. Guidelines available.

**Horsepower**
225 Industrial Parkway S., P.O. Box 670, Aurora, Ont. L4G 4J9
Phone: (905) 727-0107  Fax: (905) 841-1530
Contact: Susan Stafford, managing editor
Circulation: 20,000
Published bimonthly

Provides young riders and horse lovers with advice on horse care, feeding, and tips for riding and stable skills, plus profiles, puzzles, and contests. Pays $50 for 500 to 700 words, $75 for 1,000 words, on publication. "Our editorial focus is always on safety. Submissions must be horse-related (English or Western, all breeds), and suitable for pre-teens and young teens." Contact editor before submitting. Guidelines available.

**Horses All**
4000 – 19th Street N.E., Calgary, Alta. T2E 6P8

Phone: (403) 250-6633
Contact: Micky Dumont, editor
Circulation: 10,000
Published monthly

A tabloid carrying stories about Canadian horses and their owners, with a special section devoted to young riders. Pays on acceptance. Submissions are edited to fit the need. Fee offered is decided by editor, who sends a cheque. Writers who cash their cheques have accepted the terms – a simple system!

## Hot Water

2585 Skymark Avenue, Unit 306, Mississauga, Ont. L4W 4L5
Phone: (905) 624-8218  Fax: (905) 624-6764
Contact: Pam Cottrell, editor
Circulation: 15,000
Published quarterly

For personal watercraft owners. Carries features on newest PWC models and other jet-driven boats plus all accessories that contribute to their enjoyment. Also covers technical aspects of the sport, racing and other events, and destination stories. Preferred feature length 1,500 to 3,000 words. Pays $350 for 2,000 words plus photos, on publication. A new magazine looking for writers with an interest and knowledge of watersports.

## Impact Magazine

2007 – 2nd Street S.W., Calgary, Alta. T2S 1S4
Phone: (403) 228-0605  Fax: (403) 228-0627
Contact: Heather Ellwood-Wright, editor
Circulation: 35,000
Published bimonthly

Features health, fitness, and sports for the active and physically fit of Calgary. All content focused on Calgary and surrounds. Articles 750 to 1,000 words. Query all ideas by phone or letter before submitting. "Our budget is very limited and we pay accordingly."

## Ontario Out of Doors

777 Bay Street, 6th Floor, Toronto, Ont. M5W 1A7
Phone: (416) 596-5908  Fax: (416) 596-2517
Contact: Burton Myers, editor

Circulation: 89,000
Published 10 times a year

Established 1969. A magazine for Ontario's hunters and anglers. Carries how-to and where-to articles on topics such as boating, firearms, archery, and backroad touring. Regular columns on hunting, fishing, wildlife, camp cooking, dogs, fly fishing, scientific research, and new products. Pays on acceptance for articles of 500 to 1,500 words. Fees negotiated; average feature earns $350 to $700. Pays $500 to $750 for cover photo. Guidelines available.

## Ontario Snowmobiler

18540 Centre Street, R.R.3, Mount Albert, Ont. LOG IMO
Phone: (905) 473-7009  Fax: (905) 473-5217
Contact: Terrence Kehoe, publisher
Circulation: 80,000
Published monthly, September–January

Informs Ontario snowmobilers of industry developments, snowmobile people, clubs, programs, and travel. Pays $75 to $100 on acceptance for 400 to 800 words. Uses freelancers infrequently.

## Outdoor Canada

703 Evans Avenue, Suite 202, Toronto, Ont. M9C 5E9
Phone: (416) 695-0311  Fax: (416) 695-0381
Contact: Teddi Brown, editor
Circulation: 90,000
Published 8 times a year

A magazine dedicated to the use and conservation of Canada's outdoors. Carries articles on fishing, boating, hunting, cross-country skiing, snowmobiling, canoeing, hiking, outdoor photography, and camping. "Concentrates on destination and service stories that help readers get more out of their outdoor experiences. Canadian content only." Pays a variable rate ($200 to $450) on publication for pieces from 800 to 2,500 words. Invites on-spec submissions. Guidelines available.

## The Outdoor Edge

5829 – 97th Street, Edmonton, Alta. T6E 3J2
Phone: (403) 448-0381  Fax: (403) 438-3244
Contact: Fiona Bartel, managing editor

Circulation: 56,000
Published bimonthly

Targeting hunters and anglers, circulated among members of Western Canada's fish & game associations and wildlife federations. Articles 1,500 to 2,000 words. Pays $150 to $200 on publication for features. "Articles must be accompanied by a selection of good quality photos. Please don't send queries – we prefer to read the actual manuscript. All materials returned." Guidelines available.

### Pacific Golf Magazine

4180 Lougheed Highway, Suite 401, Burnaby, B.C. v5c 6a7
Phone: (604) 299-7311  Fax: (604) 299-9188
Contact: Bonnie Irving, editor
Circulation: 16,000
Published bimonthly

Golfing personalities and issues, equipment and course news, and feature-length stories of interest to both serious and beginning golfers. Affiliated to the B.C. PGA. Pay rates vary with project.

### Pacific Yachting

1132 Hamilton Street, Suite 202, Vancouver, B.C. v6b 2s2
Phone: (604) 687-1581  Fax: (604) 687-1925
Contact: Duart Snow, editor
Circulation: 25,000
Published monthly

Stories written from first-hand experience relating to boating on Canada's west coast for Western Canada's sailboat and powerboat owners. Carries racing reports, adventure, and articles (800 to 2,000 words) on coastal and offshore cruising, powerboat handling, and the latest technical information. "Writers must be familiar with our special-interest viewpoint, language, and orientation." Buys photos and stories together. Pays on publication.

### Power Boating Canada

2585 Skymark Avenue, Suite 306, Mississauga, Ont. l4w 4l5
Phone: (905) 624-8218  Fax: (905) 624-6764
Contact: Pam Cottrell, editor
Circulation: 40,000
Published bimonthly

Carries stories on powerboat performance and evaluates new equipment and boating techniques. Also covers waterskiing. Pays around $350 on publication for a feature of 1,500 to 2,000 words with photos. Query first with ideas.

### Recreation Canada

306 – 1600 James Naismith Drive, Gloucester, Ont. K1B 5N4
Phone: (613) 748-5651  Fax: (613) 748-5854
E-mail: cpra@cdnsport.ca
Contact: Heather Totten, managing editor
Circulation: 2,000
Published 5 times a year
Focuses on issues, research, and trends relating to innovative leisure programs and facilities, the environment, arts and culture, active living, and healthy communities. Preferred length 1,500 to 2,500 words. Cannot pay but welcomes submissions. "We rely on volunteer writers who are usually professionals or volunteers in the parks, leisure, and recreation field."

### Score: Canada's Golf Magazine

287 MacPherson Avenue, Toronto, Ont. M4V 1A4
Phone: (416) 928-2909  Fax: (416) 928-1357
Contact: Bob Weeks, managing editor
Circulation: 125,000
Published 8 times a year
A national golf magazine with regional inserts (Ontario and Western Canada). Profiles prominent golfers and golfing personalities, and reviews courses, clubs, and equipment. Also carries articles on travel and international competitions, and instructional pieces. Pays 50¢/word on acceptance for articles of 750 to 1,750 words – sometimes more for detailed stories. Guidelines available.

### Ski Canada

117 Indian Road, Toronto, Ont. M6R 2V5
Phone: (416) 538-2293  Fax: (416) 538-2475
Contact: Iain MacMillan, editor
Circulation: 57,000
Published 7 times a year
Published during the ski season, with a balanced mix of entertain-

ment and information for both the experienced and the novice-intermediate skier and snowboarder. "Published from early autumn through winter (with one summer issue), *SC* covers equipment, travel, instruction, competition, fashion, and general skiing- and alpine-related news and stories. Query letters are preferred – no phone calls. Replies will take time. Note: yearly editorial schedules are set at least six months before commencement of publishing season." Articles 400 to 2,500 words. Pays (within 30 days of publication) between $100 (news) and $500 to $800 (features), depending on length, research necessary, and writer's experience.

**Snow Goer**
130 Spy Court, Markham, Ont. L3R 5H6
Phone: (905) 475-9440  Fax: (905) 475-9560
E-mail: cknowles@fox.nstn.ca
Contact: Chris Knowles, editor
Published quarterly
   Provides information for snowmobilers about new products, touring destinations, and safe riding techniques. Pay rates vary for articles of 200 to 1,500 words. Pays on acceptance. "We're particularly interested in touring stories from experienced writers."

**Western Skier**
P.O. Box 430, 1132 – 98th Street, North Battleford, Sask. S9A 2Y5
Phone: (306) 445-7477  Fax: (306) 445-1977
Contact: Rod McDonald, publisher
Circulation: 28,000
Published 5 times a year (November to March)
   A magazine targeting ski enthusiasts from Manitoba to B.C. Articles to inform and entertain family-oriented skiers and junior and recreational racers. Covers resorts, equipment, and fashions, with fiction and racing features. Circulated to provincial alpine associations and by subscription. Pays 20¢/word on publication for articles of 1,500 to 2,500 words. Guidelines available.

**Western Sportsman**
P.O. Box 737, Regina, Sask. S4P 3A8
Phone: (306) 352-2773  Fax: (306) 565-2440
Contact: Brian Bowman, editor

Circulation: 26,000
Published bimonthly
   Provides residents of Alberta, Saskatchewan, Manitoba, and British Columbia with news and features on hunting, fishing, wildlife, camping, backpacking, canoeing, and other outdoor activities. Articles 1,800 to 2,500 words. Pays up to $300 on publication with photos. "Our requirements are seasonal and regional – hunting stories for fall, fishing stories for spring, all focusing on the western Canadian experience. Stories generally relate to personal experience rather than 'how-to' or 'where-to'." Guidelines available.

## Travel & Tourism

**Above & Beyond**
P.O. Box 2348, Yellowknife, N.W.T. X1A 2P7
Phone: (403) 873-2299  Fax: (403) 873-2295
Contact: Jake Ootes, editor
Circulation: 25,000
Published quarterly
   Glossy, full-colour inflight magazine for First Air and Air Inuit carrying articles pertaining to Arctic areas (mainly Northwest Territories, Arctic Quebec, and Greenland), its people, communities, lifestyles, tourist attractions, and commercial activities. Prefers articles 1,000 to 1,500 words. Pays $300 per article, $15 per published photo, on publication. "Assignments are not given to new freelancers. Commitment to publish provided only upon receipt of article with colour photos/slides." Guidelines available.

**Beautiful British Columbia**
929 Ellery Street, Victoria, B.C. V9A 7B4
Phone: (604) 384-5456  Fax: (604) 384-2812
Contact: Bryan McGill, editor-in-chief
Circulation: 15,000
Published bimonthly
   Established 1959. Publishes non-fiction stories about British Columbia, focusing on geography and travel. No poetry or fiction. Articles 1,500 to 2,500 words, 50¢/word, pays on acceptance. Guide-

lines available. "Almost all the freelance material we publish is by established B.C. writers."

## Canadian

199 Avenue Road, 3rd Floor, Toronto, Ont. M5R 2J3
Phone: (416) 962-9184  Fax: (416) 962-2380
Contact: Kathleen Hurd, managing editor
Published monthly

An inflight magazine for Canadian Airlines International and its affiliates. Welcomes high-quality contributions from writers and photographers. Especially interested in adventure travel and people with unusual hobbies. Articles 300 to 1,000 words. Pays top rates on publication. Mail or fax inquiries. No phone approaches, please. Guidelines available.

## Discover Vancouver and Whistler

1001 Wharf Street, 3rd Floor, Victoria, B.C. V8W 1T6
Phone: (604) 388-4324  Fax: (604) 388-6166
Contact: Cathy Leahy, editor
Circulation: 30,000
Published annually

A tourist guide targeting Japanese visitors and featuring articles on vacation activities in Vancouver and Whistler. Published in Japanese, the articles are usually written in English and then translated. Preferred length 2,500 words. Pay rates vary. Query first.

## enRoute

7 Chemin Bates, Outremont, Que. H2V 1A6
Phone: (514) 270-0688  Fax: (514) 270-4050
E-mail: info@enroute.publicor.com
Contact: Lise Ravary, editor-in-chief
Circulation: 125,000 printed, 350,000 readership
Published monthly

Air Canada's inflight magazine. Publishes strong Canadian pieces on business and technical trends, travel, successful personalities, fashion, and fine dining, aimed at the business flier. Pay rates vary depending on project. Uses published writers only. No unsolicited manuscripts; inquire first with ideas and enclose tearsheets. Guidelines available.

## Essential Victoria

1001 Wharf Street, 3rd Floor, Victoria, B.C. v8w 1t6
Phone: (604) 388-4324  Fax: (604) 388-6166
Contact: Kirsten Meincke, editor
Circulation: 8,000
Published biannually

To entertain and inform affluent, educated travellers and hotel guests in Victoria. Articles 1,000 to 3,000 words. Pays a negotiated fee on publication. Guidelines available.

## LeisureWays

2 Carlton Street, Suite 801, Toronto, Ont. m5b 1j3
Phone: (416) 595-5007  Fax: (416) 924-6308
Contact: Deborah Milton, editor
Circulation: 630,000
Published bimonthly

A Southern Ontario travel and leisure magazine financed by the CAA and circulated among Ontario members. Carries articles on personalities, interesting places, recipes, culture, current events, and ingenious entrepreneurs. Also automotive-related pieces. Articles (800 to 1,500 words) should be accompanied by suitable colour slides. Pays 50¢/word on acceptance. Line-ups for following year made in late September. Guidelines available.

## Sea'scape

1001 Wharf Street, 3rd Floor, Victoria, B.C. v8w 1t6
Phone: (604) 388-4324  Fax: (604) 388-4324
Contact: Janice Strong, director, special projects
Circulation: 100,000
Published quarterly

To entertain and inform regular and occasional travellers aboard B.C. Ferries between the mainland and B.C. islands. Articles 1,000 to 2,500 words. Pay rates may be negotiated. Pays on publication.

## Travel à la carte

136 Walton Street, Port Hope, Ont. lia in5
Phone: (905) 885-7948  Fax: (905) 885-7202
Contact: Donna Carter, editor

Circulation: 52,000
Published bimonthly

Destination travel articles both international and Canadian. Focuses on attractions, customs, and historical background where appropriate. Stories of 1,500 to 2,500 words concentrate on well-frequented destinations rather than the remote. Works with a regular group of established writers, and only rarely accepts submissions from new writers, so an initial query letter along with a sample of published writing essential. Fee negotiable. Pays within 60 days of publication. Guidelines available.

## Two Nation Vacation

1001 Wharf Street, 3rd Floor, Victoria, B.C. v8w 1t6
Phone: (604) 388-4324  Fax: (604) 388-6166
Contact: Janice Strong, director, special projects
Circulation: 60,000
Published annually

A vacation guide to promote and encourage travel to and around the region known as Cascadia, encompassing Oregon, Washington, British Columbia, and Alberta. Articles 1,000 to 2,000 words. Pay rates may be negotiated. Pays on publication. Query first.

## Westworld Magazine

4180 Lougheed Highway, Suite 401, Burnaby, B.C. v5c 6a7
Phone: (604) 299-7311  Fax: (604) 299-9188
Contact: Robin Roberts, editor
Circulation: 500,000
Published quarterly

Distributed to members of the BCAA. Features local and international travel and automotive-related articles. Pays 50¢/word on publication for articles of 800 to 1,200 words. "Query with a one-page outline of proposed article, and include published samples." Guidelines available.

## Where Calgary

1 Palliser Square, 125 – 9th Avenue S.E., Suite 250, Calgary, Alta. t2g 0p6
Phone: (403) 299-1888  Fax: (403) 299-1899
Contact: Jennifer MacLeod, editor

Circulation: 25,000
Published monthly
   News of events and attractions for visitors. Also includes restaurant and entertainment reviews, and shopping guides. Cover stories highlight things to do and see. Buys non-fiction of 500 to 800 words, and pays a $275 standard rate on publication.

## Where Halifax/Dartmouth

5475 Spring Garden Road, Box 14, Suite 302, Halifax,
   N.S. B3J 3T2
Phone: (902) 420-9943  Fax: (902) 429-9058
Contact: Karen Janik, editor
Circulation: 25,000
Published 10 times a year
   What to do and where to go in the Halifax/Dartmouth area. Shopping, sightseeing, events – anything of interest to visitors. Welcomes written inquiries with story ideas. Articles/pieces 500 to 800 words. Fees average $150 for 800 words, paid on publication.

## Where Vancouver

2208 Spruce Street, Vancouver, B.C. v6H 2P3
Phone: (604) 736-5586  Fax: (604) 736-3465
Contact: Louise Whitney, editor
Circulation: 40,000
Published monthly
   A visitors' guide incorporating entertainment listings, its aim to provide an intelligent city guide for the upscale traveller. Monthly events sections are popular features. Articles 1,200 to 1,500 words. Pay rates vary depending on project, but pays about $250 for 1,200 words. Writers should first contact editor as all assignments are commissioned.

## Where Vancouver Island

1001 Wharf Street, 3rd Floor, Victoria, B.C. v8w 1T6
Phone: (604) 388-4324  Fax: (604) 388-6166
Contact: Cathy Leahy, managing editor
Circulation: 60,000
Published annually
   A visitors' guide to the island (excluding the city of Victoria),

providing useful information on regional attractions, events, shopping, and dining. Recent feature article topics have included beachcombing and island realty. Preferred length 1,500 words. Pay rates vary with project. Pays on publication.

## Where Victoria

1001 Wharf Street, 3rd Floor, Victoria, B.C. v8w 1t6
Phone: (604) 388-4324  Fax: (604) 388-6166
Contact: Kirsten Meincke, editor
Circulation: 30,000
Published monthly

A guide for visitors and residents featuring dining, shopping, entertainment, galleries, and attractions. Articles 750 to 1,500 words. Pays a negotiated fee on publication. "We also welcome student submissions for no pay but carrying byline." Guidelines available.

## Women's

## B.C. Woman

704 Clarkson Street, New Westminster, B.C. v3m 1e2
Phone: (604) 540-8448  Fax: (604) 524-0041
Contact: Anne Brennan, editor
Circulation: 33,000
Published monthly

Designed to inspire and celebrate the achievements of B.C. women, and to inform, entertain, and provide a forum for discussion of issues of importance to B.C. women. Pays 10¢ to 30¢/word for articles of 800 to 3,000 words 30 days after publication. "We negotiate a flat fee for each story, based on length, research required, complexity of topic, and writer's skill level. Send written queries with writing samples. All stories must be targeted to the B.C. market. Spec. manuscripts are welcome, though it sometimes takes several months to respond." Guidelines available.

## Canadian Living

25 Sheppard Avenue W., North York, Ont. m2n 6s7
Phone: (416) 733-7600  Fax: (416) 733-8683

Contact: Bonnie Cowan, editor
Circulation: 586,000
Published 13 times a year

A vastly popular mass-market magazine emphasizing practical information to help Canadian families better cope with today's changing world. Also carries articles on food, beauty, fashion, decorating, crafts, contemporary living, health, and fitness. Prefers original manuscripts of 300 to 2,000 words. Pays on acceptance. Fee depends on kind of article and writer's experience. Guidelines available.

## Chatelaine

777 Bay Street, 8th Floor, Toronto, Ont. M5W 1A7
Phone: (416) 596-5425  Fax: (416) 596-5516
E-mail: ishapiro@interlog.com
Contact: Rona Maynard, editor
Circulation: 900,000
Published monthly

High-quality glossy magazine addressing the needs and preferences of Canadian women. Covers current issues, personalities, lifestyles, health, relationships, travel, and politics. Runs features of 1,500 to 2,500 words (pay rate starts at $1,250), and regular 500-word "upfront" columns on parenting, health, nutrition, and fitness (fees start at $350). "For all serious articles, deep, accurate, and thorough research and rich details are required. Features on beauty, food, fashion, and home decorating are supplied by staff writers and editors only." Buys first North American serial rights in English and French (to cover possible use in French-language edition). Pays on acceptance. Query first with brief outline. Guidelines available.

## Focus on Women

1218 Langley Street, Suite 3A, Victoria, B.C. V8W 1W2
Phone: (604) 388-7231  Fax: (604) 383-1140
E-mail: uc698@freenet.victoria.bc.ca
Contact: Kerry Slavens, editor
Circulation: 30,000
Published monthly

A magazine serving women of Vancouver Island and the West Coast. Covers political, health, and social issues, local news and profiles, and relationships. Pays 10¢/word on publication; $250 for features (2,000 to 2,500 words). "Articles should relate to West Coast women and should include photos when possible. Photo fees negotiable. We do not accept queries – only articles on spec. Allow four weeks for response."

## Homemaker's Magazine

25 Sheppard Avenue W., Suite 100, North York, Ont. M2N 6S7
Phone: (416) 733-7600  Fax: (416) 733-8683
Contact: Sally Armstrong, editor-in-chief
Circulation: 1.6 million
Published 8 times a year

Directed toward women aged 25 to 54 with children at home. Articles of 1,200 to 2,500 words address issues of particular concern to women, their families, and communities. There is a strong emphasis on relationships. Also published in French as *Madame au Foyer*. Pays a variable rate. Guidelines available.

## Today's Bride

37 Hanna Avenue, Suite 1, Toronto, Ont. M6K 1X1
Phone: (416) 537-2604  Fax: (416) 538-1794
Contact: Shirley-Anne Ohannessian, assistant editor
Circulation: 100,000
Published twice a year

Complete how-to advice on planning and co-ordinating formal weddings. Pays $200 to $300 on acceptance for 800 to 1,500 words. "Concentrate on anecdotal or unique wedding-related articles. All travel and standard planning pieces written in-house."

## You Magazine

37 Hanna Avenue, Suite 1, Toronto, Ont. M6K 1X1
Phone: (416) 537-2604  Fax: (416) 538-1794
Contact: Bettie Bradley, editor
Circulation: 226,000
Published quarterly

A magazine for the woman of the nineties who cares about how she looks, how she feels, how she eats, and her level of fitness. Pays $250 to $300 on acceptance for feature articles of 800 to 1,500 words. Guidelines available.

## Youth & Children's

### Chickadee

179 John Street, Suite 500, Toronto, Ont. M5T 3G5
Phone: (416) 971-5275  Fax: (416) 971-5294
Contact: Carolyn Meredith, managing editor
Circulation: 110,000
Published 10 times a year

A magazine focusing on science and nature that offers 3- to 8-year-olds a bright, lively look at the world. Designed to entertain and educate, each issue contains photographs, illustrations, fiction, poetry, an animal story, puzzles, a science experiment, and a pullout poster. Pays $250 on acceptance for stories of between 800 and 900 words. "Avoid anthropomorphic and religious material. Keep in mind the age range of readers, but do not talk down to them." Guidelines available.

### Kids World Magazine

108 – 93 Lombard Avenue, Winnipeg, Man. R3B 3B1
Phone: (204) 942-2214  Fax: (204) 943-8991
Contact: Stuart Slayen, editor
Circulation: 225,000
Published 5 times a year

A general interest magazine for elementary students aged 9 to 12, distributed nationally through schools, with a special emphasis on entertainment and motivation. Articles 400 to 1,000 words. Pays 45 days after acceptance. "Rates vary, depending on story. Writers are encouraged to phone editor to discuss story ideas before submitting." Guidelines available.

### OWL

179 John Street, Suite 500, Toronto, Ont. M5T 3G5
Phone: (416) 971-5275  Fax: (416) 971-5294
E-mail: owl.communications@cimtegration.com
Contact: Keltie Thomas, managing editor
Circulation: 100,000
Published 10 times a year

A discovery magazine for 8- to 12-year-olds. Sparks children's curiosity about the world around them. Topics include science, technology, animals, and the environment. Pays around $200 on publication for 500 to 800 words. Prefers submission inquiries. Strongly recommends writers check back issues (available in libraries) for a sense of *OWL*'s approach.

## TG Magazine: Voices of Today's Generation

70 University Avenue, Suite 1050, Toronto, Ont. M5J 2M4
Phone: (416) 597-8297  Fax: (416) 597-0661
Contact: Barbara McIntosh, editorial board director
Circulation: 100,000
Published quarterly

A magazine for and by Canadian teenagers, carrying articles on fashion, sports, fitness, nutrition, careers, as well as profiles of people of importance to teens. Also prints fiction. Concerned with issues of head and heart, promoting youth empowerment, and publishing student work only. Cannot pay but welcomes youth submission inquiries – no adult submissions accepted. Guidelines available.

## Tree House Family

179 John Street, Suite 500, Toronto, Ont. M5T 3G5
Phone: (416) 971-5275  Fax: (416) 971-5294
Contact: Jane Weeks, managing editor
Circulation: 180,000
Published quarterly

*Tree House Family* is sent to the parents of *OWL* and *Chickadee* readers. Written primarily for busy mothers of 3- to 12-year-olds, with quick, practical information and ideas. Stories run from 500 to 1,500 words. Fees, paid on acceptance, range from $200 up. Guidelines available.

## Watch Magazine

401 Richmond Street W., Suite 245, Toronto, Ont. M5V 1X3
Phone: (416) 595-1313  Fax: (416) 595-1312
Contact: Paul Andersen, managing editor
Circulation: 25,000
Published monthly

Promoted as "the student perspective on culture, issues, and trends," this magazine aims to provide a forum for youth to express their ideas. Features arts and entertainment (music/film/video) and social issues. Articles 200 to 1,400 words. Written by 13- to 20-year-olds, *Watch* uses some adult freelancers as editors and writing tutors for its young writers.

## What! A Magazine
108 – 93 Lombard Avenue, Winnipeg, Man. R3B 3B1
Phone: (204) 942-2214  Fax: (204) 943-8991
Contact: Stuart Slayen, editor
Circulation: 200,000
Published bimonthly

A youth magazine directed toward high school students, grade 9 and up, distributed nationally through high schools, covering a mix of news, social issues, entertainment, sports, and more. Designed to be empowering, interactive, and entertaining. Articles 700 to 2,000 words. Rates are negotiable, depending on story. Fees are paid on acceptance. Writers are encouraged to send SASE for "Query Guidelines." "Writing Guidelines" will be sent once a story is assigned. No fiction or poetry.

# 2

# LITERARY & SCHOLARLY

It's ironic that literary and scholarly journals, among the most prestigious outlets for a writer's work, can usually afford to pay their contributors the least. Many journals rely on funding from arts councils, or academic or professional sources, and still run at a loss. They have relatively small subscription lists and perhaps two or three unpaid or part-time staff, and they attract little advertising support. The upshot is that they can rarely afford to pay their contributors much. In many cases, modest funding and low revenues preclude payment altogether, or limit it to small honoraria or free copies. Contributors to scholarly journals are frequently salaried academics or professionals, who draw on current areas of research.

Writers would be unwise to look to this sector of publishing as a significant source of income. Qualified writers would be just as unwise to neglect it because of this. Publishing your work in a distinguished literary or scholarly journal can add immeasurably to your reputation, and may well open up other publishing opportunities. This chapter lists many of Canada's most notable journals and literary magazines. Use the information presented in each entry to help you choose the most appropriate publications to approach.

Before you make your submission, familiarize yourself thoroughly with the journal to which you hope to contribute. Editors take a dim view of submissions from writers who are demonstrably unfamiliar with their periodical. Study several recent issues, or better still, subscribe. Learn what you can of the editors' approach and point of view and the kind of work they favour. Determine who their readers are. Always request writer's guidelines, if they are available, and follow these closely to ensure you meet the editor's needs. (Remember to include an SASE whenever you expect a response.) Refereed journals will require several copies of your submission. Scholarly articles should be accompanied by full documentation. Fiction, poetry, reviews, and criticism must be carefully targeted and professionally presented. The extra care and attention will pay dividends.

## Acadiensis: Journal of the History of the Atlantic Region

University of New Brunswick, Campus House, Fredericton,
    N.B. E3B 5A3
Phone: (506) 453-4978  Fax: (506) 453-4599
E-mail: acadnsis@unb.ca
Contact: Gail Campbell, editor
Circulation: 900
Published twice a year

Includes original academic research, review articles, documents, notes, and a running bibliography compiled by librarians in the four Atlantic provinces. "Canada's most ambitious scholarly journal" – Michael Bliss, *Journal of Canadian Studies*. Articles published in English and in French. Cannot pay but welcomes submission inquiries. Guidelines available.

## The Antigonish Review

St. Francis Xavier University, P.O. Box 5000, Antigonish,
    N.S. B2G 2W5
Phone: (902) 867-3962  Fax: (902) 867-2389
E-mail: tar@stfx.ca
Contact: George Sanderson, editor
Circulation: 800
Published quarterly

A creative literary review featuring poetry, fiction, and critical articles from Canada and abroad. Preferred length 1,500 to 4,000 words. Pays up to $150 for articles, $50 for reviews, on publication; 2 copies for poetry and fiction. Rights remain with author. Guidelines available.

## Arachnē: A Journal of Language and Literature

Laurentian University, Ramsey Lake Road, Sudbury, Ont. P3E 2C6
Phone: (705) 675-1151, ext. 4341  Fax: (705) 675-4870
E-mail: bkrajews@nickel.laurentian.ca
Contact: Bruce Krajewski, Chair, Department of English
Published twice a year

Established 1994. An interdisciplinary journal that seeks to gauge the status quo of disciplines such as literature, film, philosophy, religion, art history, law, classics, history, and rhetoric, and to play an active role in bringing these disciplines into dialogue. Articles 5,000 to 7,500 words. Cannot pay but welcomes submission inquiries. "Freelancers will always receive more than a form letter from *Arachnē*." Guidelines available.

## ARC

P.O. Box 7368, Ottawa, Ont. KIL 8E4
Contact: Rita Donovan, co-editor
Circulation: 600
Published twice a year

Publishes poetry from Canada and abroad, as well as reviews, interviews, and articles about aspects of Canadian poetry and Canada's poetry community. Does not publish fiction or drama. Poetry submissions must be typed and include up to 6 unpublished poems. Reviews, interviews, and other articles must be queried first. Pays $25/published page on publication. Guidelines available.

## Atlantic Books Today

2085 Maitland Street, 2nd Floor, Halifax, N.S. B3K 2Z8
Phone: (902) 429-4454  Fax: (902) 429-4454
Contact: Elizabeth Eve, managing editor
Circulation: 32,000
Published quarterly

Formerly the *Atlantic Provinces Review*. Features books, writing, and related issues of the Atlantic region. Pays 20¢/word on publication for short pieces of 250 to 350 words. Welcomes inquiries by mail, fax, or phone.

## Authors

501 Cambridge Street S.E., Medicine Hat, Alta. TIA OT3

Phone: (403) 526-2524  Fax: (403) 526-2524
E-mail: authmag@aol.com
Contact: Philip Murphy, publisher/editor
Circulation: 300
Published monthly

A literary magazine that focuses on the development of its member contributors through workshops, seminars, and through publication. Every contributing member gets published, and all submissions stand to win a $50 prize and free subscription to *Authors*. Guidelines available.

## B.C. BookWorld

3516 West 13th Avenue, Vancouver, B.C. V6R 2S3
Phone: (604) 736-4011  Fax: (604) 736-4011
Contact: Alan Twigg, publisher
Circulation: 50,000
Published quarterly

Promotes B.C. books and authors. Preferred length 500 to 800 words. All fees negotiated on assignment. "Please phone or write first. We usually assign articles."

## Blood & Aphorisms

P.O. Box 702, Station P, Toronto, Ont. M5S 2Y4
Phone: (416) 972-0637
E-mail: blood@io.org
Contact: Ken Sparling, fiction editor
Circulation: 1,800
Published quarterly

Established 1990. A literary journal carrying fresh, exciting fiction by new and established writers along with reviews and interviews with emerging writers. A great market for innovative newcomers. Articles 500 to 4,000 words. Contributors receive a one-year subscription. Guidelines available. "Support literary magazines by subscribing to them. If you don't, they disappear."

## Books in Canada

130 Spadina Avenue, Suite 603, Toronto, Ont. M5V 2L4
Phone: (416) 703-9880
E-mail: binc@intacc.web.net

Contact: Dr. Norman Doidge, editor
Circulation: 8,000
Published 9 times a year

An award-winning magazine providing reviews of Canadian books, interviews with and profiles of Canadian authors, and general articles to entertain the literate reader. Carries reviews by some of the country's best-known writers and critics. Pays 12¢/word on publication. No unsolicited submissions. "All reviews and articles are assigned to our pool of freelancers, most of whom have extensive publication credits. So query first, always. Don't contact us if you've never read *BiC* – we're a very specialized market."

### Border/Lines

The Orient Building, 183 Bathurst Street, Suite 301, Toronto,
   Ont. M5T 2R7
Phone: (416) 504-5249  Fax: (416) 504-3228
Contact: Julie Jenkinson, managing editor
Circulation: 2,000
Published quarterly

An interdisciplinary magazine exploring all aspects of culture. Features articles, reviews, and visual pieces on the theory and practice of popular culture, including film, art, music, the landscape, mass communications, and political culture. Articles are between 500 and 4,000 words. Pays $50 to $250 on publication for features. Guidelines available.

### Canadian Author

27 Doxsee Avenue N., Campbellford, Ont. K0L 1L0
Phone: (705) 653-0323  Fax: (705) 653-0593
Contact: Welwyn Wilton Katz, editor
Circulation: 3,500
Published quarterly

Canada's oldest, most respected national writers' magazine, owned by the Canadian Authors Association but with an independent editorial policy. Features profiles and interviews with people who influence Canadian literature. Also publishes fiction and poetry. A valuable resource for writers. Pays $125 for fiction, $30 to $60 per published page for all other material, on publication. Written queries only. Guidelines available.

## Canadian Children's Literature

Department of English, University of Guelph, Guelph,
Ont. N1G 2W1
Phone: (519) 824-4120, ext. 3189  Fax: (519) 837-1315
E-mail: ccl@uoguelph.ca
Contact: Gay Christofides, administrator
Circulation: 900
Published quarterly

Presents in-depth criticism and reviews of Canadian literature for
children and young adults. Directed toward teachers, librarians, academics, and parents. Scholarly articles (2,000 to 8,000 words) and
reviews are supplemented by illustrations and photographs. Now
also covers film and electronic media. Cannot pay but welcomes
submissions. Guidelines available.

## Canadian Ethnic Studies

Research Unit for Canadian Ethnic Studies, University of
Calgary, 2500 University Drive N.W., Calgary, Alta. T2N 1N4
Phone: (403) 220-7257  Fax: (403) 282-8606
E-mail: frideres@acs.ucalgary.ca
Contact: Dr. J.S. Frideres, co-editor, or Mary Anne Morel, assis-
tant to the editors
Circulation: 800
Published 3 times a year

An interdisciplinary journal devoted to the study of ethnicity,
immigration, inter-group relations, and the history and cultural life
of ethnic groups in Canada. Also carries book reviews, opinions,
memoirs, creative writing, and poetry, and has an ethnic voice
section. All material should address Canadian ethnicity. "We accept
short poetry, book review queries, and ethnic memoirs. Querying
first is always helpful; we return unused manuscripts." Contributors are not paid. Guidelines available.

## Canadian Fiction Magazine

P.O. Box 1061, 240 King Street E., Kingston, Ont. K7L 4Y5
Phone: (613) 548-8429  Fax: (613) 548-1556
Contact: managing editor, Quarry Press
Circulation: 1,200
Published quarterly

Published in partnership with Quarry Press, through whom all inquiries should be made. Dedicated for 25 years to new Canadian fiction, including translations from Québécois and other languages spoken in Canada. Publishes short stories and novel excerpts, and is especially interested in innovative and experimental fiction. Also buys interviews, manifestos, graphics, and some photos. Pays $10/printed page on publication. Guidelines available.

## Canadian Journal of Philosophy

Department of Philosophy, University of Calgary, Calgary, Alta. T2N 1N4
Phone: (403) 220-5539  Fax: (403) 284-0848
E-mail: hurka@acs.ucalgary.ca
Contact: Thomas Hurka, editorial board co-ordinator
Circulation: 1,200
Published quarterly

Established 1971. A leading Canadian philosophical journal, which investigates and contributes to the scholarship, teaching, and research of the country's major philosophers. Publishes work of high quality in any field of philosophy. Articles 2,000 to 10,000 words. Cannot pay but welcomes submissions. Guidelines available.

## Canadian Literature

University of British Columbia, 2029 West Mall, Suite 225, Vancouver, B.C. v6T 1z2
Phone: (604) 822-2780  Fax: (604) 822-9452
E-mail: cdnlit@unixg.ubc.ca
Contact: E.M. Kröller, editor
Circulation: 1,500
Published quarterly

Devoted to studying all aspects of Canadian literature: fiction, non-fiction, poetry, and drama. For students and academics at all levels as well as general readers. Articles 3,000 to 6,000 words. Pays $5/printed page, $10/poem, on publication; no payment for reviews. Guidelines available.

## Canadian Modern Language Review

5201 Dufferin Street, North York, Ont. M3H 5T8
Phone: (416) 667-7782  Fax: (416) 667-7881

E-mail: cmlr@gpu.utcc.utoronto.ca
Contacts: Sharon Lapkin and Jill Bell, co-editors
Circulation: 2,100
Published quarterly

Publishes literary, linguistic, and pedagogical articles, book reviews, current advertisements, and other material of interest to teachers of French, German, Italian, Russian, Spanish, and English as a second language, at all levels of instruction. Published since 1944. All articles are voluntarily submitted rather than assigned, and are refereed. Length should not exceed 6,500 words. Contributors are not paid, but submissions are welcomed. Consult "Guide to Authors" in each issue and write to editors for further information.

## Canadian Poetry: Studies, Documents, Reviews

University of Western Ontario, Department of English, London, Ont. N6A 3K7
Phone: (519) 661-3403  Fax: (519) 661-3640
Contact: D.M.R. Bentley, editor
Circulation: 400
Published twice a year

A scholarly and critical journal devoted to the study of poetry from all periods and regions of Canada. Also prints articles, reviews, and documents directed toward university and college students and teachers. No original poetry. Cannot pay but welcomes submissions of 500 to 5,000 words. Follow *MLA Handbook* for style.

## Canadian Public Administration

150 Eglinton Avenue E., Suite 305, Toronto, Ont. M4P 1E8
Phone: (416) 932-3666  Fax: (416) 932-3667
Contact: Paul Thomas, editor
Circulation: 4,200
Published quarterly

A refereed journal, written by public administrators and academics, that examines structures, processes, and outcomes of public policy and public management related to executive, legislative, judicial, and quasi-judicial functions in municipal, provincial, and federal spheres of government. Contributors are unpaid. Guidelines available.

**Canadian Woman Studies Journal**
212 Founders College, York University, 4700 Keele Street, North
    York, Ont. M3J 1P3
Phone: (416) 736-5356  Fax: (416) 736-5765
Contact: Luciana Ricciutelli, managing editor
Circulation: 4,000
Published quarterly
    A bilingual journal featuring current writing and research on a
wide variety of feminist topics. Welcomes creative writing, experimental articles, and essays of 500 to 2,000 words, as well as book,
art, and film reviews. Contributors are unpaid. Guidelines available.

**Canadian Writer's Journal**
P.O. Box 6618, Station LCD 1, Victoria, B.C. V8P 5N7
Phone: (604) 477-8807
Contact: Gordon M. Smart, editor/publisher
Circulation: 300
Published quarterly
    Not a significant market for the writer, but freelancers are finding
it a useful source of ideas on professional, motivational, and mar-
keting aspects of the profession. Length 400 to 1,200 words.
"Queries or complete mss. welcome. Writers should present
specifics rather than generalities, and avoid overworked subjects
such as overcoming writer's block, handling rejection, etc." Runs
annual contests for poetry and short fiction. Guidelines available.

**The Capilano Review**
2055 Purcell Way, North Vancouver, B.C. V7J 3H5
Phone: (604) 984-1712  Fax: (604) 983-7520
E-mail: jhamilto@capcollege.bc.ca
Contact: Robert Sherrin, editor
Circulation: 1,000
Published 3 times a year
    Established 1972. Features poetry, prose, and fine art by some
of Canada's most innovative writers and artists *before* they become
famous. Pays $50/page, to a maximum of $200, on publication.
Carries stories up to 6,000 words. Guidelines available, but read the
magazine before submitting.

## The Challenger

441 Shepherd Avenue, Quesnel, B.C. v2J 4x1
Phone: (604) 992-6806
Contact: Dan Lukiv, editor
Circulation: 150
Published 5 times a year

Established in 1990, this small, school-based literary journal publishes poetry, mostly by teenagers, but also accepts work from adults. Experimental work welcome. No profanity or pornography. Include author details. Contributors paid in copies. Don't submit poems in June, July, or August.

## The Claremont Review

4980 Wesley Road, Victoria, B.C. v8Y 1Y9
Phone: (604) 658-5221  Fax: (604) 658-5387
E-mail: aurora@islandnet.com
Contact: Bill Stenson, co-editor
Circulation: 500
Published twice a year

Dedicated to publishing the fiction, poetry, and short drama of emerging young writers aged 13 to 19. Introduces some of the best student writing in Canada. Submissions may be between 200 and 5,000 words. Payment only if grants are available. "Our editorial board responds to all submissions with a critical evaluation." Guidelines available.

## Dalhousie Review

Dalhousie University, Sir James Dunn Building, Room 314,
    Halifax, N.S. B3H 3J5
Phone: (902) 494-2541  Fax: (902) 494-2319
E-mail: dalrev@ac.dal.ca
Contacts: Alan Andrews, editor; J.A. Wainwright, poetry/fiction
    editor
Circulation: 700
Published 3 times a year

Invites contributions of articles up to 5,000 words in such fields as history, literature, political science, and philosophy, as well as prose fiction and poetry from both new and established writers. Also carries book reviews. Prefers poetry of less than 40 lines.

Contributors to this distinguished quarterly, first published in 1921, are not usually paid. Guidelines available.

## Dandelion

922 – 9th Avenue S.E., Calgary, Alta. T2G 0S4
Phone: (403) 265-0524
Contact: Bonnie Benoit, managing editor
Circulation: 1,000
Published twice a year

Established 1974. International journal of poetry and fiction from new and established writers across Canada, plus interviews, reviews, and articles (up to 5,000 words) about the regional literary scene and local visual art. Pays on publication $125 per story, $40 per review, $15/page for poetry. Guidelines available.

## Descant

P.O. Box 314, Station P, Toronto, Ont. M5S 2S8
Phone: (416) 593-2557
Contact: Tracy Jenkins, managing editor
Circulation: 1,200
Published quarterly

Established 1970. A literary journal publishing poetry, prose, fiction, interviews, travel pieces, letters, photographs, engravings, art, and literary criticism. Pays an honorarium of $100 on publication to all contributors. "Our purpose is the critical reading of manuscripts of new and established writers. We ask for one-time publishing rights, and only use unpublished work. Turnaround time for manuscripts can be up to 4 months. Each manuscript is read three times before acceptance." Guidelines available.

## Environments: A Journal of Interdisciplinary Studies

University of Waterloo, Faculty of Environmental Studies,
    Waterloo, Ont. N2L 3G1
Phone: (519) 885-1211, ext. 2072  Fax: (519) 746-2031
Contact: Gordon Nelson, editor-in-chief
Circulation: 500
Published 2 to 3 times a year

A refereed journal for scholars and practitioners that seeks to integrate the fields of environment, development, and design. For more information, check inside front cover. Cannot pay but welcomes submission inquiries. Guidelines available.

## Essays on Canadian Writing

2120 Queen Street E., Suite 200, Toronto, Ont. M4E 1E2
Phone: (416) 694-3348  Fax: (416) 698-9906
Contacts: Jack David and Robert Lecker, editors
Circulation: 1,000
Published 3 times a year

Devoted to criticism of Canadian writers and their works. Concentrates on essays featuring contemporary authors and current critical approaches. Publishes bibliographies, interviews, and full-length book reviews of fiction, poetry, and criticism. Pays $75 to $100 on acceptance for 4,000 to 11,000 words.

## Event: The Douglas College Review

Douglas College, P.O. Box 2503, New Westminster, B.C. V3L 5B2
Phone: (604) 527-5293  Fax: (604) 527-5095
Contact: David Zieroth, editor
Circulation: 3,300
Published 3 times a year

Presents new and established Canadian and international writers through their fiction and poetry, and reviews of their work. (Features an annual $500 Creative Non-Fiction Contest each spring.) Stories to a maximum of 5,000 words or up to 8 poems per submission. Pays $22/page on publication. Guidelines available.

## Exile

P.O. Box 67, Station B, Toronto, Ont. M5T 2C0
Phone: (416) 969-8877  Fax: (416) 966-9556
Contact: Barry Callaghan, publisher
Circulation: 1,200
Published quarterly

Devoted to fine fiction, poetry, and drama on the edge from Canada and abroad. Pays on publication. Mail typed inquiries. Study journal first.

## The Fiddlehead

Campus House, University of New Brunswick, P.O. Box 4400, Fredericton, N.B. E3B 5A3

Phone: (506) 453-3501  Fax: (506) 453-4599

Contact: Don McKay, editor

Circulation: 900

Published quarterly

A highly respected literary journal, established in 1945, publishing fine poetry, prose, book reviews, and art work, with a focus on freshness and vitality. While retaining a special interest in writers of Atlantic Canada, it is open to outstanding work from all over the country. Prose submissions may be 100 up to 4,000 words ($10/page). Poetry submissions, 3 to 10 poems. Pays on publication.

## Grain

P.O. Box 1154, Regina, Sask. S4P 3B4

Phone: (306) 244-2828  Fax: (306) 565-8554

E-mail: grain@bailey2.unibase.com

Contact: J. Jill Robinson, editor

Circulation: 1,500

Published quarterly

A literary journal of national and international scope published by the Saskatchewan Writers' Guild. Prints high-quality literary and visual art, both traditional and experimental, with the aim of presenting new and challenging writing by established and emerging writers. Original, unpublished fiction, poetry, essays, creative non-fiction, and occasional excerpts from plays considered. Pays $30 to $100 on publication for poetry and fiction. Guidelines available.

## Journal of Canadian Studies

Trent University, P.O. Box 4800, Peterborough, Ont. K9J 7B8

Contact: Michèle Lacombe, editor

Circulation: 1,300

Published quarterly

Publishes a variety of scholarly articles, critical comment, and book reviews pertaining to Canadian history, politics, the economy, education, literature and the arts, public policy, communications, anthropology, and sociology. Accepts articles of between 3,000 and

10,000 words. Cannot pay but welcomes submission inquiries. Guidelines available.

## Labour/Le travail

Memorial University, Department of History, St. John's, Nfld. A1C 5S7

Phone: (709) 737-2144   Fax: (709) 737-4342

E-mail: joanb@plato.usc.mun.ca

Contact: Gregory S. Kealey, editor

Circulation: 1,200

Published twice a year

A bilingual, interdisciplinary, historical journal concerned with work, workers, and the labour movement. Includes articles of 5,000 to 10,000 words, book notes, archival notes, and an annual bibliography of Canadian labour studies. Cannot pay but welcomes submission inquiries. Guidelines available.

## The Literary Review of Canada

3266 Yonge Street, P.O. Box 1830, Toronto, Ont. M4N 3P6

Fax: (416) 322-4852

Contact: Pat Dutil, editor

Circulation: 2,000

Published 11 times a year

A scholarly tabloid, in the style of *The New York Review of Books*, carrying substantive book reviews of Canadian non-fiction. Intriguing, incisively written, and informative, it attracts a highly educated readership. Reviews are 3,000 to 5,000 words. Cannot yet pay contributors, but hopes to in the future. Warmly welcomes faxed or mailed proposals and outlines, but study review first.

## The Malahat Review

University of Victoria, P.O. Box 1700, MS 8524, Victoria, B.C. V8W 2Y2

Phone: (604) 721-8524   Fax: (604) 721-7212

Contact: Derk Wynand, editor

Circulation: 1,800

Published quarterly

A distinguished, award-winning literary journal publishing Canada's best poets and short story writers. Pays $25 per estimated published page on acceptance. Don't send queries first. For poetry, submit 6 to 10 pages of poems; for fiction, send one complete story.

## Matrix

1400 de Maisonneuve W., Suite 514-8, Montreal, Que. H3G 1M8
Phone: (514) 848-2340  Fax: (514) 848-4501
Contact: Robert Allen, editor
Circulation: 1,800
Published 3 times a year

A literary/cultural magazine rooted in Quebec but open to writers from across Canada, the United States, and abroad. Seeks out the best contemporary fiction, non-fiction, articles, and artwork. Described by Bill Katz, in *Library Journal*, as "a northern combination of *The New Yorker* and *Atlantic Monthly*." Publishes original prose and poetry by new and established writers. Length 1,500 to 5,000 words. Articles/fiction receive $100 to $200; poetry $15 to $100. Pays on publication. Guidelines available.

## McGill Street Magazine

193 Bellwoods Avenue, Toronto, Ont. M6J 2P8
Phone: (416) 538-0559
Contact: Chris Garbutt, publisher
Circulation: 1,500
Published quarterly

Established 1992. A quarterly dedicated to publishing the work of emerging writers, including poetry, short stories, and excerpts from longer works and plays (to a maximum 4,000 words). Cannot pay but welcomes submissions. Two copies of magazine on publication. Guidelines available.

## Mosaic: A Journal for the Interdisciplinary Study of Literature

208 Tier Building, University of Manitoba, Winnipeg, Man. R3T 2N2
Phone: (204) 474-9763  Fax: (204) 261-9086
E-mail: ejhinz@bildgarts.lanl.umanitoba.ca
Contact: Dr. Evelyn J. Hinz, editor
Circulation: 900
Published quarterly

For scholars, educators, students, and the sophisticated general reader. Combining reader-friendly prose and current research, essays use insights from a wide variety of disciplines to highlight the practical and cultural relevance of literary works. Essays are 5,000 to 6,000 words. Contributors are unpaid. Submission inquiries welcome. "We strongly encourage potential contributors to subscribe to *Mosaic* in order to become familiar with our format, editorial mandate, and interdisciplinary requirements." Guidelines available.

## The Muse Journal
226 Lisgar Street, Toronto, Ont. M6J 3G7
Phone: (416) 539-9517  Fax: (416) 539-0047
E-mail: egoncalves@ablelink.org
Contact: Emanuel Goncalves, editor
Circulation: 1,000
Published once or twice a year

A journal for writers, poets, and visual artists open to all topics, themes, and genres but emphasizing the metaphysical, philosophical, and humorous. Preferred length 800 to 1,600 words. Generally only pays for solicited works. "*The Muse Journal* serves, supports, and publishes poets, writers, and artists of exceptional talent, whether known or unknown." Guidelines available. Conducts a poetry and a prose contest each year – send SASE for details.

## The Mystery Review
P.O. Box 233, Colborne, Ont. KOK 1SO
Phone: (613) 475-4440  Fax: (613) 475-3400
E-mail: 71554.551@compuserve.com
Contact: Barbara Davey, editor
Circulation: 5,000
Published quarterly

For readers of mystery and suspense. Carries information on new mystery titles, book reviews, interviews with authors, real-life unsolved mysteries, puzzles, and word games relating to the genre. Pays honorarium on publication. Contact editor for guidelines. Query before submitting an article or review.

## The New Quarterly
University of Waterloo, English Language Proficiency Program,
PAS 2082, Waterloo, Ont. N2L 3GI
Phone: (519) 885-1211, ext. 2837
E-mail: mmerikle@watarts.uwaterloo.ca
Contact: Mary Merikle, managing editor
Circulation: 500

Publishes poetry, short fiction, and excerpts from novels, while encouraging "new voices and directions" in Canadian writing. "New features include essays on the writer's craft and very short fiction (sometimes called postcard or flash fiction)." Prose should be about 20 pages. Pays $100 for a short story or novel extract, $20 for a poem, on publication. Guidelines available.

## ON SPEC: The Canadian Magazine of Speculative Writing
P.O. Box 4727, Edmonton, Alta. T6E 5G6
Phone: (403) 413-0215
Contact: Cath Jackel, administrator
Circulation: 2,000
Published quarterly

Specializes in Canadian science fiction, fantasy, horror, and magic realism in stories and poetry. Stories up to 6,000 words are paid 2½¢/word, stories under 1,000 words earn $25, poems up to 100 lines earn $15 per poem. Pays on acceptance. "Read the magazine (samples $6 including tax and postage), and send for guidelines before submitting – we have unusual format requirements."

## Ontario History
34 Parkview Avenue, Willowdale, Ont. M2N 3Y2
Phone: (416) 226-9011  Fax: (416) 226-2740
Contact: Jean Burnet, editor
Circulation: 1,200
Published quarterly

A regional journal of current scholarly writing on various aspects of the province's past, directed toward academics, professional and amateur historians, libraries, and universities. Articles should be 6,000 to 7,000 words. Cannot pay but welcomes submission inquiries. Guidelines available.

## Other Voices

Garneau P.O. Box 52059, 8210 – 109th Street, Edmonton,
Alta. T6G 2T5
Contact: editorial collective
Published twice a year

A small literary journal, published in the spring and fall, seeks submissions of fiction, poetry, black and white prints, and artwork. Submission deadlines March 15 and September 15. Payment by one-year subscription and small honorarium.

## Pacific Affairs

University of British Columbia, 2029 West Mall, Vancouver,
B.C. V6T 1Z2
Phone: (604) 822-6504  Fax: (604) 822-9452
Contact: Bernie Chisholm, business manager
Circulation: 2,800
Published quarterly

A source of scholarly insight into the social, cultural, political, and economic issues of the Pacific region, directed toward universities, institutions, embassies, and consulates. Runs articles, review articles, and research notes contributed by authors from around the world. Also reviews about 60 books each issue. Preferred length 6,000 to 6,250 words. Contributors are not paid. Submission inquiries welcome. See inside back cover for guidelines.

## paperplates

19 Kenwood Avenue, Toronto, Ont. M6C 2R8
Phone: (416) 651-2551
E-mail: beekelly@hookup.net
Contact: Bernard Kelly, publisher/editor
Circulation: 350
Published quarterly

Established 1991. Publishes poetry, fiction, plays, travel pieces, essays, interviews, memoirs. Length 2,500 to 15,000 words. Cannot pay, but inquiries are welcomed. Guidelines available.

## Poetry Canada

P.O. Box 1061, Kingston, Ont. K7L 4Y5
Phone: (613) 548-8429  Fax: (613) 548-1556

Contact: the editor
Circulation: 1,500
Published quarterly

The nation's only magazine devoted entirely to publishing poetry, criticism of poetry, and poetry news. Carries about 30 poems each issue, some by Canada's best poets, others by new writers. Aims to discover the best new work by established and emerging poets in Canada. Includes essays and in-depth interviews of 1,750 to 3,500 words. Pays $20/poem, $100/page, $50/review, after publication. "Please read the magazine first to get a sense of what we publish."

## Possibilitiis Literary Arts Magazine

109 – 2100 Scott Street, Ottawa, Ont. KIZ IA3
Phone: (613) 761-1177
Contact: Maureen Henry, publisher
Circulation: 600
Published quarterly

Established 1993. Provides a forum for emerging and established writers of colour or those writing from particular minority cultural perspectives. Seeks adult and children's fiction, poetry, stories, and other creative work written from the writer's distinct cultural perspective. Preferred length 500 to 3,000 words. A short (50-word) abstract and a brief biographical note should accompany submissions. Cannot pay but welcomes submission inquiries. Preference given to previously unpublished material. Guidelines available.

## Prairie Fire

100 Arthur Street, Suite 423, Winnipeg, Man. R3B IH3
Phone: (204) 943-9066  Fax: (204) 942-1555
Contact: Andris Taskans, managing editor
Circulation: 1,500
Published quarterly

Publishes poetry, fiction, essays, interviews, reviews, commentary, satire, and literary and other arts criticism. Submissions may be from 150 to 5,000 words. Pays on publication: for fiction, $40/first page, then $35/page; for articles, $35/first page, then $30/page; for reviews/interviews, $20–$25/first page, then $15–$20/page. Guidelines and full payment schedule available.

## PRISM international

Department of Creative Writing, University of British Columbia,
   1866 Main Mall – Buch E462, Vancouver, B.C. V6T 1Z1
Phone: (604) 822-2514  Fax: (604) 822-3616
E-mail: prism@unixg.ubc.ca
Contact: Leah Postman, editor
Circulation: 1,000
Published quarterly

   Features innovative new fiction, poetry, drama, creative non-fiction, and translation from Canada and around the world. The oldest literary journal in the West. Welcomes submissions of 500 to 5,000 words from established and unknown writers. "We print work on any subject, in any style; our only criteria are originality and quality." No multiple submissions. Pays $20/published page plus one year's subscription on publication. Guidelines available.

## Public

192 Spadina Avenue, Suite 307, Toronto, Ont. M5T 2C2
Phone: (416) 703-1161  Fax: (416) 703-7975
Contact: Tom Taylor, collective member
Circulation: 1,500
Published twice a year

   An interdisciplinary journal combining scholarly and critical writing in cultural studies, focusing on the visual arts, performance, and literature. Dedicated to providing a forum in which artists, critics, and theorists exchange ideas on topics previously segregated by ideological boundaries of discipline. Pays $500 on publication for contributions of 3,000 to 6,000 words.

## Quarry

P.O. Box 1061, Kingston, Ont. K7L 4Y5
Phone: (613) 548-8429
Contact: Mary Cameron, editor
Circulation: 1,200
Published quarterly

   For more than 45 years this literary magazine has been publishing new, innovative fiction, poetry, and essays by established and emerging Canadian writers. Also carries translations, travel writing, and reviews. Committed to discovering talented new writers. Pays $10 per published page for fiction, $15 per poem, after publication.

## Queen's Quarterly

184 Union Street, Kingston, Ont. K7L 3N6
Phone: (613) 545-2667  Fax: (613) 545-6822
E-mail: qquartly@qucdn.bitnet
Contact: Boris Castel, editor
Circulation: 2,700
Published quarterly

   A distinctive and authoritative university-based review with a Canadian focus and an international outlook. First published in 1893. Features scholarly articles (2,500 to 5,000 words) of general interest on politics, history, science, the humanities, and arts and letters, plus regular music and science columns, original poetry, fiction, and extensive book reviews. Fees, paid on publication, vary and are sometimes negotiated. Guidelines available.

## Quill & Quire

70 The Esplanade, 2nd Floor, Toronto, Ont. M5E 1R2
Phone: (416) 360-0044  Fax: (416) 955-0794
Contact: Ted Mumford, editor
Circulation: 7,000
Published monthly

   The news journal of the Canadian book trade – for booksellers, librarians, educators, publishers, and writers. Prints news, reviews, lists of recently published and upcoming books, and profiles of authors and publishing houses. Includes the biannual supplement, *Canadian Publishers Directory*. Pays a variable fee on acceptance.

## Raddle Moon

2239 Stephens Street, Vancouver, B.C. V6K 3W5
Contacts: Susan Clark, Catriona Strang, and Lisa Robertson, editors
Published twice a year

   An international literary review featuring mostly Canadian and U.S. poetry and criticism as well as previously untranslated writing from many countries. Welcomes submission inquiries from those who have familiarized themselves with the journal.

## Rampike

95 Rivercrest Road, Toronto, Ont. M6S 4H7
Phone: (416) 767-6713
Contact: Karl Jirgens, publisher
Published twice a year

Features poetry, fiction, one-act plays, and cinema and video scripts. Innovative work by writers, theorists, and artists from around the world. There's never a shortage of stimulating contributors to this visually arresting and highly regarded magazine. But contact editors regarding upcoming themes and you may be able to offer them something they need. Pays a nominal fee.

## The Reader

1701 West 3rd Avenue, Vancouver, B.C. V6J 1K7
Phone: (604) 732-7631  Fax: (604) 732-3765
Contact: Celia Duthie, publisher
Circulation: 11,000
Published quarterly

A free-circulation book review selection of new titles of interest to the general reader. Preferred length 200 to 800 words. Pays on publication with a $100 gift certificate for major reviews, a $50 gift certificate for brief reviews. Welcomes unsolicited reviews, but acceptance not guaranteed. "Submissions should be succinct, interesting, and positive." Guidelines available.

## The Readers Showcase

17317 – 107th Avenue, Edmonton, Alta. T5S 1E5
Phone: (403) 486-5802  Fax: (403) 481-9276
E-mail: suggitt@earth.orbital.net
Contact: David Suggitt, managing editor
Circulation: 40,000
Published monthly

Book reviews, author interviews, etc. Preferred length up to 800 words. Pay rates vary and may be negotiated.

## Resources for Feminist Research

OISE, 252 Bloor Street W., Toronto, Ont. M5S 1V6
Phone: (416) 923-6641, ext. 2277  Fax: (416) 926-4725

Contact: Philinda Masters, co-ordinating editor
Circulation: 2,000
Published quarterly

A journal of feminist scholarship containing papers, abstracts, reviews, reports of work in progress, and bibliographies. Preferred length 3,000 to 5,000 words. Cannot pay but welcomes submissions. Guidelines are outlined on inside back cover.

### Room of One's Own

P.O. Box 46160, Station D, Vancouver, B.C. v6j 5g5
Contact: the growing room collective
Circulation: 900
Published quarterly

An irregular quarterly, established 1975. Solicits fine writing and editing from Canada's best women authors, both well-known and unknown. Features original poetry, fiction, criticism, and reviews. Articles 2,000 to 2,500 words. Pays $25 honorarium plus 2 copies of issue. Guidelines are available, but reading recent back issues will provide best guidance.

### Rotunda

Royal Ontario Museum, 100 Queen's Park, Toronto, Ont. m5s 2c6
Phone: (416) 586-5590  Fax: (416) 586-5827
Contact: Sandra Shaul, executive editor
Circulation: 20,000
Published quarterly

A semi-scholarly magazine, published by the Royal Ontario Museum, carrying authoritative pieces on art, archaeology, the earth and life sciences, astronomy, and museology, addressing the research of rom scholars and their associates worldwide. Preferred length 2,000 to 2,500 words. Occasionally buys articles from professional journalists. Academics receive honoraria.

### Scholarly Publishing

University of Toronto Press, 10 St. Mary Street, Suite 700, Toronto, Ont. m4y 2w8
Phone: (416) 978-2232  Fax: (416) 978-4738
Contact: Hamish Cameron, editor

Circulation: 1,500

Published quarterly

Concerned with the "pleasure and perils" of publishing. Coverage ranges from the classic concerns of manuscript editing and list building to such contemporary issues as on-demand publishing and computer applications. Also explores the delicate balance of author–editor relations, and the intricacies of production and budgeting. Carries articles with a unique blend of philosophical analysis and practical advice. Contributors unpaid, but submission inquiries welcome. Guidelines available.

## Studies in Canadian Literature

University of New Brunswick, English Department, Hut 5,
 P.O. Box 4400, Fredericton, N.B. E3B 5A3

Phone: (506) 453-3501  Fax: (506) 453-4599

Contact: Sabine Campbell, editor

Circulation: 550

Published twice a year

A bilingual, refereed journal of Canadian literary criticism. Carries essays of 8,000 to 10,000 words. Contributors are not paid. Guidelines in journal. Use *MLA Handbook* for style.

## sub-TERRAIN Magazine

175 East Broadway, Suite 204A, Vancouver, B.C. V5T 1W2

Phone: (604) 876-8710  Fax: (604) 879-2667

E-mail: subter@pinc.com

Contact: Brian Kaufman, managing editor

Circulation: 3,000

Published quarterly

Publishes new and established writers from across North America. Interested in contemporary fiction and poetry from original voices. Preferred length 1,000 to 4,000 words. Pays in copies. Read the magazine before submitting. Send 4 to 6 poems at a time. Guidelines available.

## Tessera

c/o Lianne Moyes, Dépt. d'études anglaises, Université de
 Montréal, C.P. 6128, Succ. A, Montréal, Que. H3C 3J7

Phone: (514) 343-7926
Contacts: Lianne Moyes, Jennifer Henderson, editorial collective
Circulation: 250
Published twice a year

Established 1982. A bilingual journal of experimental writing, feminist theory, and cultural critique. "We encourage play along borders, especially crossings of the boundary between creative and theoretical texts." Issues are organized by topic; consult the editors for forthcoming topics. Pays $10/page on publication. Contributions, which should include a biographical note, must be supplied on diskette. Guidelines available.

### The Toronto Review (of Contemporary Writing Abroad)

P.O. Box 6996, Station A, Toronto, Ont. M5W 1X7
Contact: Ms. Nurjehan Aziz, editorial board
Published 3 times a year

Carries poetry, fiction, drama, criticism, and book reviews by writers who originate from the Indian subcontinent, Africa, and the Caribbean. A bias toward diasporic and Third World subjects. Prose 2,000 to 4,000 words. Cash payment for solicited material only; other contributors receive free subscriptions. Published in English and in translation.

### Urban History Review

Becker Associates, P.O. Box 507, Station Q, Toronto,
   Ont. M4T 2M5
Phone: (416) 483-7282  Fax: (416) 489-1713
Contact: John Becker, managing editor
Circulation: 500
Published twice a year

A bilingual interdisciplinary and refereed journal presenting lively articles covering such topics as architecture, heritage, urbanization, housing, and planning – all in a generously illustrated format. Regular features include in-depth articles, research notes, two annual bibliographies covering Canadian and international publications, comprehensive book reviews, and notes and comments on conferences, urban policy, and publications. Contributors are unpaid.

**West Coast Line**
2027 East Annex, Simon Fraser University, Burnaby, B.C. v5a 1s6
Phone: (604) 291-4287  Fax: (604) 291-5737
Contact: Jacqueline Larson, managing editor
Circulation: 600
Published 3 times a year

A creative arts magazine featuring contemporary poetry, short fiction, visual art, critical essays, and photography. Devoted to "contemporary writers who are experimenting with, or expanding the boundaries of, conventional forms of poetry, fiction, and criticism. . . . We encourage western Canadian writers but also publish occasional international features. Read back issues (available at $10/copy) for an idea of our interests." Fiction up to 7,000 words. Pay rates vary but average $8/page, paid after publication. Query first. Guidelines available.

# 3

# TRADE, BUSINESS, FARM, & PROFESSIONAL PUBLICATIONS

This is a potentially lucrative sector of the writer's market that is often overlooked. Although trade publications rarely pay more than $500 for a full-length article, and usually less, the writing may require considerably fewer sources than are needed for consumer magazine features. An article can often be completed in a day or two, sometimes after research and interviews conducted solely by telephone. In terms of hours spent, therefore, the pay is generally relatively good. What's more, trade editors are often keen to find competent new writers. Writers living in remote areas can find themselves at an unexpected advantage, as editors seek regional balance, and copy can always readily be sent long distance.

The secret to making money from these publications is to work frequently for as many as possible, always bearing in mind that they may want a degree of technical detail that will inform readers already well acquainted with the specific fields they serve. Most trade periodicals, however, deliberately avoid becoming *too* technical, and aim to appeal to a wide readership. If you're not well informed on your subject, become so through research. It bears repeating that before submitting, you *must* familiarize yourself with the magazine thoroughly by reading back issues and related periodicals.

Magazines in each of the following categories carry pieces about new products and developments, unusual marketing and promotion ideas, innovative management techniques, and prominent people and events specific to the industry, trade, or profession they serve. In many cases, staff writers produce the bulk of the feature writing, and call on outside "experts" to provide specific material. But they will often utilize freelancers when there is an editorial shortfall. Some editors cultivate long-term relationships with regular freelancers, who produce much of their copy.

Often one editor is involved in several magazines, so that making yourself and your work known to him or her can lead to further commissions, especially if you show yourself to be reliable and adaptable. Chapter 10, Book Resources, lists some of the larger publishers of trade magazines in Canada, who can be contacted for a list of their publications. If you have an area of technical or specialist knowledge, you have a significant advantage. If not, you would do well to familiarize yourself with at least one trade or business area and the publications that serve it.

This chapter offers a broadly representative selection of trade publications across a wide range of industrial and professional areas, including many well-established, dependable employment sources, and provides a solid resource for the freelance writer looking to break into a new market. However, this is perhaps the most fluid sector in publishing: periodicals appear and disappear, and reappear under a new masthead; editors move from job to job relatively often in response to industry and structural changes. For a monthly updated reference source, consult Maclean-Hunter's *CARD* directory, or refer to *Matthews Media Directory*, published three times a year by Canadian Corporate News, at your library. Check *CARD*, too, for upcoming editorial themes, media profiles, circulation figures, and other useful information.

Lastly, please note that we have an expanded listing of business publications in this section. These regional business journals offer valuable potential for the freelance writer with business knowledge, often paying top dollar for timely and well-informed contributions. Those writers who have found markets through the main business section in Chapter 1 may profitably pursue this specialty further in the business listing below.

## Advertising, Marketing, & Sales

**Canadian Purchasing Journal**
235 Yorkland Boulevard, 3rd Floor, North York, Ont. M2J 4Y8
Phone: (416) 494-2960, ext. 243  Fax: (416) 491-2757
Contact: Susan Lee, editor
Published bimonthly

**Canadian Retailer**
200 – 388 Donald Street, Winnipeg, Man. R3B 2J4
Phone: (204) 957-0265  Fax: (204) 957-0217
Contact: Andrea Kuch, editor
Published bimonthly

**Government Purchasing Guide**
10 Gateway Boulevard, Suite 490, North York, Ont. M3C 3T4
Phone: (416) 696-5488  Fax: (416) 696-7395
Contact: Margaret Williamson, editor
Published monthly

**Marketnews**
364 Supertest Road, 2nd Floor, North York, Ont. M3J 2M2
Phone: (416) 667-9945  Fax: (416) 667-0609
Contact: Robert Franner, editor
Published monthly

**Meetings Monthly**
P.O. Box 365, Montreal, Que. H2Y 3H1
Phone: (514) 274-0004  Fax: (514) 274-5884
Contact: Guy Jonkman, publisher/editor
Published 10 times a year

**Modern Purchasing**
777 Bay Street, Toronto, Ont. M5W 1A7
Phone: (416) 596-5704  Fax: (416) 596-5866
Contact: Joe Terrett, editor
Published 10 times a year

## Pool & Spa Marketing
270 Esna Park Drive, Unit 12, Markham, Ont. L3R 1H3
Phone: (905) 513-0090  Fax: (905) 513-1377
Contact: David Barnsley, editor
Published 7 times a year

## Strategy
366 Adelaide Street W., Suite 500, Toronto, Ont. M5V 1R9
Phone: (416) 408-2300  Fax: (416) 408-0870
Contact: Mark Smyka, editor
Published biweekly

# Automotive (see also Transportation & Cargo)

## Automotive Retailer
120 – 4281 Canada Way, Burnaby, B.C. V5G 4P1
Phone: (604) 432-7987  Fax: (604) 432-1756
Contact: Reg Romero, editor
Published 10 times a year

## Bodyshop
1450 Don Mills Road, Don Mills, Ont. M3B 2X7
Phone: (416) 445-6641  Fax: (416) 442-2213
Contact: Brian Harper, editor
Published bimonthly

## Canadian Auto World
1200 Markham Road, Suite 220, Scarborough, Ont. M1H 3C3
Phone: (416) 438-7777  Fax: (416) 438-5333
Contact: Michael Goetz, editor
Published monthly

## Canadian Automotive Fleet
152 Parliament Street, Toronto, Ont. M5A 2Z1
Phone: (416) 864-1700  Fax: (416) 864-1498
Contact: Kevin Sheehy, managing editor
Published bimonthly

**Jobber News**
1450 Don Mills Road, Don Mills, Ont. M3B 2X7
Phone: (416) 442-4101  Fax: (416) 442-2077
Contact: Bob Blans, editor
Published monthly

**Octane**
101 – 6th Avenue S.W., Suite 2450, Calgary, Alta. T2P 3P4
Phone: (403) 266-8700  Fax: (403) 266-6634
Contact: David Coll, editor
Published quarterly

**Service Station & Garage Management**
1450 Don Mills Road, Don Mills, Ont. M3B 2X7
Phone: (416) 445-6641  Fax: (416) 442-2077
Contact: Gary Kenez, editor
Published monthly

**Taxi News**
38 Fairmount Crescent, Toronto, Ont. M4L 2H4
Phone: (416) 466-2328  Fax: (416) 466-4220
Contact: John Q. Duffy, publisher
Published monthly

**Thunder Bay Car & Truck News**
1145 Barton Street, Thunder Bay, Ont. P7B 5N3
Phone: (807) 623-2348  Fax: (807) 623-7515
Contact: Scott Sumner, publisher
Published biweekly

**Western Automotive Repair**
P.O. Box 64011, Winnipeg, Man. R2K 2Z4
Phone: (204) 654-3573  Fax: (204) 667-8922
Contact: Dan Proudley, editor
Published bimonthly

## Aviation & Aerospace

**Airforce**
100 Metcalfe Street, Ottawa, Ont. KIP 5W6
Phone: (613) 992-5184  Fax: (613) 992-5184
Contact: Vic Johnson, editor
Published quarterly

**The Canadian Aircraft Operator**
P.O. Box 149, Mississauga, Ont. L4W IV5
Phone: (905) 625-9660  Fax: (905) 625-9604
Contact: Edward Belitsky, editor
Published twice a month

**Canadian Flight**
P.O. Box 563, Station B, Ottawa, Ont. KIP 5P7
Phone: (613) 565-0881  Fax: (613) 236-8646
Contact: Doris Ohlmann, managing editor
Published monthly

**Helicopters**
1224 Aviation Park N.E., Suite 158, Calgary, Alta. T2E 7E2
Phone: (403) 275-9457  Fax: (403) 275-3925
Contact: Paul Skinner, editor/publisher
Published quarterly

**ICAO Journal**
Published by the International Civil Aviation Organization, 1000
    Sherbrooke Street W., Suite 327, Montreal, Que. H3A 2R2
Phone: (514) 285-8222  Fax: (514) 288-4772
Contact: Eric MacBurnie, editor
Published 10 times a year

**Wings Magazine**
1224 Aviation Park N.E., Suite 158, Calgary, Alta. T2E 7E2
Phone: (403) 275-9457  Fax: (403) 275-3925
Contact: Paul Skinner, editor/publisher
Published bimonthly

# Building, Engineering, & Heavy Construction

**Alberta Construction**
100 Sutherland Avenue, Winnipeg, Man. R2W 3C7
Phone: (204) 947-0222  Fax: (204) 947-2047
Contact: Wendy Melanson, editor
Published quarterly

**AlumiNews**
P.O. Box 400, Victoria Station, Westmount, Que. H3Z 2V8
Phone: (514) 489-4941  Fax: (514) 489-5505
Contact: Nachmi Artzy, publisher
Published bimonthly

**Atlantic Construction Journal**
6029 Cunard Street, Halifax, N.S. B3K 1E5
Phone: (902) 420-0437  Fax: (902) 423-8212
Contact: Ken Partridge, editor
Published quarterly

**Award**
4180 Lougheed Highway, Suite 401, Burnaby, B.C. V5C 6A7
Phone: (604) 299-7311  Fax: (604) 299-9188
Contact: Marisa Paterson, editor
Published 5 times a year

**B.C. Professional Engineer**
6400 Roberts Street, Burnaby, B.C. V5G 4C9
Phone: (604) 929-6733  Fax: (604) 929-6753
Contact: Wayne Gibson, editor
Published 10 times a year

**Building Magazine**
360 Dupont Street, Toronto, Ont. M5R 1B9
Phone: (416) 966-9944  Fax: (416) 966-9946
Contact: John Fennell, editor
Published bimonthly

## Building Management & Design
136 Coleridge Avenue, Toronto, Ont. M4C 4H6
Phone: (416) 424-2152  Fax: (416) 424-2624
Contact: Cindy Woods, publisher/editor
Published bimonthly

## Canadian Architect
1450 Don Mills Road, Don Mills, Ont. M3B 2X7
Phone: (416) 445-6641  Fax: (416) 442-2214
Contact: Bronwen Ledger, managing editor
Published monthly

## Canadian Consulting Engineer
1450 Don Mills Road, Don Mills, Ont. M3B 2X7
Phone: (416) 445-6641  Fax: (416) 442-2214
Contact: Sophie Kneisel, editor
Published bimonthly

## Canadian Masonry Contractor
1735 Bayly Street, Suite 7A, Pickering, Ont. L1W 3G7
Phone: (905) 831-4711
Contact: Tanja Nowotny, editor
Published quarterly

## Canadian Roofing Contractor
1735 Bayly Street, Suite 7A, Pickering, Ont. L1W 3G7
Phone: (905) 831-4711
Contact: Tanja Nowotny, editor
Published quarterly

## Construction Alberta News
10536 – 106th Street, Edmonton, Alta. T5H 2X6
Phone: (403) 424-1146  Fax: (403) 425-5886
Contact: Don Coates, editor
Published twice a week

## Construction Canada
316 Adelaide Street W., Toronto, Ont. M5V 1R1

Phone: (416) 977-8104  Fax: (416) 598-0658
Contact: Jim Tobros, executive editor
Published bimonthly

## Construction Comment

920 Yonge Street, 6th Floor, Toronto, Ont. M4W 3C7
Phone: (416) 961-1028  Fax: (416) 924-4408
Contact: Lori Knowles, editor
Published twice a year

## Daily Commercial News & Construction Record

280 Yorkland Boulevard, North York, Ont. M2J 4Z6
Phone: (416) 494-4990  Fax: (416) 756-2767
Contact: Scott Button, editor

## Design Engineering

777 Bay Street, Toronto, Ont. M5W 1A7
Phone: (416) 596-5833  Fax: (416) 596-5881
Contact: Steve Purwitsky, editor
Published 8 times a year

## Engineering Dimensions

25 Sheppard Avenue W., Suite 1000, North York, Ont. M2N 6S9
Phone: (416) 224-1100  Fax: (416) 224-8168
Contact: Connie Mucklestone, managing editor
Published bimonthly

## Heavy Construction News

777 Bay Street, Toronto, Ont. M5W 1A7
Phone: (416) 596-5844  Fax: (416) 593-3193
Contact: Russ Noble, editor
Published monthly

## Home Builder Magazine

P.O. Box 400, Victoria Station, Westmount, Que. H3Z 2V8
Phone: (514) 489-4941  Fax: (514) 489-5505
Contact: Nachmi Artzy, publisher/editor
Published bimonthly

## Northpoint
10 Four Seasons Place, Suite 404, Etobicoke, Ont. M9B 6H7
Phone: (416) 621-9621  Fax: (416) 621-8694
Contact: Robert Fowler, editor
Published quarterly

## Ontario Home Builder
1455 Lakeshore Road, Suite 205s, Burlington, Ont. L7S 2J1
Phone: (905) 634-5770  Fax: (905) 634-8335
Contact: Mary Anne Crooker, publisher
Published 5 times a year

## The Pegg
10060 Jasper Avenue, 15th Floor, Tower One, Scotia Place,
    Edmonton, Alta. T5J 4A2
Phone: (403) 426-3990  Fax: (403) 426-1877
Contact: Trevor Maine, managing editor
Published 10 times a year

## Toronto Construction News
280 Yorkland Boulevard, North York, Ont. M2J 4Z6
Phone: (416) 494-4990  Fax: (416) 756-2767
Contact: Randy Threndyle, managing editor
Published bimonthly

## What's New in Welding
777 Bay Street, Toronto, Ont. M5W 1A7
Phone: (416) 596-5000  Fax: (416) 596-5881
Contact: Glen Alton, publisher
Published bimonthly

# Business, Commerce, Banking, Law, Insurance, & Pensions

## Acumen
199 Avenue Road, 3rd Floor, Toronto, Ont. M5R 2J3
Phone: (416) 962-9184  Fax: (416) 962-2380

Contact: Kathleen Hurd, managing editor
Published bimonthly

## Alberta Business
2207 Hanselman Court, Saskatoon, Sask. S7L 6A8
Phone: (306) 244-5668  Fax: (306) 653-4515
Contact: Heather Sterling, editor
Published bimonthly

## Atlantic Chamber Journal
309 Amirault Street, Dieppe, N.B. E1A 1G1
Phone: (506) 858-8710  Fax: (586) 858-1707
Contact: Elie Richard, publisher
Published bimonthly

## Benefits Canada
777 Bay Street, Toronto, Ont. M5W 1A7
Phone: (416) 596-5958  Fax: (416) 593-3166
Contact: Paul Williams, editor
Published 11 times a year

## Benefits and Pensions Monitor
245 Fairview Mall Drive, 3rd Floor, North York, Ont. M2J 4T1
Phone: (416) 494-1066  Fax: (416) 946-8931
Contact: Mary DiSpalatro, managing editor
Published bimonthly

## The Bottom Line
75 Clegg Road, Suite 200, Markham, Ont. L6G 1A1
Phone: (905) 415-5803  Fax: (905) 479-3758
Contact: Michael Lewis, editor
Published monthly

## The Business Advocate
244 Pall Mall Street, Box 3295, London, Ont. N6A 5P6
Phone: (519) 432-7551  Fax: (519) 432-8063
Contact: John Redmond, editor
Published monthly

### The Business & Professional Woman
95 Leeward Glenway, Unit 121, Don Mills, Ont. M3C 2Z6
Phone: (416) 424-1393  Fax: (416) 467-8262
Contact: Valerie Dunn, editor
Published quarterly

### Business in Vancouver
1155 West Pender Street, Suite 500, Vancouver, B.C. V6E 2P4
Phone: (604) 688-2398  Fax: (604) 688-1963
Contact: Peter Ladner, editor/publisher
Published weekly

### Business People Magazine
232 Henderson Highway, Winnipeg, Man. R2L 1L9
Phone: (204) 982-4002  Fax: (204) 982-4001
Contact: Al Davies, editor/associate publisher
Published quarterly

### The Business Times
231 Dundas Street, Suite 203, London, Ont. N6A 1H1
Phone: (519) 679-4901  Fax: (519) 434-7842
Contact: Nadia Shousher, managing editor
Published monthly

### CA Magazine
Published by the Canadian Institute of Chartered Accountants,
    277 Wellington Street W., Toronto, Ont. M5V 3H2
Phone: (416) 977-3222  Fax: (416) 204-3409
Contact: Nelson Luscombe, editor/publisher
Published 10 times a year

### CGA Magazine
Published by the Certified General Accountants' Association
    of Canada, 1188 West Georgia Street, Suite 700, Vancouver,
    B.C. V6E 4E2
Phone: (604) 669-3555  Fax: (604) 689-5845
Contact: Lesley Wood, editor
Published monthly

**CMA Magazine**
Published by the Society of Management Accountants of Canada,
    P.O. Box 176, Hamilton, Ont. L8N 3C3
Phone: (905) 525-4100  Fax: (905) 525-4533
Contact: Kevin Graham, associate publisher
Published 10 times a year

**Canada Japan Business Journal**
220 Cambie Street, Suite 370, Vancouver, B.C. V6B 2M9
Phone: (604) 688-2486  Fax: (604) 688-1487
Contact: Taka Aoki, editor
Published monthly

**Canadian Banker**
Commerce Court West, 199 Bay Street, Suite 3000, Toronto,
    Ont. M5L 1G2
Phone: (416) 362-6092  Fax: (416) 362-7705
Contact: Simon Hally, editor
Published bimonthly

**Canadian Bar Review**
50 O'Connor Street, Suite 902, Ottawa, Ont. KIP 6L2
Phone: (613) 237-2925  Fax: (613) 237-0185
Contact: A. J. McClean, editor
Published quarterly

**Canadian Insurance**
111 Peter Street, Suite 202, Toronto, Ont. M5V 2HI
Phone: (416) 599-0772  Fax: (416) 599-0867
Contact: Craig Harris, editor
Published monthly

**The Canadian Manager**
2175 Sheppard Avenue E., Suite 110, Willowdale, Ont. M2J 1W8
Phone: (416) 493-0155  Fax: (416) 491-1670
Contact: Ruth Max, editor
Published quarterly

## Canadian Underwriter

1450 Don Mills Road, Don Mills, Ont. M5B 2X7
Phone: (416) 445-6641  Fax: (416) 442-2213
Contact: Larry Welsh, managing editor
Published monthly

## Church Business

4040 Creditview Road, Unit 11, P.O. Box 6900, Mississauga,
    Ont. L5C 3Y8
Phone: (905) 569-1800  Fax: (905) 569-1818
Contact: Eleanor Parkinson, editor
Published bimonthly

## Commerce News

10123 – 99th Street, Suite 600, Edmonton, Alta. T5J 3G9
Phone: (403) 426-4620  Fax: (403) 424-7946
Contact: Gretchen Ziegler, editor
Published 9 times a year

## Equity

1178 West Pender Street, Suite 200, Vancouver, B.C. V6E 2R5
Phone: (604) 684-1414  Fax: (604) 684-6907
Contact: Peter Waal, editor
Published 10 times a year

## Exchange

75 King Street S., Waterloo, Ont. N2J 1P2
Phone: (519) 886-2831  Fax: (519) 886-9383
Contact: Rick Campbell, executive editor
Published monthly

## The Financial Post

333 King Street E., Toronto, Ont. M5A 4N2
Phone: (416) 350-6000  Fax: (416) 350-6080
Contact: Diane Francis, editor
Published daily and weekly

## Hamilton Business Report

875 Main Street W., Hamilton, Ont. L8S 4R1

Phone: (905) 522-6117  Fax: (905) 529-2242
Contact: Elizabeth Kelly, editor-in-chief
Published quarterly

## Head Office at Home
44 Carleton Road, Unionville, Ont. L3R 1Z5
Phone: (905) 477-4349
Contact: Elizabeth Harris, publisher/editor
Published bimonthly

## Human Resources Professional
2 Bloor Street W., Suite 1902, Toronto, Ont. M4W 3E2
Phone: (416) 923-2324, ext. 319  Fax: (416) 923-7264
Contact: Ruta Lovett, editor
Published monthly

## Huronia Business Times
24 Dunlop Street E., 2nd Floor, Barrie, Ont. L4M 1A3
Phone: (705) 721-1450  Fax: (705) 721-1449
Contact: Eric Skelton, editor
Published 10 times a year

## Journal of Commerce
4285 Canada Way, Burnaby, B.C. V5G 1H2
Phone: (604) 433-8164  Fax: (604) 433-9549
Contact: Frank Lillquist, editor
Published twice a week

## Kootenay Business Journal
P.O. Box 784, Nelson, B.C. V1L 5P5
Phone: (604) 352-6397  Fax: (604) 352-2588
Contact: Jeff Shecter, publisher/editor
Published monthly

## Kootenay Business Magazine
1510 – 2nd Street N., Cranbrook, B.C. V1C 3L2
Phone: (604) 426-7253  Fax: (604) 489-3743
Contact: Daryl Shellborn, publisher
Published monthly

## LUAC Forum
Published by the Life Underwriters' Association of Canada,
   41 Lesmill Road, Don Mills, Ont. M3B 2T3
Phone: (416) 444-5251  Fax: (416) 444-8031
Contact: Val Osborne, editor
Published 10 times a year

## Law Times
240 Edward Street, Aurora, Ont. L4G 3S9
Phone: (905) 841-6481  Fax: (905) 841-5078
Contact: Beth Marlin, managing editor
Published weekly

## The Lawyers Weekly
75 Clegg Road, Markham, Ont. L6G 1A1
Phone: (905) 415-5804  Fax: (905) 479-3758
Contact: Don Brillinger, editor

## London Business Magazine
P.O. Box 7400, London, Ont. N5Y 4X3
Phone: (519) 472-7601  Fax: (519) 473-2256
Contact: Janine Foster, managing editor
Published monthly

## Manitoba Business
8 Donald Street, Winnipeg, Man. R3L 2T8
Phone: (204) 477-4620  Fax: (204) 284-3255
Contact: Ritchie Gage, editor
Published 10 times a year

## Marketing Magazine
777 Bay Street, 5th Floor, Toronto, Ont. M5W 1A7
Phone: (416) 596-5858  Fax: (416) 593-3170
Contact: Wayne Gooding, editor
Published weekly

## Mississauga Business Times
1606 Sedlescomb Drive, Unit 8, Mississauga, Ont. L4X 1M6
Phone: (905) 625-7070  Fax: (905) 625-4856

Contact: Adam Gutteridge, managing editor
Published 10 times a year

## Montreal Business Magazine
275 St. Jacques Street W., Suite 43, Montreal, Que. H2Y 1M9
Phone: (514) 286-8038
Contact: Mark Weller, publisher
Published bimonthly

## Muskoka Focus on Business
P.O. Box 1600, Bracebridge, Ont. P1L 1V6
Phone: (705) 645-4463  Fax: (705) 645-3928
Contact: Donald Smith, publisher
Published quarterly

## National (The Canadian Bar Foundation)
777 Bay Street, 5th Floor, Toronto, Ont. M5W 1A7
Phone: (416) 596-5247  Fax: (416) 593-3162
Contact: J. Stuart Langford, editor
Published 8 times a year

## Niagara Business Report
4309 Central Avenue, Box 400, Beamsville, Ont. L0R 1B0
Phone: (905) 563-1629/6165  Fax: (905) 563-7977
Contact: Molly Harding, editor
Published quarterly

## Northern Ontario Business
158 Elgin Street, Sudbury, Ont. P3E 3N5
Phone: (705) 673-5705  Fax: (705) 673-9542
Contact: Mark Sandford, publisher/editor
Published monthly

## Northwest Business
P.O. Box 22082, Grande Prairie, Alta. T8V 6X1
Phone: (403) 887-4781  Fax: (403) 887-4717
Contact: Donald Sylvester, publisher/editor
Published bimonthly

## Okanagan Business Magazine

P.O. Box 1479, Station A, Kelowna, B.C. V1Y 7V8
Phone: (604) 861-5399  Fax: (604) 868-3040
Contact: J. Paul Byrne, publisher/managing editor
Published 8 times a year

## Ottawa Business Magazine

192 Bank Street, Ottawa, Ont. K2P 1W8
Phone: (613) 234-7751  Fax: (613) 234-9226
Contact: Mark Sutcliffe, editor
Published bimonthly

## Ottawa Business News

77 Auriga Drive, Unit 3, Nepean, Ont. K2E 7Z7
Phone: (613) 727-1400  Fax: (613) 727-1010
Contact: Darrin Denne, editor
Published biweekly

## Profiles

Published by York University, Suite 280, York Lanes, 4700 Keele
    Street, North York, Ont. M3J 1P3
Phone: (416) 736-2100, ext. 33160  Fax: (416) 736-5681
Contact: Michael Todd, managing editor
Published quarterly

## Saskatchewan Business

2207 Hanselman Court, Saskatoon, Sask. S7L 6A8
Phone: (306) 244-5668  Fax: (306) 653-4515
Contact: Heather Sterling, editor
Published bimonthly

## Sports Business

501 Oakdale Road, Downsview, Ont. M3N 1W7
Phone: (416) 746-7360  Fax: (416) 746-1421
Contact: Bruce Etheridge, editor
Published bimonthly

## This Week in Business

250 St. Antoine Street W., Montreal, Que. H2Y 3R7

Phone: (514) 987-2512  Fax: (514) 987-2433
Contact: Michael Goldbloom, publisher
Published weekly

**Today's Woman in Business**
Grandview Industrial Park, 113 Old Black River Road, P.O. Box
    1291, Saint John, N.B. E2L 4H8
Phone: (506) 658-0754  Fax: (506) 633-0868
Contact: Carol Maber, publisher/editor
Published quarterly

**Toronto Business Magazine**
Zanny Ltd., 11966 Woodbine Avenue, Gormley, Ont. L0H 1G0
Phone: (905) 887-4813  Fax: (905) 479-4834
Contact: Kate Flemming, editor
Published bimonthly

**Western Commerce & Industry**
945 King Edward Street, Winnipeg, Man. R3H 0P8
Phone: (204) 775-0387  Fax: (204) 775-7830
Contact: Kelly Gray, editor
Published bimonthly

**Worldbusiness**
5480 Canotek Road, Suite 14, Ottawa, Ont. K1J 9H6
Phone: (613) 747-2732  Fax: (613) 747-2735
Contact: Douglas MacArthur, publisher/editor
Published monthly

## Data Processing

**CAD Systems**
395 Matheson Boulevard E., Mississauga, Ont. L4Z 2H2
Phone: (905) 890-1846  Fax: (905) 890-5769
Contact: Karen Dalton, editor
Published bimonthly

## CIO Canada
501 Oakdale Road, North York, Ont. M3N 1W7
Phone: (416) 746-7360  Fax: (416) 746-1421
Contact: John Pickett, editor-in-chief
Published 10 times a year

## Canadian Computer Reseller
777 Bay Street, Toronto, Ont. M5W 1A7
Phone: (416) 596-2668  Fax: (416) 593-3166
Contact: Kathryn Swan, publisher
Published twice a month

## Computer & Entertainment Retailing
2005 Sheppard Avenue E., Willowdale, Ont. M2J 5B1
Phone: (416) 497-9562  Fax: (416) 497-9427
Contact: Pamela Addo, managing editor
Published 10 times a year

## Computer Dealer News
2005 Sheppard Avenue E., 4th Floor, Willowdale, Ont. M2J 5B1
Phone: (416) 497-9562  Fax: (416) 497-9427
Contact: Paul Plesman, publisher/president
Published twice a month

## The Computer Paper
3661 West 4th Avenue, Suite 8, Vancouver, B.C. V6R 1P2
Phone: (604) 733-5596  Fax: (604) 732-4280
Contact: Graeme Bennett, managing editor
Published monthly

## The Computer Post
68 Higgins Avenue, 3rd Floor, Winnipeg, Man. R3B 0A5
Phone: (204) 947-9766  Fax: (204) 947-9767
Contact: Robert Li, managing editor
Published monthly

## ComputerWorld Canada
501 Oakdale Road, North York, Ont. M3N 1W7
Phone: (416) 746-7360  Fax: (416) 746-1421

Contact: John Pickett, editor-in-chief
Published twice a month

## Computing Canada
2005 Sheppard Avenue E., 4th Floor, Willowdale, Ont. M2J 5B1
Phone: (416) 497-9562  Fax: (416) 497-9427
Contact: Gordon Campbell, editor
Published twice a month

## Government Computing Digest
132 Adrian Crescent, Markham, Ont. L3P 7B3
Phone: (905) 472-2801  Fax: (905) 472-3091
Contact: Nick Stephens, editor
Published bimonthly

## Hum: The Government Computing Magazine
202 – 557 Cambridge Street S., Ottawa, Ont. KIS 4J4
Phone: (613) 237-4862  Fax: (613) 237-4232
Contact: Lee Hunter, publisher
Published 11 times a year

## Info Canada
501 Oakdale Road, North York, Ont. M3N 1W7
Phone: (416) 746-7360  Fax: (416) 746-1421
Contact: John Pickett, editor-in-chief
Published monthly

## Network World
501 Oakdale Road, North York, Ont. M3N 1W7
Phone: (416) 746-7360  Fax: (416) 746-1421
Contact: John Pickett, editor-in-chief
Published monthly

# Education & School Management

## The ATA Magazine (Alberta Teachers' Association)
11010 – 142nd Street, Edmonton, Alta. T5N 2R1
Phone: (403) 453-2411

Contact: Timothy Johnston, editor
Published quarterly

## The Canadian School Executive
P.O. Box 48265, Bentall Court, Vancouver, B.C. V7X 1A1
Phone: (604) 739-8600  Fax: (604) 739-8200
Contact: Dr. Joe Fris, editor
Published 10 times a year

## Educational Digest
Zanny Ltd., 11966 Woodbine Avenue, Gormley, Ont. L0H 1G0
Phone: (905) 887-5048  Fax: (905) 479-4834
Contact: Janet Gardiner, publisher
Published 5 times a year

## Education Today
439 University Avenue, 18th Floor, Toronto, Ont. M5G 1V8
Phone: (416) 340-2540  Fax: (416) 340-7571
Contact: Heather Dion, editor
Published 5 times a year

## Quebec Home & School News
3285 Cavendish Boulevard, Suite 562, Montreal, Que. H4B 2L9
Phone: (514) 481-5619
Contact: Dorothy Nixon, editor
Published 5 times a year

## The Reporter
65 St. Clair Avenue E., Toronto, Ont. M4T 2Y8
Phone: (416) 925-2493  Fax: (416) 925-7764
Contact: Aleda O'Connor, editor
Published 5 times a year

## The School Trustee
2222 – 13th Avenue, Suite 400, Regina, Sask. S4P 3M7
Phone: (306) 569-0750
Contact: Leslie Anderson, editor
Published 5 times a year

**University Affairs**
600 – 350 Albert Street, Ottawa, Ont. K1R 1B1
Phone: (613) 563-1236  Fax: (613) 563-9745
Contact: Christine Tausig Ford, editor
Published 10 times a year

**University Manager**
388 Donald Street, Suite 200, Winnipeg, Man. R3B 2J4
Phone: (204) 957-0265  Fax: (204) 957-0217
Contact: Andrea Kuch, editor
Published quarterly

## Electronics & Electrical

**Canadian Electronics**
135 Spy Court, Markham, Ont. L3R 5H6
Phone: (905) 447-3222  Fax: (905) 477-4320
Contact: Peter Thorne, editor
Published 7 times a year

**Electrical Business**
395 Matheson Boulevard E., Mississauga, Ont. L4Z 2H2
Phone: (905) 890-1846  Fax: (905) 890-5769
Contact: Roger Burford Mason, editor
Published monthly

**Electrical Equipment News**
1450 Don Mills Road, Don Mills, Ont. M3B 2X7
Phone: (416) 445-6641  Fax: (416) 442-2214
Contact: Olga Markovich, editor/associate publisher
Published bimonthly

**Electricity Today**
345 Kingston Road, Suite 101, Pickering, Ont. L1V 1A1
Phone: (905) 509-4448  Fax: (905) 509-4451
Contact: Randolph Hurst, publisher/executive editor
Published 10 times a year

**Electronic Products & Technology**
1200 Aerowood Drive, Unit 27, Mississauga, Ont. L4W 2S7
Phone: (905) 624-8100  Fax: (905) 624-1760
Contact: David Kerfoot, editor
Published 8 times a year

## Energy, Mining, Forestry, Lumber, Pulp & Paper, & Fisheries

**Atlantic Fisherman**
1127 Barrington Street, Suite 107, Halifax, N.S. B3H 2P8
Phone: (902) 422-4990  Fax: (902) 422-4728
Contact: Karen Fulton, editor
Published monthly

**Canadian Forest Industries**
1, rue Pacifique, Ste.-Anne-de-Bellevue, Que. H9X 1C5
Phone: (514) 457-2211  Fax: (514) 457-2558
Contact: Scott Jamieson, editor
Published 8 times a year

**Canadian Mining Journal**
1450 Don Mills Road, Don Mills, Ont. M3B 2X7
Phone: (416) 445-6641  Fax: (416) 442-2272
Contact: Patrick Whiteway, editor
Published bimonthly

**Canadian Papermaker**
777 Bay Street, Toronto, Ont. M5W 1A7
Phone: (416) 596-5832  Fax: (416) 593-3193
Contact: Wayne Karl, editor
Published monthly

**Canadian Wood Products**
1, rue Pacifique, Ste.-Anne-de-Bellevue, Que. H9X 1C5
Phone: (514) 457-2211  Fax: (514) 457-2558
Contact: Scott Jamieson, editor
Published bimonthly

## Energy Processing/Canada
700 – 4th Avenue S.W., Suite 1600, Calgary, Alta. T2P 3J4
Phone: (403) 263-6881  Fax: (403) 263-6886
Contact: Scott Jeffrey, publisher
Published bimonthly

## The Fisherman
111 Victoria Drive, Suite 160, Vancouver, B.C. V5L 4C4
Phone: (604) 255-1366  Fax: (604) 255-3162
Contact: Sean Griffin, editor
Published monthly

## The Forestry Chronicle
151 Slater Street, Suite 606, Ottawa, Ont. KIP 5H3
Phone: (613) 234-2242  Fax: (613) 234-6181
Contacts: V.J. Nordin, D. Burgess, editors
Published bimonthly

## Hiballer Forest Magazine
106 – 14th Street E., Suite 11, North Vancouver, B.C. V7L 2N3
Phone: (604) 984-2002  Fax: (604) 984-2820
Contact: Paul Young, managing editor/publisher
Published bimonthly

## Logging & Sawmilling Journal
P.O. Box 86670, North Vancouver, B.C. V74 4L2
Phone: (604) 944-6146  Fax: (604) 990-9971
Contact: Norm Poole, editor
Published 9 times a year

## Mining Review
100 Sutherland Avenue, Winnipeg, Man. R2W 3C7
Phone: (204) 947-0222  Fax: (204) 947-2047
Contact: Wendy Melanson, editor
Published quarterly

## The Northern Miner
1450 Don Mills Road, Don Mills, Ont. M3B 2X7
Phone: (416) 445-6641  Fax: (416) 442-2272

Contact: Doug Donnelly, publisher
Published weekly

### Oil Patch Magazine
17560 – 107th Avenue, 2nd Floor, Edmonton, Alta. T5S IE9
Phone: (403) 486-1295  Fax: (403) 484-0884
Contact: L.M. Hyman, publisher/editor
Published bimonthly

### Oilweek
101 – 6th Avenue S.W., Suite 2450, Calgary, Alta. T2P 3P4
Phone: (403) 266-8700  Fax: (403) 266-6634
Contact: David Coll, editor/associate publisher
Published monthly

### Propane/Canada
700 – 4th Avenue S.W., Suite 1600, Calgary, Alta. T2P 3J4
Phone: (403) 263-6881  Fax: (403) 263-6886
Contact: Scott Jeffrey, publisher
Published bimonthly

### Pulp & Paper Canada
3300 Côte Vertu, Suite 410, St. Laurent, Que. H4R 2B7
Phone: (514) 339-1399  Fax: (514) 339-1396
Contact: Graeme Rodden, editor
Published monthly

### The Roughneck
700 – 4th Avenue S.W., Suite 1600, Calgary, Alta. T2P 3J4
Phone: (403) 263-6881  Fax: (403) 263-6886
Contact: Scott Jeffrey, publisher
Published monthly

### The Sou'Wester
P.O. Box 128, Yarmouth, N.S. B5A 4BI
Phone: (902) 742-7111  Fax: (902) 742-2311
Contact: Alain Meuse, editor
Published biweekly

**Truck Logger Magazine**
815 West Hastings Street, Suite 725, Vancouver, B.C. v6c 1B4
Phone: (604) 682-4080  Fax: (604) 682-3775
Contact: David Webster, editor/publisher
Published bimonthly

**The Westcoast Fisherman**
1496 West 72nd Avenue, Vancouver, B.C. v6P 3c8
Phone: (604) 266-7433  Fax: (604) 263-8620
Contact: David Rahn, publisher
Published monthly

# Environmental Science & Management

**Canadian Environmental Protection**
1625 Ingleton Avenue, Burnaby, B.C. v5c 4L8
Phone: (604) 291-9900  Fax: (604) 291-1906
Contact: Dan Kennedy, editor
Published 9 times a year

**Environmental Science & Engineering**
220 Industrial Parkway, Unit 30, Aurora, Ont. L4G 3V6
Phone: (905) 727-4666  Fax: (905) 841-7271
Contact: Tom Davey, publisher/editor
Published bimonthly

**Hazardous Materials Management**
401 Richmond Street W., Suite 139, Toronto, Ont. M5V 1X3
Phone: (416) 348-9922  Fax: (416) 348-9744
Contact: Guy Crittenden, editor
Published bimonthly

**Recycling Product News**
1625 Ingleton Avenue, Burnaby, B.C. v5c 4L8
Phone: (604) 291-9900  Fax: (604) 291-1906
Contact: Dan Kennedy, editor
Published bimonthly

**Waste Business Magazine**
85 Somerset Avenue, Suite 200, Toronto, Ont. M6H 2R3
Phone: (416) 658-7519  Fax: (416) 658-9708
Contact: Matthew Keegan, publisher/editor
Published bimonthly

**Water & Pollution Control**
Zanny Ltd., 11966 Woodbine Avenue, Gormley, Ont. L0H 1G0
Phone: (905) 887-4813  Fax: (905) 479-4834
Contact: Amy Margaret, editor
Published bimonthly

## Farming

**B.C. Farmer**
4383 Seldon Road, Abbotsford, B.C. V2S 7X3
Phone: (604) 855-6000  Fax: (604) 855-6002
Contact: Phil Hood, publisher
Published monthly

**Canada Poultryman**
9547 – 152nd Street, Suite 105B, Surrey, B.C. V3R 5Y5
Phone: (604) 585-3131  Fax: (604) 585-1504
Contact: Tony Greaves, editor and manager
Published monthly

**Canadian Fruitgrower**
222 Argyle Avenue, Delhi, Ont. N4B 2Y2
Phone: (519) 582-2513  Fax: (519) 582-4040
Contact: Blair Adams, editor
Published 9 times a year

**Canadian Guernsey Journal**
368 Woolwich Street, Guelph, Ont. N1H 3W6
Phone: (519) 836-2141
Contact: V. Macdonald, editor
Published bimonthly

**Canadian Hereford Digest**
5160 Skyline Way N.E., Calgary, Alta. T2E 6VI
Phone: (403) 274-1734
Contact: Kurt Gilmore, editor
Published monthly

**Canadian Jersey Breeder**
350 Speedvale Avenue W., Unit 9, Guelph, Ont. NIH 7M7
Phone: (519) 821-9150  Fax: (519) 821-2723
Contact: Betty Clements, editor
Published 10 times a year

**Canola Guide**
P.O. Box 6600, Winnipeg, Man. R3C 3A7
Phone: (204) 944-5760  Fax: (204) 942-8463
Contact: Ray Wytink, editor
Published 9 times a year

**Cattlemen**
P.O. Box 6600, Winnipeg, Man. R3C 3A7
Phone: (204) 944-5763  Fax: (204) 942-8463
Contact: Gren Winslow, editor
Published monthly

**Corn-Soy Guide**
P.O. Box 6600, Winnipeg, Man. R3C 3A7
Phone: (204) 944-5760  Fax: (204) 942-8463
Contact: Dave Wreford, editor
Published 10 times a year

**Country Guide**
P.O. Box 6600, Winnipeg, Man. R3C 3A7
Phone: (204) 944-5760  Fax: (204) 942-8463
Contact: Dave Wreford, editor
Published 11 times a year

**Country Life in B.C.**
3308 King George Highway, Surrey, B.C. V4P IA8
Phone: (604) 536-7622  Fax: (604) 536-5677

Contact: Allen F. Parr, publisher/editor
Published monthly

## Dairy Contact

P.O. Box 549, 4917 – 50th Street, Onoway, Alta. TOE IVO
Phone: (403) 967-2922  Fax: (403) 967-2930
Contact: Allen F. Parr, publisher/editor
Published monthly

## Dairy Guide

P.O. Box 6600, Winnipeg, Man. R3C 3A7
Phone: (204) 944-5760  Fax: (204) 942-8463
Contact: D. Wilkins, editor
Published 5 times a year

## Farm & Country

100 Broadview Avenue, Suite 402, Toronto, Ont. M4M 3H3
Phone: (416) 463-8080  Fax: (416) 463-1075
Contact: John Muggeridge, managing editor
Published 18 times a year

## Farm Focus

P.O. Box 128, Yarmouth, N.S. B5A 4B1
Phone: (902) 742-7111  Fax: (902) 742-2311
Contact: Heather Jones, editor
Published biweekly

## The Farm Gate

15 King Street, Elmira, Ont. N3B 2R1
Phone: (519) 669-5155
Contact: Bob Verdun, editor/publisher
Published monthly

## Farm Light & Power

2330 – 15th Avenue, Regina, Sask. S4P 1A2
Phone: (306) 525-3305  Fax: (306) 757-1810
Contact: L.T. Bradley, publisher
Published 10 times a year

**Farm Review**
41 Dundas Street E., Napanee, Ont. K7R 1H7
Phone: (613) 354-6648  Fax: (613) 354-6708
Contact: Kathleen Clark, editor
Published monthly

**Farmers' Choice**
2950 Bremner Avenue, Bag 5200, Red Deer, Alta. T4N 5G3
Phone: (403) 343-2400  Fax: (403) 342-4051
Contact: Howard Janzen, publisher
Published monthly

**Grainews**
P.O. Box 6600, Winnipeg, Man. R3C 3A7
Phone: (204) 944-5569  Fax: (204) 944-5416
Contact: Roger Olson, editor
Published 16 times a year

**The Grower**
355 Elmira Road, Suite 103, Guelph, Ont. N1K 1S5
Phone: (519) 763-8728  Fax: (519) 763-6604
Contact: Michael Mazur, publisher
Published monthly

**Holstein Journal**
9120 Leslie Street, Unit 105, Richmond Hill, Ont. L4B 3S9
Phone: (905) 886-4222  Fax: (905) 886-0037
Contact: Bonnie Cooper, editor
Published monthly

**The Manitoba Co-operator**
P.O. Box 9800, Winnipeg, Man. R3C 3K7
Phone: (204) 934-0401  Fax: (204) 934-0480
Contact: John Morriss, publisher/editor
Published weekly

**Niagara Farmers' Monthly**
P.O. Box 52, Smithville, Ont. L0R 2A0
Phone: (905) 957-3751  Fax: (905) 957-0088

Contact: Ivan Carruthers, publisher
Published 11 times a year

## Ontario Corn Producer

90 Woodlawn Road W., Guelph, Ont. NIH IB2
Phone: (519) 837-1660  Fax: (519) 837-1674
Contact: Terry Boland, editor-in-chief
Published 10 times a year

## Ontario Dairy Farmer

P.O. Box 7400, London, Ont. N5Y 4X3
Phone: (519) 473-0010  Fax: (519) 473-2256
Contact: Paul Mahon, editor
Published bimonthly

## Ontario Farmer

P.O. Box 7400, London, Ont. N5Y 4X3
Phone: (519) 473-0010  Fax: (519) 473-2256
Contact: Paul Mahon, editor
Published weekly

## Ontario Milk Producer

6780 Campobello Road, Mississauga, Ont. L5N 2L8
Phone: (905) 821-8970  Fax: (905) 821-3160
Contact: Bill Dimmick, editor
Published monthly

## Quebec Farmers' Advocate

P.O. Box 80, Ste.-Anne-de-Bellevue, Que. H9X 3L4
Phone: (514) 457-2010  Fax: (514) 398-7972
Contact: Hugh Maynard, editor
Published 10 times a year

## Rural Roots

30 – 10th Street E., P.O. Box 550, Prince Albert, Sask. S6V 5R9
Phone: (306) 764-4276  Fax: (306) 763-3331
Contact: Barb Gustafson, editor
Published weekly

**Saskatchewan Farm Life**
4 – 75 Lenore Drive, Saskatoon, Sask. S7K 7Y1
Phone: (306) 242-5723  Fax: (306) 244-6656
Contact: Larry Hyatt, manager
Published biweekly

**Simmental Country**
13, 4101 – 19th Street N.E., Calgary, Alta. T2E 7C4
Phone: (403) 250-5255  Fax: (403) 250-5279
Contact: Ted Pritchett, publisher/editor
Published monthly

**Western Hog Journal**
10319 Princess Elizabeth Avenue, Edmonton, Alta. T5G 0Y5
Phone: (403) 474-8288  Fax: (403) 471-8065
Contact: Ed Schultz, editor
Published quarterly

**The Western Producer**
P.O. Box 2500, Saskatoon, Sask. S7K 2C4
Phone: (306) 665-3500  Fax: (306) 653-8750
Contact: Garry Fairbairn, editor
Published weekly

## Food, Drink, & Hostelry

**Bakers Journal**
106 Lakeshore Road E., Suite 209, Port Credit, Ont. L5G 1E2
Phone: (905) 271-1366  Fax: (905) 271-6373
Contact: Carol Horseman, editor
Published 10 times a year

**Canadian Grocer**
777 Bay Street, Toronto, Ont. M5W 1A7
Phone: (416) 596-5772  Fax: (416) 593-3162
Contact: G.H. Condon, editor
Published monthly

**Food in Canada**
777 Bay Street, Toronto, Ont. M5W 1A7
Phone: (416) 596-5477  Fax: (416) 593-3189
Contact: Catherine Wilson, editor
Published 9 times a year

**Foodservice & Hospitality**
23 Lesmill Road, Suite 202, Don Mills, Ont. M3B 3P6
Phone: (416) 447-0888  Fax: (416) 447-5333
Contact: Rosanna Caira, editor
Published monthly

**Grocer Today**
401 – 4180 Lougheed Highway, Burnaby, B.C. V5C 6A7
Phone: (604) 299-7311  Fax: (604) 299-9188
Contact: Marisa Paterson, editor
Published 10 times a year

**Inn Business**
Zanny Ltd., 11966 Woodbine Avenue, Gormley, Ont. L0H 1G0
Phone: (905) 887-4813  Fax: (905) 479-4834
Contact: Amy Margaret, editor
Published bimonthly

**Modern Dairy**
3269 Bloor Street W., Suite 205, Toronto, Ont. M8X 1E2
Phone: (416) 239-8423
Contact: Iain Macnab, editor/publisher
Published 5 times a year

**Ontario Restaurant News**
2065 Dundas Street E., Suite 101, Mississauga, Ont. L4X 2W1
Phone: (905) 206-0150  Fax: (905) 206-9972
Contact: Stephen Law, editor
Published monthly

**Western Grocer**
945 King Edward Street, Winnipeg, Man. R3H 0P8

Phone: (204) 775-0387  Fax: (204) 775-7830
Contact: Kelly Gray, editor
Published bimonthly

# Health, Dentistry, Medicine, Pharmacy, & Nursing

**Canadian Family Physician**
2630 Skymark Avenue, Mississauga, Ont. L4W 5A4
Phone: (905) 629-0900  Fax: (905) 629-0893
Contact: Dr. Reg Perkin, editorial director
Published monthly

**Canadian Journal of Continuing Medical Education**
955, boulevard St.-Jean, Suite 306, Pointe Claire, Que. H9R 5K3
Phone: (514) 695-7623  Fax: (514) 695-8554
Contact: Paul Brand, executive editor
Published monthly

**Canadian Journal of Hospital Pharmacy**
1145 Hunt Club Road, Suite 350, Ottawa, Ont. KIV OY3
Phone: (613) 736-9733  Fax: (613) 736-5660
Contact: Scott Walker, editor
Published bimonthly

**The Canadian Nurse**
50 The Driveway, Ottawa, Ont. K2P IE2
Phone: (613) 237-2133  Fax: (613) 237-3520
Contact: Heather Broughton, editor-in-chief
Published monthly

**Canadian Pharmaceutical Journal**
1382 Hurontario Street, Mississauga, Ont. L5G 3H4
Phone: (905) 278-6700  Fax: (905) 278-4850
Contact: Andrew Reinboldt, editor
Published 10 times a year

**The Care Connection**
Published by the Ontario Association of Registered Nursing
    Assistants, 5025 Orbitor Drive, Building 4, Suite 200,
    Mississauga, Ont. L4W 4Y5
Phone: (905) 602-4664  Fax: (905) 602-4666
Contact: Kelly Zimmer, editor
Published quarterly

**Dental Practice Management**
1450 Don Mills Road, Don Mills, Ont. M3B 2X7
Phone: (416) 445-6641  Fax: (416) 442-2214
Contact: Janet Bonellie, managing editor
Published quarterly

**Dentist's Guide**
1120 Bichmount Road, Suite 200, Scarborough, Ont. M1K 5G4
Phone: (416) 750-8900  Fax: (416) 751-8126
Contact: Frank Lederer, publisher
Published quarterly

**Doctor's Review**
400 McGill Street, 3rd Floor, Montreal, Que. H2Y 2G1
Phone: (514) 397-8833  Fax: (514) 397-0228
Contact: Madeleine Partous, editor
Published monthly

**Family Practice**
1120 Birchmount Road, Suite 200, Scarborough, Ont. M1K 5G4
Phone: (416) 750-8900  Fax: (416) 751-8126
Contact: John Shaughnessy, editor
Published 32 times a year

**Hospital News**
23 Apex Road, Toronto, Ont. M6A 2V6
Phone: (416) 781-5516  Fax: (416) 781-5499
Contact: Donna Kell, editor
Published monthly

**The Journal**
Published by the Addiction Research Foundation, 33 Russell
    Street, Toronto, Ont. M5S 2S1
Phone: (416) 595-6059  Fax: (416) 593-4694
Contact: Ian Kinross, editor
Published bimonthly

**Journal of the Canadian Dental Association**
1815 Alta Vista Drive, Ottawa, Ont. K1G 3Y6
Phone: (613) 523-1770  Fax: (613) 523-7736
Contact: Terence Davis, managing editor
Published monthly

**The Medical Post**
777 Bay Street, Toronto, Ont. M5W 1A7
Phone: (416) 596-5770  Fax: (416) 593-3177
Contact: Derek Cassels, editor
Published 44 times a year

**Medicine North America**
400 McGill Street, 3rd Floor, Montreal, Que. H2Y 2G1
Phone: (514) 397-9393  Fax: (514) 397-0228
Contact: Dr. Ian R. Hart, editor
Published monthly

**Nursing B.C.**
2855 Arbutus Street, Vancouver, B.C. V6J 3Y8
Phone: (604) 736-7331  Fax: (604) 738-2272
Contact: Bruce Wells, editor
Published 5 times a year

**Ontario Dentist**
4 New Street, Toronto, Ont. M5R 1P6
Phone: (416) 922-3900  Fax: (416) 922-9005
Contact: Jim Shosenberg, editor
Published 10 times a year

## Ontario Medical Review
525 University Avenue, Suite 300, Toronto, Ont. M5G 2K7
Phone: (416) 599-2580  Fax: (416) 599-9309
Contact: Jeff Henry, managing editor
Published monthly

## Oral Health
1450 Don Mills Road, Don Mills, Ont. M3B 2X7
Phone: (416) 442-2046  Fax: (416) 442-2201
Contact: Erla Kay, publisher
Published monthly

## Patient Care
1120 Birchmount Road, Suite 200, Scarborough, Ont. M1K 5G4
Phone: (416) 750-8900  Fax: (416) 751-8126
Contact: Vil Meere, editor
Published 10 times a year

## Pharmacist News
777 Bay Street, Toronto, Ont. M5W 1A7
Phone: (416) 596-5950  Fax: (416) 593-3162
Contact: Polly Thompson, editor
Published 14 times a year

## Pharmacy Practice
1120 Birchmount Road, Suite 200, Scarborough, Ont. M1K 5G4
Phone: (416) 750-8900  Fax: (416) 751-8126
Contact: Anne Bokma, editor
Published 10 times a year

## Rehab and Community Care Management
101 Thorncliffe Park Drive, Toronto, Ont. M4H 1M2
Phone: (416) 421-7944  Fax: (416) 421-0966
Contact: Helmut Dostal, managing editor
Published quarterly

## Wellness MD
344 Edgeley Boulevard, Unit 16-17, Concord, Ont. L4K 4B7
Phone: (905) 738-9086  Fax: (905) 738-4994

Contact: Gordon Bagley, editor
Published bimonthly

## Industrial & Design

**Canadian Facility Management & Design**
62 Olsen Drive, Don Mills, Ont. M3A 3J3
Phone: (416) 447-3417  Fax: (416) 447-4410
Contact: Victor von Buchstab, editor
Published bimonthly

**Canadian Industrial Equipment News**
1450 Don Mills Road, Don Mills, Ont. M3B 2X7
Phone: (416) 445-6641  Fax: (416) 442-2214
Contact: Olga Markovich, editor/associate publisher
Published monthly

**Canadian Machinery & Metalworking**
777 Bay Street, Toronto, Ont. M5W 1A7
Phone: (416) 596-5714  Fax: (416) 596-5881
Contact: Mike Overment, editor
Published 8 times a year

**Canadian Occupational Safety**
Royal Life Building, Suite 209, 277 Lakeshore Road E., Oakville,
    Ont. L6J 6J3
Phone: (905) 842-2884  Fax: (905) 842-8226
Contact: Jackie Roth, editor
Published bimonthly

**Canadian Packaging**
777 Bay Street, Toronto, Ont. M5W 1A7
Phone: (416) 596-5746  Fax: (416) 596-5810
Contact: Douglas Faulkner, editor
Published 11 times a year

**Canadian Plastics**
1450 Don Mills Road, Don Mills, Ont. M3B 2X7

Phone: (416) 445-6641  Fax: (416) 442-2213
Contact: Michael Shelley, editor
Published 8 times a year

## Canadian Textile Journal

1, rue Pacifique, Ste.-Anne-de-Bellevue, Que. H9X 1C5
Phone: (514) 457-2347  Fax: (514) 457-2147
Contact: Gillian Crosby, editor
Published 7 times a year

## Equipment Journal

150 Lakeshore Road W., Suite 36, Mississauga, Ont. L5H 3R2
Phone: (905) 274-4883  Fax: (905) 274-8686
Contact: E.E. Abel, publisher/editor
Published 17 times a year

## Heating–Plumbing–Air Conditioning

1370 Don Mills Road, Suite 300, Don Mills, Ont. M3B 3N7
Phone: (416) 759-9595  Fax: (416) 442-2214
Contact: Bruce Cole, editor
Published 7 times a year

## Laboratory Product News

1450 Don Mills Road, Don Mills, Ont. M3B 2X7
Phone: (416) 442-2052  Fax: (416) 442-2201
Contact: Rita Tate, publisher/editor
Published bimonthly

## Machinery & Equipment MRO

1450 Don Mills Road, Don Mills, Ont. M3B 2X7
Phone: (416) 442-2089  Fax: (416) 442-2214
Contact: William Roebuck, editor
Published bimonthly

## Metalworking Production & Purchasing

135 Spy Court, Markham, Ont. L3R 5H6
Phone: (905) 477-3222  Fax: (905) 477-4320
Contact: Maurice Holtham, editor
Published bimonthly

**New Equipment News**
204 Richmond Street W., Toronto, Ont. M5V 1V6
Phone: (416) 599-3737  Fax: (416) 599-3730
Contact: Barrie Lehman, editor
Published monthly

**Occupational Health & Safety**
1450 Don Mills Road, Don Mills, Ont. M3B 2X7
Phone: (416) 445-6641  Fax: (416) 442-2200
Contact: Margaret Nearing, editor
Published 7 times a year

**Plant**
777 Bay Street, Toronto, Ont. M5W 1A7
Phone: (416) 596-5776  Fax: (416) 596-5552
Contact: Wayne Karl, editor
Published 18 times a year

**Plant Engineering & Maintenance**
277 Lakeshore Road E., Suite 209, Oakville, Ont. L6J 6J3
Phone: (905) 842-2884  Fax: (905) 842-8226
Contact: Rae Robb, editor
Published 7 times a year

**Plastics Business**
1450 Don Mills Road, Don Mills, Ont. M3B 2X7
Phone: (416) 445-6641  Fax: (416) 442-2213
Contact: Michael Shelley, editor
Published quarterly

## Landscaping & Horticulture

**Canadian Florist, Greenhouse & Nursery**
1090 Aerowood Drive, Unit 1, Mississauga, Ont. L4W 1Y5
Phone: (905) 625-2730  Fax: (905) 625-1355
Contact: Peter Heywood, editor/publisher
Published monthly

**Greenhouse Canada**
222 Argyle Avenue, Delhi, Ont. N4B 2Y2
Phone: (519) 582-2513  Fax: (519) 582-4040
Contact: Ben Steidman, editor
Published monthly

**GreenMaster**
80 West Beaver Creek, Suite 18, Richmond Hill, Ont. L4B 1H3
Phone: (905) 771-7333  Fax: (905) 771-7336
Contact: Dennis Mellersh, editor
Published bimonthly

**Hortwest**
5830 – 176A Street, Suite 101, Surrey, B.C. V3S 4E3
Phone: (604) 574-7772  Fax: (604) 574-7773
Contact: Jane Stock, managing editor
Published bimonthly

**Landmark**
1000 – 1777 Victoria Avenue, Regina, Sask. S4P 4K5
Phone: (306) 584-1000  Fax: (306) 584-2824
Contact: Tom Steve, editor
Published bimonthly

**Landscape Trades**
7856 Fifth Line South, R.R.4, Milton, Ont. L9T 2X8
Phone: (905) 875-1805  Fax: (905) 875-3942
Contact: Linda Erskine, editor
Published 9 times a year

**The Ontario Land Surveyor**
1043 McNicoll Avenue, Scarborough, Ont. M1W 3W6
Phone: (416) 491-9020  Fax: (416) 491-2576
Contact: Brian Munday, editor
Published quarterly

**Prairie Landscape Magazine**
1000 – 1777 Victoria Avenue, Regina, Sask. S4P 4K5
Phone: (306) 584-1000  Fax: (306) 352-4110

Contact: Tara August, editor
Published bimonthly

**Turf & Recreation**
123B King Street, Delhi, Ont. N4B 1X9
Phone: (519) 582-8873  Fax: (519) 582-8877
Contact: Mike Jiggens, editor
Published bimonthly

## Media, Music, & Communications

**Broadcast Technology**
P.O. Box 420, Bolton, Ont. L7E 5T3
Phone: (905) 857-6076  Fax: (905) 857-6045
Contact: Doug Loney, publisher/editor
Published 10 times a year

**Broadcaster**
1450 Don Mills Road, Don Mills, Ont. M3B 2X7
Phone: (416) 445-6641  Fax: (416) 442-2213
Contact: John Bugailiskis, editor
Published 10 times a year

**Cable Communications Magazine**
57 Peachwood Court, Kitchener, Ont. N2B 1S7
Phone: (519) 744-4111  Fax: (519) 744-1261
Contact: Udo Salewsky, publisher/editor
Published bimonthly

**Cablecaster**
1450 Don Mills Road, Don Mills, Ont. M3B 2X7
Phone: (416) 445-6641  Fax: (416) 442-2213
Contact: Steve Pawlett, editor
Published 8 times a year

**Canada on Location**
366 Adelaide Street W., Suite 500, Toronto, Ont. M5V 1R9
Phone: (416) 408-2300  Fax: (416) 408-0870

Contact: Mary Maddever, editor
Published twice a year

## Canadian Music Trade
23 Hannover Drive, Unit 7, St. Catharines, Ont. L2W 1A3
Phone: (905) 641-1512  Fax: (905) 641-1648
Contact: Jim Norris, publisher
Published bimonthly

## Masthead: The Magazine about Magazines
1606 Sedlescomb Drive, Unit 8, Mississauga, Ont. L4X 1M6
Phone: (905) 625-7070  Fax: (905) 625-4856
Contact: Doug Bennet, editor
Published 10 times a year

## Playback
366 Adelaide Street W., Suite 500, Toronto, Ont. M5V 1R9
Phone: (416) 408-2300  Fax: (416) 408-0870
Contact: Mary Maddever, editor
Published biweekly

## Playback International
366 Adelaide Street W., Suite 500, Toronto, Ont. M5V 1R9
Phone: (416) 408-2300  Fax: (416) 408-0870
Contact: Mary Maddever, editor
Published twice a year

## Premiere Video Magazine
1314 Britannia Road E., Mississauga, Ont. L4W 1C8
Phone: (905) 564-1033  Fax: (905) 564-3398
Contact: Salah Bachir, editor
Published monthly

## Press Review
P.O. Box 368, Station A, Toronto, Ont. M5W 1C2
Phone: (416) 368-0512  Fax: (416) 366-0104
Contact: Sheila Johnston, managing editor
Published quarterly

## Professional Sound

23 Hannover Drive, Unit 7, St. Catharines, Ont. L2W 1A3
Phone: (905) 641-3471  Fax: (905) 641-1648
Contact: Jim Norris, publisher
Published quarterly

## The Publisher

90 Eglinton Avenue E., Suite 206, Toronto, Ont. M4P 2Y3
Phone: (416) 482-1090  Fax: (416) 482-1908
Contact: Dave de Yong, editor
Published 10 times a year

## RPM Weekly

6 Brentcliffe Road, Toronto, Ont. M4G 3Y2
Phone: (416) 425-0257  Fax: (416) 425-8629
Contact: Walter Grealis, publisher

# Miscellaneous Trade & Professional

## Apparel

1, rue Pacifique, Ste.-Anne-de-Bellevue, Que. H9X 1C5
Phone: (514) 457-2347  Fax: (514) 457-2147
Contact: Gillian Crosby, editor
Published monthly

## Canadian Ceramics Quarterly

2175 Sheppard Avenue E., Suite 110, Willowdale, Ont. M2J 1W8
Phone: (416) 491-2886  Fax: (416) 491-1670
Contact: M. Sayer, editor
Published quarterly

## The Canadian Firefighter

P.O. Box 95, Station D, Etobicoke, Ont. M9A 4X1
Phone: (416) 233-2516  Fax: (416) 233-2051
Contact: Lorne Campbell, editor/publisher
Published bimonthly

## Canadian Footwear Journal
1, rue Pacifique, Ste.-Anne-de-Bellevue, Que. H9X 1C5
Phone: (514) 457-2423  Fax: (514) 457-2577
Contact: Barbara McLeish, managing editor
Published 8 times a year

## Canadian Funeral Director
174 Harwood Avenue S., Suite 206, Ajax, Ont. L1S 2H7
Phone: (905) 427-6121  Fax: (905) 427-6121
Contact: Scott Hillier, editor
Published monthly

## Canadian Funeral News
237 – 8th Avenue S.E., Suite 600, Calgary, Alta. T2G 5C3
Phone: (403) 264-3270  Fax: (403) 264-3276
Contact: Natika Sunstrom, editor
Published monthly

## Canadian Home Style Magazine
598 Stillwater Court, Burlington, Ont. L7T 4G7
Phone: (905) 681-7932  Fax: (905) 681-2141
Contact: Laurie O'Halloran, publisher/editorial director
Published bimonthly

## Canadian Interiors
360 Dupont Street, Toronto, Ont. M5R 1V9
Phone: (416) 966-9944  Fax: (416) 966-9946
Contact: Sheri Craig, publisher/editor
Published bimonthly

## Canadian Jeweller
1448 Lawrence Avenue W., Suite 302, Toronto, Ont. M4A 2V6
Phone: (416) 755-5199  Fax: (416) 755-9123
Contact: Carol Besler, editor
Published 7 times a year

## Canadian Property Management
33 Fraser Avenue, Suite 208, Toronto, Ont. M6K 3J9
Phone: (416) 588-6220  Fax: (416) 588-5217

Contact: Kim Morningstar, editor
Published 7 times a year

## Canadian Realtor News

320 Queen Street, Suite 2100, Ottawa, Ont. KIR 5A3
Phone: (613) 234-3372  Fax: (613) 234-2567
Contact: Jim McCarthy, editor
Published monthly

## Canadian Rental Service

145 Thames Road W., Exeter, Ont. NOM 1S3
Phone: (519) 235-2400  Fax: (519) 235-0798
Contact: Peter Darbishire, managing editor
Published 8 times a year

## Canadian Security

46 Crockford Boulevard, Scarborough, Ont. MIR 3C3
Phone: (416) 755-4343  Fax: (416) 755-7487
Contact: Robert Robinson, editor
Published 7 times a year

## Canadian Veterinary Journal

339 Booth Street, Ottawa, Ont. KIR 7KI
Phone: (613) 236-1162  Fax: (613) 236-9681
Contact: Dr. Doug Hare, editor
Published monthly

## Condominium Magazine

33 Fraser Avenue, Suite 208, Toronto, Ont. M6K 3J9
Phone: (416) 588-6220  Fax: (416) 588-5217
Contact: Kim Morningstar, managing editor
Published monthly

## Cosmetics

777 Bay Street, 5th Floor, Toronto, Ont. M5W IA7
Phone: (416) 596-5246  Fax: (416) 596-5179
Contact: Ron Wood, editor
Published bimonthly

## Fire Fighting in Canada
222 Argyle Avenue, Delhi, Ont. N4B 2Y2
Phone: (519) 582-2513  Fax: (519) 582-4040
Contact: James Haley, editor
Published 10 times a year

## Footwear Forum
1448 Lawrence Avenue E., Suite 302, Toronto, Ont. M4A 2V6
Phone: (416) 755-5199  Fax: (416) 755-9123
Contact: Victoria Curran, editor
Published 7 times a year

## Gifts & Tablewares
1450 Don Mills Road, Don Mills, Ont. M3B 2X7
Phone: (416) 442-2996  Fax: (416) 442-2213
Contact: Dawn Dickinson, editor
Published 7 times a year

## Lighting Magazine
395 Matheson Boulevard E., Mississauga, Ont. L4Z 2H2
Phone: (905) 890-1846  Fax: (905) 890-5769
Contact: Bryan Rogers, editor
Published bimonthly

## Luggage, Leathergoods & Accessories
501 Oakdale Road, Downsview, Ont. M3N 1W7
Phone: (416) 746-7360  Fax: (416) 746-1421
Contact: Virginia Hutton, publisher/editor
Published quarterly

## Materials Management & Distribution
777 Bay Street, Toronto, Ont. M5W 1A7
Phone: (416) 596-5709  Fax: (416) 596-5554
Contact: Rob Robertson, editor
Published monthly

## Municipal World
P.O. Box 399, St. Thomas, Ont. N5P 3V3
Phone: (519) 633-0031  Fax: (519) 633-1001

Contact: Michael Smither, editor
Published monthly

## The Ontario Technologist
10 Four Seasons Place, Suite 404, Etobicoke, Ont. M9B 6H7
Phone: (416) 621-9621  Fax: (416) 621-8694
Contact: Ruth Klein, editor
Published bimonthly

## Optical Prism
31 Hastings Drive, Unionville, Ont. L3R 4Y5
Phone: (905) 475-9343  Fax: (905) 477-2821
Contact: Allan Vezina, editor/publisher
Published 9 times a year

## Physics in Canada
151 Slater Street, Suite 903, Ottawa, Ont. KIP 5H3
Phone: (613) 237-3392  Fax: (613) 238-1677
Contact: J.S.C. McKee, editor
Published bimonthly

## Salon Magazine
411 Richmond Street E., Suite 300, Toronto, Ont. M5A 3S5
Phone: (416) 869-3131  Fax: (416) 869-3008
Contact: Alison Wood, editor
Published bimonthly

## Style
1448 Lawrence Avenue E., Suite 302, Toronto, Ont. M4A 2V6
Phone: (416) 755-5199  Fax: (416) 755-9123
Contact: Marsha Ross, editor
Published 14 times a year

## Toys & Games
501 Oakdale Road, Downsview, Ont. M3N IW7
Phone: (416) 746-7360  Fax: (416) 746-1421
Contact: Lynn Winston, editor
Published bimonthly

**Woodworking**
135 Spy Court, Markham, Ont. L3R 5H6
Phone: (905) 477-3222  Fax: (905) 477-4320
Contact: Maurice Holtham, editor
Published 7 times a year

## Printing & Photography

**Canadian Printer**
777 Bay Street, Toronto, Ont. M5W 1A7
Phone: (416) 596-5781  Fax: (416) 596-5965
Contact: Nick Hancock, editor
Published 10 times a year

**The Graphic Monthly**
1606 Sedlescomb Drive, Unit 8, Mississauga, Ont. L4X 1M6
Phone: (905) 625-7070  Fax: (905) 625-4856
Contact: Nancy Clark, managing editor
Published bimonthly

**Photo Dealer News**
130 Spy Court, Markham, Ont. L3R 5H6
Phone: (905) 475-8440  Fax: (905) 475-9246
Contact: Jim Dominey, editor
Published bimonthly

**Photo Retailer**
185 St. Paul, Quebec, Que. G1K 3W2
Phone: (418) 692-2110  Fax: (418) 692-3392
Contact: Don Long, editor
Published quarterly

**Photonews**
101 Thorncliffe Park Drive, Toronto, Ont. M4H 1M2
Phone: (416) 421-7944  Fax: (416) 421-0966
Contact: Gunter Ott, editor
Published 3 times a year

**PrintAction**
2240 Midland Avenue, Suite 201, Scarborough, Ont. MIP 4R8
Phone: (416) 299-6007  Fax: (416) 299-6674
Contact: Julian Mills, editor
Published monthly

# Transportation & Cargo

**Atlantic Transportation Journal**
6029 Cunard Street, Halifax, N.S. B3K IE5
Phone: (902) 420-0437  Fax: (902) 423-8212
Contact: Ken Partridge, managing editor
Published quarterly

**Canadian Shipper**
777 Bay Street, Toronto, Ont. M5W IA7
Phone: (416) 596-5709  Fax: (416) 596-5881
Contact: Robert Robertson, editor
Published bimonthly

**Canadian Transportation Logistics**
1450 Don Mills Road, Don Mills, Ont. M3B 2X7
Phone: (416) 442-2228  Fax: (416) 442-2214
Contact: Bonnie Toews, editor
Published monthly

**Harbour & Shipping**
1765 Bellevue Avenue, West Vancouver, B.C. V7V IA8
Phone: (604) 922-6717  Fax: (604) 922-1739
Contact: Liz Bennett, editor
Published monthly

**Motor Truck**
1450 Don Mills Road, Don Mills, Ont. M3B 2X7
Phone: (416) 445-6641  Fax: (416) 442-2213
Contact: Barry Holmes, executive editor
Published monthly

**Today's Trucking**
452 Attwell Drive, Suite 100, Etobicoke, Ont. M9W 5C3
Phone: (416) 798-2977  Fax: (416) 798-3017
Contact: Rolf Lockwood, editor
Published 10 times a year

**Truck News**
1450 Don Mills Road, Don Mills, Ont. M3B 2X7
Phone: (416) 442-2062  Fax: (416) 442-2092
Contact: Brenda Yarrow, editor
Published monthly

**Truck West**
1555 Dublin Avenue, Unit 9, Winnipeg, Man. R3E 3M8
Phone: (204) 831-8814  Fax: (204) 888-3853
Contact: Patrick Munro, publisher
Published monthly

**Truck World**
11 – 106 East 14th Street, North Vancouver, B.C. V7L 2N3
Phone: (604) 984-2002  Fax: (604) 984-2820
Contact: Ken Barnsohn, managing editor
Published bimonthly

## Travel

**Canadian Travel Press**
310 Dupont Street, Toronto, Ont. M5R 1V9
Phone: (416) 968-7252  Fax: (416) 968-2377
Contact: Edith Baxter, editor
Published weekly

**Canadian Traveller**
5200 Miller Road, Suite 115, Richmond, B.C. V7B 1K5
Phone: (604) 276-0818  Fax: (604) 276-0843
Contact: Doreen Ormiston, editor
Published monthly

## Meetings & Incentive Travel
777 Bay Street, 5th Floor, Toronto, Ont. M5W 1A7
Phone: (416) 596-2697  Fax: (416) 596-5810
Contact: Lori Bak, editor
Published 8 times a year

## Tours on Motorcoach
C.P. 365, Montreal, Que. H2Y 3H1
Phone: (514) 274-0004  Fax: (514) 274-5884
Contact: Guy Jonkman, publisher/editor
Published monthly

## Travel Courier
310 Dupont Street, Toronto, Ont. M5R 1V9
Phone: (416) 968-7252  Fax: (416) 968-2377
Contact: Edith Baxter, editor-in-chief
Published weekly

## Travelweek Bulletin
282 Richmond Street E., Suite 100, Toronto, Ont. M5A 1P4
Phone: (416) 365-1500  Fax: (416) 365-1504
Contact: Patrick Dineen, editor
Published twice a week

# 4

# DAILY NEWSPAPERS

Many a successful writing career began in the pages of a small community newspaper. High-profile, high-circulation magazines are alluring, but top-quality magazine pieces are among the most difficult of literary forms, and many of these publications are disinclined to try out inexperienced writers. Discouragement mounts with each rejection slip, often to the point where a promising writing career is abandoned. A planned approach to becoming a published writer is the surest road to success.

Weekly community newspapers are a good starting point. With small staffs and low budgets, their editors are often pleased to accept outside contributions, particularly feature articles that cover the local scene. And since payment is modest, there is little competition from more experienced writers. Many established writers began by writing for no pay for their local paper.

Always remember that news loses its value as quickly as it changes, and it is therefore usually gathered hurriedly – on large papers and small – by staff reporters. Therefore, it is to your advantage to concentrate on background stories about ongoing issues, or to write profiles of prominent, interesting, or unusual local citizens and institutions. Stories about travel, hobbies, lifestyles, personal finance, and business are particularly welcome. So are strong human-interest pieces – always among the best-read articles in any newspaper. Most editors like to build a stash of timely articles that do not have to be used immediately.

Writers do not propose ideas to newspapers in the same way as they do for magazines. On newspapers, time is a much more crucial factor. So rather than craft a written proposal, it is perfectly acceptable to solicit a go-ahead decision from the editor of one of the paper's sections with a quick telephone call. Initially, however, they will probably want to see tearsheets of published work. If they have published your letters, it may be worth including clippings of these, too.

If you are considering this market, your best preparation is to read critically several issues of the paper. Note the style, the story lengths preferred, the use of photographs, the paper's editorial policy, and the difference in content, construction, and tone of news stories and feature articles. If you have never studied journalism, you might need a reference book, such as *News Reporting and Writing*, by Melvin Mencher, a professor at Columbia University's School of Journalism (see Chapter 10, Book Resources).

Naturally, it will take more experience to sell to large, well-staffed metropolitan dailies like the *Toronto Star* or the *Winnipeg Free Press*. But even here, the outside contributor has a chance, provided he or she has some specialized knowledge, can handle human-interest material deftly, and can write full-bodied issue stories with conviction and authority. For a well-written, well-researched article on an important or intriguing subject, many of the bigger city dailies pay as much or more than the average consumer magazine. And they settle faster: most pay at the end of the month, some even on acceptance.

Freelance writers submit their manuscripts to newspapers in much the same way as they do for magazines, and many write successfully for both. They meet deadlines even when it means losing sleep. They are always aware that for the daily press, accuracy and reliability are two virtues worth cultivating, even under pressure. While the news story is essentially factual and must have a strong sense of immediacy, the feature article needs body and strength as well as originality and freshness. Timing is a key element. Keep a calendar of dates for seasonal stories – Hallowe'en, Thanksgiving, Chinese New Year, Canada Day, and so on – and read behind the news for feature ideas.

Besides writing for your city paper, look for opportunities to act as a correspondent, or stringer, for one published elsewhere. The full listing of English-language Canadian daily newspapers that follows will prove useful. For suburban weeklies, check the *CARD* directory. Canadian newspapers are also listed in *Matthews Media Directory* and annual publications such as the *Canadian Almanac & Directory* and *Corpus Almanac and Canadian Sourcebook* (see Chapter 10, Book Resources).

## Alberta

**Calgary Herald**
215 – 16th Street S.E., Calgary, Alta. T2P 0W8
Phone: (403) 235-7388   Fax: (403) 235-8668

**Calgary Sun**
2615 – 12th Street N.E., Calgary, Alta. T2E 7W9
Phone: (403) 250-4200   Fax: (403) 250-8439

**Daily Herald Tribune**
10604 – 100th Street, Grande Prairie, Alta. T8V 2M5
Phone: (403) 532-1110   Fax: (403) 532-2120

**Edmonton Journal**
10006 – 101st Street, Edmonton, Alta. T5J 2S6
Phone: (403) 429-5400

**Edmonton Sun**
4990 – 92nd Avenue, Suite 250, Edmonton, Alta. T6B 3A1
Phone: (403) 468-0181   Fax: (403) 468-0128

**Fort McMurray Today**
8550 Franklin Avenue, Bag 4008, Fort McMurray, Alta. T9H 3G1
Phone: (403) 743-8186   Fax: (403) 790-1006

**Lethbridge Herald**
504 – 7th Street S., Lethbridge, Alta. T1J 3Z7
Phone: (403) 328-4411   Fax: (403) 328-4536

**Medicine Hat News**
3257 Dunmore Road S.E., P.O. Box 10, Medicine Hat, Alta. T1A 7E6
Phone: (403) 527-1101   Fax: (403) 527-6029

**Red Deer Advocate**
2950 Bremner Avenue, Bag 5200, P.O. Box 250, Red Deer,
    Alta. T4N 5G3
Phone: (403) 343-2400  Fax: (403) 342-4051

## British Columbia

**Alaska Highway News**
9916 – 98th Street, Fort St. John, B.C. V1J 3T8
Phone: (604) 785-5631  Fax: (604) 785-3522

**Alberni Valley Times**
4918 Napier Street, P.O. Box 400, Port Alberni, B.C. V9Y 7N1
Phone: (604) 723-8171  Fax: (604) 723-0586

**Cranbrook Daily Townsman**
822 Cranbrook Street N., Cranbrook, B.C. V1C 3R9
Phone: (604) 426-5201  Fax: (604) 426-5003

**Kamloops Daily News**
393 Seymour Street, Kamloops, B.C. V2C 6P6
Phone: (604) 372-2331  Fax: (604) 372-0823

**Kelowna Daily Courier**
550 Doyle Avenue, Kelowna, B.C. V1Y 7V1
Phone: (604) 762-4445  Fax: (604) 762-3866

**Kimberley Daily Bulletin**
335 Spokane Street, Kimberley, B.C. V1A 1Y9
Phone: (604) 427-5333

**Nanaimo Daily Free Press**
223 Commercial Street, Box 69, Nanaimo, B.C. V9R 5K5
Phone: (604) 753-3451  Fax: (604) 753-8730

**Nelson Daily News**
266 Baker Street, Nelson, B.C. V1L 4H3
Phone: (604) 352-3552  Fax: (604) 352-2418

**Peace River Block News**
901 – 100th Avenue, P.O. Box 180, Dawson Creek, B.C. V1G 4G6
Phone: (604) 782-4888  Fax: (604) 782-6770

**Penticton Herald**
186 Nanaimo Avenue W., Penticton, B.C. V2A 1N4
Phone: (604) 492-4002  Fax: (604) 492-2403

**Prince George Citizen**
150 Brunswick Street, P.O. Box 5700, Prince George,
   B.C. V2L 5K9
Phone: (604) 562-2441  Fax: (604) 562-9201

**Prince Rupert Daily News**
P.O. Box 580, Prince Rupert, B.C. V8J 3R9
Phone: (604) 624-6781  Fax: (604) 624-2851

**Trail Times**
1163 Cedar Avenue, Trail, B.C. V1R 4B8
Phone: (604) 364-1416  Fax: (604) 368-8550

**Vancouver Sun Province**
2250 Granville Street, Vancouver, B.C. V6H 3G2
Phone: (604) 732-2478  Fax: (604) 732-2704

**Vernon Daily News**
3309 – 31st Avenue, Vernon, B.C. V1T 6N8
Phone: (604) 545-0671  Fax: (604) 545-7193

**Victoria Times–Colonist**
2621 Douglas Street, Box 300, Victoria, B.C. V8W 2N4
Phone: (604) 380-5211  Fax: (604) 380-5255

## Manitoba

**Brandon Sun**
501 Rosser Avenue, Brandon, Man. R7A 5Z6
Phone: (204) 727-2451  Fax: (204) 725-0976

**Daily Graphic**
1941 Saskatchewan Avenue W., P.O. Box 130, Portage La Prairie,
Man. R1N 3B4
Phone: (204) 857-3427  Fax: (204) 239-1270

**Flin Flon Reminder**
P.O. Box 727, 10 North Avenue, Flin Flon, Man. R8A 1N5
Phone: (204) 687-3454  Fax: (204) 687-4473

**Winnipeg Free Press**
1355 Mountain Avenue, Winnipeg, Man. R2X 3B6
Phone: (204) 697-7000  Fax: (204) 697-7370

**Winnipeg Sun**
1700 Church Avenue, Winnipeg, Man. R2X 3A2
Phone: (204) 694-2022  Fax: (204) 632-8709

## New Brunswick

**Fredericton Daily Gleaner**
Prospect Street at Smythe, P.O. Box 3370, Fredericton,
N.B. E3B 5A2
Phone: (506) 452-6671  Fax: (506) 452-7405

**Moncton Times–Transcript**
939 Main Street, P.O. Box 1001, Moncton, N.B. E1C 8P3
Phone: (506) 859-4900  Fax: 859-4899

**Telegraph–Journal & Evening Times–Globe**
210 Crown Street, P.O. Box 2350, Saint John, N.B. E2L 3V8
Phone: (506) 632-8888  Fax: (506) 648-2661

## Newfoundland

**St. John's Telegram**
P.O. Box 5970, St. John's, Nfld. A1C 5X7
Phone: (709) 364-6300  Fax: (709) 364-9333

**Western Star**
West Street, P.O. Box 460, Corner Brook, Nfld. A2H 6E7
Phone: (709) 634-4348  Fax: (709) 634-9824

## Nova Scotia

**Amherst Daily News**
P.O. Box 280, Amherst, N.S. B4H 3Z2
Phone: (902) 667-5102  Fax: (902) 667-0419

**Cape Breton Post**
255 George Street, Box 1500, Sydney, N.S. B1P 6K6
Phone: (902) 564-5451  Fax: (902) 562-7077

**Chronicle–Herald & Mail-Star**
1650 Argyle Street, Halifax, N.S. B3J 2T2
Phone: (902) 426-2898  Fax: (902) 426-3382

**Evening News**
352 East River Road, New Glasgow, N.S. B2H 5E2
Phone: (902) 752-3000  Fax: (902) 752-1945

**Halifax Daily News**
P.O. Box 8330, Station A, Halifax, N.S. B3K 5M1
Phone: (902) 468-2288  Fax: (902) 468-3609

**Truro Daily News**
6 Louise Street, P.O. Box 220, Truro, N.S. B2N 5C3
Phone: (902) 893-9405  Fax: (902) 893-0518

## Ontario

**Barrie Examiner**
16 Bayfield Street, Barrie, Ont. L4M 4T6
Phone: (705) 728-2414  Fax: (705) 726-7245

**Belleville Intelligencer**
45 Bridge Street E., Belleville, Ont. K8N IL5
Phone: (613) 962-9171  Fax: (613) 962-9652

**Brantford Expositor**
53 Dalhousie Street, Brantford, Ont. N3T 5S8
Phone: (519) 756-2020  Fax: (519) 756-4911

**Brockville Recorder & Times**
23 King Street W., Box 10, Brockville, Ont. K6V 5T8
Phone: (613) 342-4441  Fax: (613) 342-4456

**Cambridge Reporter**
26 Ainslie Street S., Cambridge, Ont. NIR 3KI
Phone: (519) 621-3810  Fax: (519) 621-8239

**Chatham Daily News**
45 – 4th Street, Box 2007, Chatham, Ont. N7M 2G4
Phone: (519) 354-2000  Fax: (519) 436-0949

**Cobourg Daily Star**
415 King Street W., Box 400, Cobourg, Ont. K9A 4LI
Phone: (905) 372-0131  Fax: (905) 372-4966

**Cornwall Standard–Freeholder**
44 Pitt Street, Cornwall, Ont. K6J 3P3
Phone: (613) 933-3160  Fax: (613) 933-7521

**The Financial Post**
333 King Street E., Toronto, Ont. M5A 4N2
Phone: (416) 350-6000  Fax: (416) 350-6031

**Fort Frances Daily Bulletin**
P.O. Box 339, Fort Frances, Ont. P9A 3M7
Phone: (807) 274-5373  Fax: (807) 274-7286

**Globe and Mail**
444 Front Street W., Toronto, Ont. M5V 2S9
Phone: (416) 585-5600  Fax: (416) 585-5275

**Guelph Mercury**
14 Macdonell Street, Suite 8, Guelph, Ont. NIH 6P7
Phone: (519) 822-4310   Fax: (519) 767-1681

**Hamilton Spectator**
44 Frid Street, Hamilton, Ont. L8N 3G3
Phone: (416) 526-3333   Fax: (416) 522-1696

**Kenora Daily Miner & News**
33 Main Street S., P.O. Box 1620, Kenora, Ont. P9N 3X7
Phone: (807) 468-5555   Fax: (807) 468-4318

**Kingston Whig–Standard**
306 King Street E., Kingston, Ont. K7L 4Z7
Phone: (613) 544-5000   Fax: (613) 530-4122

**Kitchener–Waterloo Record**
225 Fairway Road, Kitchener, Ont. N2G 4E5
Phone: (519) 894-2231   Fax: (519) 894-3912

**Lindsay Daily Post**
15 William Street N., Lindsay, Ont. K9V 3Z8
Phone: (705) 324-2114   Fax: (705) 324-0174

**London Free Press**
369 York Street, Box 2280, London, Ont. N6A 4G1
Phone: (519) 679-1111   Fax: (519) 667-4523

**Niagara Falls Review**
4801 Valley Way, Box 270, Niagara Falls, Ont. L2E 6T6
Phone: (416) 358-5711   Fax: (416) 356-0785

**North Bay Nugget**
259 Worthington Street W., P.O. Box 570, North Bay, Ont. P1B 8J6
Phone: (705) 472-3200   Fax: (705) 472-1438

**Northern Daily News**
8 Duncan Avenue, Kirkland Lake, Ont. P2N 3L4
Phone: (705) 567-5321   Fax: (705) 567-6162

## Orillia Packet & Times

31 Colborne Street E., Orillia, Ont. L3V 1T4
Phone: (705) 325-1355  Fax: (705) 325-7691

## Ottawa Citizen

1101 Baxter Road, Box 5020, Ottawa, Ont. K2C 3M4
Phone: (613) 829-9100  Fax: (613) 726-1198

## Ottawa Sun

380 Hunt Club Road, Ottawa, Ont. K1G 5H7
Phone: (613) 739-7100

## Owen Sound Sun–Times

290 – 9th Street E., Owen Sound, Ont. N4K 5P2
Phone: (519) 376-2250  Fax: (519) 376-7190

## Pembroke Daily News

86 Pembroke Street W., Box 10, Pembroke, Ont. K8A 6X1
Phone: (613) 735-3141  Fax: (613) 732-7214

## Pembroke Observer

186 Alexander Street, Pembroke, Ont. K8A 4L9
Phone: (613) 732-3691  Fax: (613) 732-2645

## Peterborough Examiner

400 Water Street, P.O. Box 3890, Peterborough, Ont. K9J 8L4
Phone: (705) 745-4641  Fax: (705) 741-3217

## Port Hope Guide

415 King Street W., Box 400, Cobourg, Ont. K9A 4L1
Phone: (905) 372-0131  Fax: (905) 372-4966

## St. Catharines Standard

17 Queen Street, St. Catharines, Ont. L2R 5G5
Phone: (416) 684-7251  Fax: (416) 684-8011

## St. Thomas Times–Journal

16 Hincks Street, St. Thomas, Ont. N5P 3W6
Phone: (519) 631-2790  Fax: (519) 631-5653

**Sarnia Observer**
140 South Front Street, Sarnia, Ont. N7T 7M8
Phone: (519) 344-3641   Fax: (519) 332-2951

**Sault Ste. Marie Star**
145 Old Garden River Road, Sault Ste. Marie, Ont. P6A 5M5
Phone: (705) 759-3030   Fax: (705) 942-8690

**Simcoe Reformer**
105 Donly Drive, Simcoe, Ont. N3Y 4L2
Phone: (519) 426-5710   Fax: (519) 426-9255

**Stratford Beacon Herald**
108 Ontario Street, P.O. Box 430, Stratford, Ont. N5A 6T6
Phone: (519) 271-2220   Fax: (519) 271-1026

**Sudbury Star**
33 Mackenzie Street, Sudbury, Ont. P3C 4Y1
Phone: (705) 674-5271   Fax: (705) 674-0624

**Thunder Bay Times–News & Chronical–Journal**
75 South Cumberland Street, Thunder Bay, Ont. P7B 1A3
Phone: (807) 343-6200   Fax: (807) 345-5991

**Timmins Daily Press**
187 Cedar Street S., Timmins, Ont. P4N 2G9
Phone: (705) 268-5050   Fax: (705) 268-7373

**Toronto Star**
1 Yonge Street, Suite 300, Toronto, Ont. M5E 1E6
Phone: (416) 869-4321   Fax: (416) 869-4416

**Toronto Sun**
333 King Street E., Toronto, Ont. M5A 3X5
Phone: (416) 947-2333   Fax: (416) 361-1205

**Welland–Port Colborne Tribune**
228 East Main Street, Welland, Ont. L3B 3W8
Phone: (416) 732-2411   Fax: (416) 732-4883

**Windsor Star**
167 Ferry Street, Windsor, Ont. N9A 4M5
Phone: (519) 255-5711  Fax: (519) 255-5778

**Woodstock–Ingersoll Daily Sentinel Review**
16 Brock Street, Woodstock, Ont. N4S 8A5
Phone: (519) 537-2341  Fax: (519) 537-3049

## Prince Edward Island

**Guardian & Evening Patriot**
165 Prince Street., Charlottetown, P.E.I. C1A 4R7
Phone: (902) 629-6000  Fax: (902) 566-3808

**Journal Pioneer**
4 Queen Street, Box 2480, Summerside, P.E.I. C1N 4K5
Phone: (902) 436-2121  Fax: (902) 436-3027

## Quebec

**The Gazette**
250 St. Antoine Street W., Montreal, Que. H2Y 3R7
Phone: (514) 987-2399  Fax: (514) 987-2323

**Sherbrooke Record**
2850 Delorme Street, Sherbrooke, Que. J1K 1A1
Phone: (819) 569-9525  Fax: (819) 569-3945

## Saskatchewan

**LeaderPost**
1964 Park Street, Regina, Sask. S4P 3G4
Phone: (306) 565-8211  Fax: (306) 565-8350

**Prince Albert Herald**
30 – 10th Street E., Prince Albert, Sask. S6V 5R9
Phone: (306) 764-4276  Fax: (306) 763-6747

**StarPhoenix**
204 – 5th Avenue N., Saskatoon, Sask. s7k 2p1
Phone: (306) 664-8340  Fax: (306) 664-8208

**Times–Herald**
44 Fairford Street W., Moose Jaw, Sask. s6h 6e4
Phone: (306) 692-6441  Fax: (306) 692-2101

## Yukon

**Whitehorse Star**
2149 – 2nd Avenue, Whitehorse, Yukon y1a 1c5
Phone: (403) 668-2060  Fax: (403) 668-7130

# 5

# BOOK PUBLISHERS

Unless they are crafting novels or writing on subjects deeply personal to them, professionals rarely produce books on speculation. The hard work involved – research and revisions stretched over months or years – is better invested in a firm commitment from a publisher. This follows a full proposal on how the book will be shaped, what each chapter will include, and how it will be written. Where an unpublished writer is concerned, however, most publishers will not make a final commitment until they have read the finished manuscript.

The first-time author should be under no illusions about the difficulties of breaking into the book publishing market – still less, unless you are phenomenally talented or hit on that rare winning formula, of making a living from the slender proceeds. Nonetheless, every year brings a new success story – another brilliant unknown author takes the publishing world by storm. Every writer must be a realist, *and* an optimist.

Professional writers will attest that writing books is a little easier after having consistently fed well-tailored articles to top magazines. As opposed to a long newspaper story, the magazine piece, in design, content, tone, and colour, conforms more closely to a short book, and can be a logical stepping-stone to longer, more substantial works. On the other hand, some publishers put greater trust in the newcomer than the journalist-turned-author. Certainly the disciplines are very different, though there are plenty of professional writers who have worked successfully across these boundaries. Many experienced Canadian authors supplement their royalty cheques with earnings from their magazine contributions.

Canada has all kinds of book publishers – from small presses producing two or three titles a year to large houses that turn out as many as sixty to a hundred. Most larger houses can offer authors an advance against royalties on acceptance of their proposal, though this is seldom the case with small and scholarly presses. Depending on the author and the book's potential in the marketplace, an advance can range from $500 to tens of thousands, although there are not so many of these. After publication, and once the advance has been earned, the author receives a royalty cheque every six or twelve months for the life of his or her book. An average royalty on a hardcover book is 10 per cent of the selling price. At this rate, a 3,000-copy sale of a $25 book would eventually yield the writer $7,500. Usually, authors can expect an 8 per cent royalty on the paperback version, but because it is cheaper than a hardcover, the paperback is likely to sell through in larger quantities so may be a bigger money-spinner. Some small presses offer royalties in copies, usually 10 per cent of the print run for adult books.

Small presses are more likely to take an interest in an unpublished writer, and are generally more receptive to unsolicited manuscripts. They also may be more accessible, offer more personal attention to their authors, and be more willing to take a risk. Nino Ricci's prize-winning first novel, *Lives of the Saints*, was published by Cormorant Press, having been rejected by a raft of the larger players. But he had no difficulty placing his eagerly awaited second novel with McClelland & Stewart. Small presses almost always work with un-agented writers. On the down side, small publishers can rarely offer an advance, their print runs tend to be low, and their distribution systems cannot match those of the big houses.

While editors are always on the lookout for high-quality fiction, non-fiction books are far easier to market. Books are normally bought well in advance of publication. Fall books, for example, are usually required to be on an editor's desk by the previous January or February. The contract for each book will have been signed a year or eighteen months prior to publication. Occasionally a title rejected by a publisher one year will be bought a couple of years later, when it fits better with the publisher's current needs. A book may be turned down because the publisher has a similar one underway. If you study a big trade publisher's list for one season, you'll notice that it does not publish a random selection of books so much as an editorial program of releases likely to satisfy a range of tastes.

You can save yourself much wasted time and dashed hopes by undertaking a little research into the Canadian publishing scene *before* you submit your proposal or manuscript. Use this chapter to draw up a shortlist of publishers whose programs seem most compatible with your own work, then check out some of their books at a good bookstore. If this is not practical, write to their publicity departments to request recent catalogues (always include a large SASE with this request). Familiarity with the programs of several houses can help you develop an attractive proposal as well as target the most appropriate potential publishers.

Given how difficult it is to place a manuscript, it's worth re-emphasizing the importance of an attractive, interesting, well-presented proposal. Editors simply do not have the time to unravel an ill-prepared proposal or to sift through unwieldy, indifferently written manuscripts that arrive unannounced. It's always best to know the name of the editor or publisher to whom you are submitting. Manuscripts addressed to "The Editor" often end up in the slush pile, where they can languish for years. The sad truth is that most of the unsolicited material that crosses the editors' desks is unpublishable. Your aim must be to present a submission that will stand out dramatically from the rest. Generally, a detailed outline together with a sample chapter and a covering letter will be received best. *Always* include an SASE if you want your material returned, and prepare for a wait of up to two or three months for the editor's response. What the editor will be looking for is originality, a strong central idea, intelligent organization, clarity, an engaging writing style, and, of course, "saleability." Marketing information can be useful. Enclose a list of recent books on similar subjects with your submission (check *Books in Print* at the library). Think about your audience and how the publisher might reach it.

It is a truism that would-be authors must learn to cope with rejection. First-timers might draw comfort from the knowledge of how many great writers could paper their walls with publishers' rejection letters received early in their careers. (Faulkner's great work *The Sound and the Fury* was rejected thirteen times before finding a publisher, as was William Kennedy's Pulitzer Prize-winning *Ironweed*. On an altogether different scale, big-selling English crime writer John Creasey is said to have received no fewer than 744 rejections during his career!) Since editors usually don't have time to issue more than a standard rejection note, take heart if the rejection is sugared with qualified praise or, better still, specific constructive criticism. Chances are the editor is not simply letting you down gently, but genuinely sees redeeming value in your work. Be open to suggestions, and consider reworking your manuscript if the advice seems sensible. You may even be able to resubmit to the same editor.

Writing is an isolating occupation, and it is good for morale as well as immensely practical to tap into one or more of the many writers' groups that exist in the community – a list of provincial associations is provided in Chapter 9. For professional writers with at least one published book behind them, valuable support is available from the Writers' Union of Canada, which offers members an impressive array of services and resources, from assistance with contracts and grievances with publishers to a manuscript evaluation service, and a range of practical publications, a custom-designed insurance plan, and other benefits. Some of the union's professional guides that may be ordered by non-members for a small cost are *Model Trade Book Contract*, *Help Yourself to a Better Contract*, *Anthology Rates and Contracts*, *Income Tax Guide for Writers*, *Writers' Guide to Canadian Publishers*, *Writers' Guide to Grants*, *Writers' Guide to Electronic Publishing Rights*, *Ghost Writing*, and *Libel: A Handbook for Canadian Publishers, Editors and Writers*. Above all, the Writers' Union of Canada gives its members the opportunity to share their concerns and experiences with fellow writers, providing a forum for collective action to support their interests.

Many of these services are also available to members of the Canadian Authors Association, which has branches across the country. Founded in Montreal in 1921, the CAA has represented the interests of Canadian writers on many fronts, from championing improved copyright protection and the Public Lending Right to helping individual writers improve their contracts with publishers. (The Public Lending Right provides published writers with income from books held in libraries by compensating them according to how often their books are borrowed. In 1993, according to *Masthead* magazine,

8,393 authors received an average of $821 each – it may come as no surprise that federal cuts are expected to reduce this benefit.) They publish the quarterly magazine *Canadian Author* and *The Canadian Writer's Guide*, a handbook for freelance writers. They also administer several major literary awards. Local branches hold writing classes, workshops, and literary competitions, and organize author tours.

Specialist writers' organizations, too, offer resources and support to writers in their field. The Canadian Society of Children's Authors, Illustrators and Performers (CANSCAIP), through its newsletter, regular meetings, and other organized activities, offers practical advice, moral support, and useful contacts to writers of children's books. The Canadian Children's Book Centre in Toronto also offers writers and illustrators of children's books a range of resources and services. The centre has a comprehensive reference library of children's books and promotes children's writers and titles through author tours and book readings. Their publication *Get Published: The Writing for Children Kit* is particularly useful for aspiring children's authors.

Before outlining what we do cover in this chapter, perhaps it's worth clarifying what we don't. Educational publishers are not listed unless they have a significant trade publishing arm. Today more than ever, educational publishers are commissioning their books in close collaboration with schools and colleges to meet specific curricular needs. These texts are nearly always written by specialists in the field. Very few educational publishers consider unsolicited manuscripts or proposals, and fewer still are likely to look favourably upon them, unless their author has a proven track record in the area.

Neither, with a couple of exceptions, have we included publishers that specialize entirely in poetry. For a comprehensive listing, consult *Poetry Markets for Canadians* (6th edition), published by the League of Canadian Poets. Also, as mentioned in the introduction, we have again focused on English-language publishing houses only. Finally, several substantial publishers (most notably perhaps, Random House and Knopf Canada) have chosen not to be included in this edition.

The inventory that follows, then, includes almost all the major and many of the smaller English-language trade publishers currently operating in Canada. Some have large general interest lists; others are more specialized, either in their subject areas or in their regional concerns; all offer market opportunities for your work.

## The Anglican Book Centre

600 Jarvis Street, Toronto, Ont. M4Y 2J6
Phone: (416) 924-9192  Fax: (416) 924-2760
Contact: Robert Maclennan, editor

Publishes manuscripts by Canadians on religious and contemporary issues, such as theology, spirituality, life crises, peace, justice, and feminism. Produced 12 new titles in 1995. No unsolicited manuscripts. Accepts written inquiries, with outline and sample chapter, in the stated areas of interest.

Notable 1995 title: *For All the Saints*, compiled by Stephen Reynolds.

## Annick Press

15 Patricia Avenue, Willowdale, Ont. M2M 1H9
Phone: (416) 221-4802  Fax: (416) 221-8400
Contact: Rick Wilks or Anne Millyard, co-directors

Established 1975. Publishes children's literature, mainly picture books with some pre-teen novels and non-fiction – books to "project supportive and positive messages to young readers while also entertaining and enthralling them." Released 22 new titles in 1994. Accepts unsolicited manuscripts, but first send sample chapters. "Be sure your submission is appropriate to our list and that you include an SASE." No faxed submissions accepted. Guidelines available.

Notable 1995 title: *From Far Away*, Robert Munsch and Saoussan Askar.

## Anvil Press

175 East Broadway, Suite 204A, Vancouver, B.C. V5T 1W2
Phone: (604) 876-8710  Fax: (604) 879-2667
Contact: Brian Kaufman, managing editor

A small literary press fostering new Canadian talent in all genres. Publishes two books a year. Send synopsis with sample chapter or two. Expect a wait of 3 to 4 months for reply. Send #10 SASE for reply without ms. Guidelines available.

Notable 1995 title: *Monday Night Man*, Grant Buday.

## Arsenal Pulp Press

101 – 1013 Homer Street, Vancouver, B.C. v6b 2w9
Phone: (604) 687-4233  Fax: (604) 669-8250
Contact: Linda Field, editor
    Established 1971. Publishes fiction, culture, politics, regional, Native subjects, and humour. Released 13 titles in 1995. "Our mandate is to publish provocative books that challenge the status quo, regardless of the subject matter." Accepts unsolicited manuscripts, but first send inquiry. Guidelines available.
    Notable 1995 title: *Altered Statements*, Marion Farrant.

## Aurora Editions

1184 Garfield Street N., Winnipeg, Man. r3e 2p1
Phone: (204) 783-7113  Fax: (204) 786-6188
Contact: Roma Quapp, editor/publisher
    Established 1993. A small publisher seeking original fiction and non-fiction representing a women's perspective on the world, including literary fiction, biography, and social critique by, for, and/or about women. "We are looking for writing that is literary in style, daring in its use of language, challenging in its view of the world, and yet accessible to a broad spectrum of society." Published 5 titles in 1995. Send entire manuscript for fiction, outline with sample chapter for non-fiction. Guidelines available for sase.
    Notable 1995 title: *A Slice of Life*, Marie Barton.

## Bantam Books Canada

105 Bond Street, 4th Floor, Toronto, Ont. m5b 1y3
Phone: (416) 340-0777  Fax: (416) 340-1069
Contact: editorial department
    Publishes mass-market fiction and non-fiction. Will not accept unsolicited manuscripts.

## Beach Holme Publishers

4252 Commerce Circle, Victoria, B.C. v8z 4m2
Phone: (604) 727-6514  Fax: (604) 727-6418
Contact: Antonia Banyard, managing editor
    Formerly Porcépic Books, established 1971. Specializes in wicca (no occult) non-fiction, regional (west of Winnipeg and North), young adult and historical fiction, and poetry. Publishes 8 to 10 titles

a year. Accepts unsolicited manuscripts, but first send an inquiry. Response time 4 to 6 months. Accepted manuscripts must be made available electronically. Guidelines available.

Notable 1995 title: *Shabash!*, Ann Walsh.

## Between the Lines
720 Bathurst Street, Suite 404, Toronto, Ont. M5S 2R4
Phone: (416) 535-9914  Fax: (416) 535-1484
Contact: Marg Anne Morrison, managing editor

Established 1977. Publishes non-fiction books on Canadian social and political issues, culture, Third World development, gender politics, and the media. Produced 6 new titles in 1994. Send full proposal with outline before submitting manuscript.

Notable 1995 title: *Wheel of Fortune: Work and Life in the Age of Falling Expectations*, Jamie Swift.

## Blizzard Publishing
73 Furby Street, Winnipeg, Man. R3C 2A2
Phone: (204) 775-2923  Fax: (204) 775-2947
Contact: Anna Synenko, acquisitions editor

Established 1985. A literary publisher specializing in contemporary drama and theatre-related books. New imprint (Bain & Cox) publishes prose and non-fiction, including children's and young adult. Publishes 12 new titles a year. Accepts unsolicited manuscripts, but first send an outline and sample chapters. Guidelines available.

Notable 1995 title: *The Trials of Ezra Pound*, Timothy Findley.

## Borealis/Tecumseh Presses
9 Ashburn Drive, Ottawa, Ont. K2E 6N4
Phone: (613) 224-6837  Fax: (613) 829-7783
Contact: Glenn Clever, editor

Established 1972. Publishes poetry, fiction, and general trade with Canadian authorship or interest. Releases about 10 new books each year. "We do not consider multiple submissions or unsolicited material. Query first, including synopsis and a sample chapter or equivalent, together with return postage or international postal coupons and adequate-sized envelope or package." Guidelines available.

Notable 1995 title: *Menominee: The Wild River People*, Douella Knobel.

## The Boston Mills Press

132 Main Street, Erin, Ont. NOB ITO
Phone: (519) 833-2407  Fax: (519) 833-2195
Contact: John Denison, publisher

Established 1974. Specializes in historical works. Publishes local or regional history, guidebooks, and large-format pictorials. Releases about 20 new titles a year. Accepts unsolicited manuscripts, but first send an inquiry with outline and sample chapter.

Notable 1995 title: *Gift of Wings*, Carl Hiebert.

## Breakwater Books

100 Water Street, P.O. Box 2188, St. John's, Nfld. AIC 6E6
Phone: (709) 722-6680  Fax: (709) 753-0708
Contact: Michele Cable, executive assistant

Established 1973. Publishes educational materials and a wide selection of manuscripts about Atlantic Canada, including plays, poetry, satire, biography, songbooks, cookbooks, and fiction. Main areas of interest include environmental science, enterprise education, and language arts. Publishes about 15 new books a year. "We are especially interested in Canadian writers with experience in writing for the school market." No unsolicited manuscripts. Send outline and writing sample.

Notable 1995 title: *Waiting for Time*, Bernice Morgan.

## Brick Books

431 Boler Road, P.O. Box 20081, London, Ont. N6K 4G6
Phone: (519) 657-8579  Fax: (519) 657-8579
Contact: Kitty Lewis, general manager

Established 1975. Publishes Canadian poetry only. Released 6 new titles during 1995. Accepts unsolicited manuscripts. Guidelines available.

Notable 1995 title: *Hologram: A Book of Glosas*, P.K. Page.

## Broadview Press

P.O. Box 1243, Peterborough, Ont. K9J 7H5
Phone: (705) 743-8990  Fax: (705) 743-8353

604 – 1st Street S.W., Suite 627, Calgary, Alta. T2P 1M7
Phone: (403) 232-6863  Fax: (403) 232-6863
Contact: Michael Harrison, vice-president
Established 1985. Publishes university and college texts, specializing in the arts and social sciences, and some general trade nonfiction. Subject areas include Canadian politics, history, philosophy, English literature, ethics, and medieval studies. Covers a broad range of political and philosophical viewpoints. About 25 new titles a year. Catalogues available on request. No unsolicited manuscripts.

Notable 1995 title: *Theories of Human Nature*, Peter Lopston.

## Butterworths Canada

75 Clegg Road, Markham, Ont. L6G 1A1
Phone: (905) 479-2665  Fax: (905) 479-6266
Contact: Ruth Epstein, publishing director
Established 1912. Specializes mainly in legal works; also business and accounting materials for the professional market. Publishes about 30 new titles a year, as well as ongoing looseleaf materials. Welcomes inquiries within these designated areas. Send an outline and sample chapters.

Notable 1995 title: *The Law of Confidential Communications in Canada*, Michael Silver and Ron Manes.

## The Caitlin Press

P.O. Box 2387, Station B, Prince George, B.C. V2N 2S6
Phone: (604) 964-4953  Fax: (604) 964-4970
Contact: Cynthia Wilson, managing editor
Established 1977. A small regional publisher specializing in trade books by B.C. Interior authors. Some literary titles by B.C. authors. Published 7 new titles in 1995. "We are interested primarily in Canada's North – more particularly, northern British Columbia." Accepts unsolicited manuscripts that meet these criteria. Send inquiry, outline, and sample chapters. Guidelines available.

## Camden House Publishing

25 Sheppard Avenue W., Suite 100, North York, Ont. M2N 6S7
Phone: (416) 733-7600  Fax: (416) 733-7981
Contact: Michael Warwick, director of book publishing
Established 1976. Publishes anthologies from *Harrowsmith*

*Country Living* magazine and books on gardening, cooking, do-it-yourself furniture and garden building, the natural sciences, astronomy, wildlife, and natural history. Averages 5 new titles a year. No unsolicited manuscripts. Query in designated areas only.

Notable 1995 title: *The Best of Pantry*, a *Harrowsmith* anthology.

## Canadian Arctic Resources Committee

1 Nicholas Street, Suite 1100, Ottawa, Ont. KIP 7B7
Phone: (613) 241-7379  Fax: (613) 241-2244
E-mail: ay385@freenet.carleton.ca
Contact: C.A. Samhaber, office manager

Established 1971. Publishes mostly scholarly non-fiction, usually related to Canada's North: its people, environment, and resource development. Particularly concerned with environmental issues. Also aboriginal rights, self-government, and international matters pertaining to northern Canada and the circumpolar world. Produces 4 to 6 new titles a year. Accepts unsolicited manuscripts.

## Canadian Stage and Arts Publications

104 Glenrose Avenue, Toronto, Ont. M4T 1K8
Phone: (416) 484-4534  Fax: (416) 484-6214
Contact: Karen Bell, editor

Established 1975. Publishes an average of 4 new arts, Canadiana, and children's books each year. No unsolicited manuscripts.

Notable 1995 title: *For the Love of Simple Linework*, Arvind Narale.

## Carleton University Press

1125 Colonel By Drive, Suite 1400, CTTC, Ottawa, Ont. KIS 5RI
Phone: (613) 520-3740  Fax: (613) 520-2893
Contact: John Flood, director and general editor

Established 1963. Publishes scholarly and trade books focusing on Canadian studies. Subject areas include women's studies, geography, history, sociology, anthropology and aboriginal peoples, media studies, political science, law, economics, public administration, literature, art, philosophy, and the classics. Releases an average of 18 new books a year. Accepts full manuscripts in declared areas of interest. Guidelines available.

Notable 1995 title: *How Ottawa Spends: Midlife Crisis*, ed. Susan D. Phillips.

## Coach House Press

50 Prince Arthur Avenue, Suite 107, Toronto, Ont. M5R 1B5

Phone: (416) 921-3910  Fax: (416) 921-4403

Established 1965. Publishes fiction, visual arts, drama, poetry, and essays. Released 22 new titles in 1995. Inquire before sending manuscripts.

Notable 1995 title: *Exotica*, Atom Egoyan.

## Cormorant Books

R.R.1, Dunvegan, Ont. K0C 1J0

Phone: (613) 527-3348  Fax: (613) 527-2262

Contact: Jan Geddes, publisher

Established 1986. Publishes adult fiction, short and long, featuring work from the literary mainstream and from ethnic minorities; also some non-fiction. Looks for a unique voice rather than particular content. Released 9 new titles in 1995. Accepts unsolicited manuscripts (send sample chapters). There's a 4- to 6-month response delay for submissions.

Notable 1995 title: *Guerrilla Beach*, Oakland Ross.

## Coteau Books

2206 Dewdney Avenue, Suite 401, Regina, Sask. S4R 1H3

Phone: (306) 777-0170  Fax: (306) 522-5152

Contact: Shelley Sopher, managing editor

Established 1975. Publishes poetry, short stories, novels, books on writers and writing, anthologies, children's stories, women's issues, and drama. Averages 12 new titles a year. Internet users can sample some of the work published by Coteau on the www: http://coteau.unibase.com. Reviews unsolicited manuscripts by Canadian writers. "We will not accept multiple/simultaneous submissions. We consider children's manuscripts only by Prairie authors." Guidelines available.

Notable 1995 title: *Crosswinds*, Byrna Barclay.

## Crabtree Publishing Co.

360 York Road, R.R.4, Niagara-on-the-Lake, Ont. L0S 1J0

Phone: (905) 682-5221  Fax: (905) 262-5890

Contact: Lynda Hale, managing editor

Established 1978. Publishes children's illustrated non-fiction series written at a specific reading level to meet educational demands for the children's library market. Main subjects are social studies and science. Releases about 20 new titles a year. "We do not accept unsolicited manuscripts and discourage fiction, as it is not our market. Ideas for series that are accompanied by photos are considered."

Notable 1995 title: *Ballet School*, Bobbie Kalman.

## Creative Publishers
P.O. Box 8660, St. John's, Nfld. A1B 3T7
Phone: (709) 722-8500  Fax: (709) 722-2228
Contact: Donald Morgan, manager

Established 1983. Publishes mainly local history and biography by Newfoundland writers. The Killick Press imprint specializes in literary books: novels, short stories, poetry, creative non-fiction, and drama. Released 12 titles in 1995. Query first. Guidelines available.

Notable 1995 title: *Their Lives and Times, Women in Newfoundland and Labrador: A Collage*, eds. Carmelita McGrath, Barbara Neis, and Marilyn Porter.

## Detselig Enterprises
1220 Kensington Road N.W., Suite 210, Calgary, Alta. T2N 3P5
Phone: (403) 283-0900  Fax: (403) 283-6947
Contact: T. Gregg, editor

Established 1975. Publishes academic, professional, and trade books. Half the list is academic/scholarly, the other half general interest non-fiction. Averages 22 new books each year. Accepts unsolicited manuscripts, but first send inquiry letter with outline and sample chapters. Guidelines available.

Notable 1995 title: *The Grizzly Kingdom*, Thomas and Enns.

## Doubleday Canada
105 Bond Street, Toronto, Ont. M5B 1Y3
Phone: (416) 340-0777, ext. 402  Fax: (416) 977-8488
Contact: John Pearce, editor-in-chief

Established 1944. Interested in children's books and a wide range of adult fiction and non-fiction by Canadian and international authors. Published 50 new titles in 1995. No unsolicited manuscripts. Inquiries only.

Notable 1995 title: *My Times*, Pierre Berton.

## Douglas & McIntyre

1615 Venables Street, Vancouver, B.C. V5L 2H1
Phone: (604) 254-7191  Fax: (604) 254-9099
Contact: editorial department
Toronto office: 585 Bloor Street W., 2nd Floor, Toronto,
  Ont. M6G 1K5
Phone: (416) 537-2501  Fax: (416) 537-4647
Contact: Lucy Fraser, editor
  Established 1964. Publishes general trade books but specializes in history, biography, art, outdoors and recreation, and Native subjects. Imprints are Greystone Books and Groundwood Books. Produces 50 new titles annually. Toronto office handles all children's books. A submission including an outline with two or three sample chapters preferred.

## Dundurn Press

2181 Queen Street E., Suite 301, Toronto, Ont. M4E 1E5
Phone: (416) 698-0454  Fax: (416) 698-1102
Contact: Nadine Stoikoff, assistant to the publisher
  Established 1973. Publishes Canadian history (notably of Ontario), biography, art, and literary criticism. Averages 50 new titles annually. Accepts unsolicited manuscripts, but first send outline and sample chapters, and identify your prospective market. Allow 4 to 12 weeks for reply. Guidelines available.
  Notable 1995 title: *Toronto Sketches 3*, Mike Filey.

## ECW Press

2120 Queen Street E., Suite 200, Toronto, Ont. M4E 1E2
Phone: (416) 694-3348  Fax: (416) 698-9906
Contact: Jack David, president
  Established 1974. Publishes reference books, literary criticism on Canadian writers and their works, and biography. Released 30 titles in 1995. Accepts unsolicited manuscripts, but send a query first. Guidelines available.
  Notable 1995 title: *The Healthy Barmaid*, Dr. W. Gifford Jones.

## Ekstasis Editions

P.O. Box 8474, Main Postal Outlet, Victoria, B.C. V8W 3S1

Phone: (604) 385-3378
Contact: Carol Ann Sokoloff, editor

Established 1982. A literary press publishing elegant editions of poetry, novels, short story collections, children's stories (under the Cherubim imprint), and criticism, along with general environmental and New Age trade books. Averages 12 new books each year. Accepts written inquiries with outlines or sample chapters. Guidelines available.

Notable 1995 title: *The Ogre of Grand Remous*, Robert Lalonde.

**Exile Editions**
P.O. Box 67, Station B, Toronto, Ont. M5T 2CO
Phone: (416) 969-8877  Fax: (416) 966-9556
Contact: Barry Callaghan, president

Established 1976. Publishes fiction, drama, poetry, and fiction and poetry in translation. Produces about 10 new titles a year. Rarely accepts unsolicited manuscripts. Be sure to study both *Exile* quarterly and the Exile Editions list before deciding to submit.

**Fifth House Publishers**
620 Duchess Street, Saskatoon, Sask. S7K ORI
Phone: (306) 242-4936  Fax: (306) 242-7667
Contact: Charlene Dobmeier, managing editor

Established 1982. Publishes general trade non-fiction (especially western Canadiana), emphasizing history and biography, with some children's books and a strong Native list. Releases 16 to 18 books a year. Accepts unsolicited manuscripts, but first send an outline, sample chapter, and author background. No phone calls please. Guidelines available.

Notable 1995 title: *The Golden Age of the Canadian Cowboy*, Hugh A. Dempsey.

**Fitzhenry & Whiteside & Little Brown**
195 Allstate Parkway, Markham, Ont. L3R 4T8
Phone: (905) 477-9700  Fax: (905) 477-9179
Contact: Robert Read, senior vice-president

Established 1966. Publishes a wide selection of general trade and education books, especially Canadian adult non-fiction and children's books. Releases about 30 titles a year. Reviews unsolicited manuscripts, but first send an outline or sample chapters.

## Formac Publishing Co.

5502 Atlantic Street, Halifax, N.S. B3H 1G4
Phone: (902) 421-7022  Fax: (902) 425-0166
Contact: Carolyn MacGregor, publisher

Established 1977. Publishes regional titles, including history, folklore, cookbooks, and guidebooks, Canadian biography, and children's books. Accepts unsolicited manuscripts, but first send an outline or sample chapter.

Notable 1995 title: *Halifax Colour Guidebook*, Stephen Poole.

## The Frederick Harris Music Co.

529 Speers Road, Oakville, Ont. L6K 2G4
Phone: (905) 845-3487  Fax: (905) 845-1208
Contact: Trish Sauerbrei, publishing manager

Established 1904. A not-for-profit publisher of music education materials, particularly curriculum material for the Royal Conservatory of Music. Released 40 new titles in 1995. Accepts unsolicited manuscripts. Guidelines available.

Notable 1995 title: *Celebration Series Handbook for Teachers*, Cathy Albergo, Reid Alexander, and Marvin Blickenstaff.

## Garamond Press

77 Mowat Avenue, Suite 403, Toronto, Ont. M6K 3E3
Phone: (416) 516-2709  Fax: (416) 516-0571
E-mail: garamon@web.apc.org
Contact: Peter Saunders, director

Established 1981. Publishes academic and university texts. Subject areas include women's studies, cultural and labour studies, education, Third World topics, and ethnicity. Releases 6 to 8 new titles a year. No unsolicited manuscripts. Please note that this is a very specialized house. Written inquiries only. Very specific submission guidelines available.

Notable 1995 title: *Globalization and the Decline of Social Reform*, Gary Teeple.

## General Store Publishing House

1 Main Street, Burnstown, Ont. KOJ IGO
Phone: (613) 432-7697  Fax: (613) 432-7184
Contact: Tim Gordon, publisher

Established 1980. Publishes history, military, cookbooks, regional titles pertaining to the Ottawa Valley, sports, and some children's books. Released 30 titles in 1995. Accepts unsolicited manuscripts.

Notable 1995 title: *Missing the Kisses of Elephants*, Michael Dennis.

## Goose Lane Editions/Fiddlehead Poetry Books

469 King Street, Fredericton, N.B. E3B IE5
Phone: (506) 450-4251  Fax: (506) 459-4991
Contact: Laurel Boone, acquisitions editor

Established 1958. Publishes Canadian adult literary fiction, non-fiction, and poetry. Produced 14 new titles in 1995. Accepts unsolicited manuscripts. "Query first for poetry, story collections, and non-fiction. Send outline or synopsis and 30- to 50-page sample for novels." Guidelines available with SASE.

Notable 1995 title: *Something Drastic*, Colleen Curran.

## Guernica Editions

P.O. Box 117, Station P, Toronto, Ont. M5S 2S6
Phone: (416) 657-8885  Fax: (416) 657-8885
Contact: Antonio D'Alfonso, editor

Established 1978. Specializes in prose and poetry addressing the Italian/North American experience. Also translates Québécois authors. Publishes about 20 titles a year. No unsolicited manuscripts. Inquiries welcome. "We want writers interested in ethnicity and a new world vision."

Notable 1995 title: *Mediating Culture: Representation of Culture*, William Anselmi and Kosta Gouliamos.

## Gutter Press

50 Baldwin Street, Suite 100, Toronto, Ont. M5T IL4
Phone: (416) 977-7187
Contact: Sam Hiyate, publisher

Specializes in literary fiction and avant-garde writing. "We want nothing less than to rewrite the literary canon. And we want your best work. Check out the literary magazine *The Quarterly* plus our backlist for an idea of what we might like." Produces 4 to 8 titles a year. Welcomes work by new writers, but first send a query plus sample chapters.

Notable 1995 title: *The Necrofiles*, Donna Lypchuk.

## HMS Press

P.O. Box 340, Station B, London, Ont. N6A 4W1
Phone: (519) 433-8994  Fax: (519) 432-6199
Contact: Wayne Ray, president

Specializes in books on diskette. Averages 30 new titles a year. Interested in any well-written manuscript, any genre, any style: poetry, essays, history, biography, etc. Sold on computer diskette. Payment takes the form of a 20 per cent royalty. Accepts unsolicited works. "Do not send hard copy. Submit on disk in ASCII or Word Perfect." Guidelines available.

Notable 1995 title: *False Pretences*, Michael C. McPherson.

## Hancock House Publishers

19313 Zero Avenue, Surrey, B.C. V4P 1M7
Phone: (604) 538-1114  Fax: (604) 538-2262
Contact: David Hancock, editor

Established 1970. Specializes in Pacific Northwest history and biography, Native culture, nature guides, and natural history. Publishes about 25 titles a year. No unsolicited manuscripts. Send a one- or two-page synopsis, a sample chapter, and biographical/marketing support material. Guidelines available.

Notable 1995 title: *Understanding the Bird of Prey*, Nick Fox.

## Harbour Publishing

P.O. Box 219, Madeira Park, B.C. VON 2HO
Phone: (604) 883-2730  Fax: (604) 883-9451
Contact: Howard White, president

Established 1974. Publishes books on West Coast regional history and culture, both literary and non-fiction, as well as poetry and guides. Specializes in B.C. authors and women's issues. Published 20 titles in 1995. Accepts unsolicited manuscripts, but send letter of inquiry first. Guidelines available.

Notable 1995 title: *Starting from Ameliasburgh: The Collected Prose of Al Purdy*, ed. Sam Solecki.

## Harlequin Enterprises

225 Duncan Mill Road, Don Mills, Ont. M3B 3K9
Phone: (416) 445-5860  Fax: (416) 445-8655
Contact: Candy Lee, publisher and vice-president, retail marketing and editorial

Established 1949. Each year publishes more than 700 mass-market paperback series romances (Harlequin and Silhouette imprints), single title women's fiction (Mira Books), and mystery and action adventures (Golden Eagle and Worldwide Library imprints). Interested in receiving manuscript outlines, particularly those with series potential, in either fiction or non-fiction. Accepts unsolicited manuscripts, but initial inquiry preferred. Tip sheets available. New authors are contracted only on full manuscript.

## HarperCollins Publishers

55 Avenue Road, Suite 2900, West Tower at Hazelton Lanes,
    Toronto, Ont. M5R 3L2
Phone: (416) 975-9334  Fax: (416) 975-9884
Contact: Harold Hill, acquisitions editor

Publishes a wide range of fiction, non-fiction, business, young adult and children's books, and collections. Produces over 100 titles each year. No unsolicited manuscripts.

Notable 1995 title: *The Piano Man's Daughter*, Timothy Findley.

## Harry Cuff Publications

94 LeMarchant Road, St. John's, Nfld. A1C 2H2
Phone: (709) 726-6590  Fax: (709) 726-0902
Contact: Robert Cuff, managing editor

Established 1981. Publishes an average of 8 books a year on Newfoundland and/or by Newfoundlanders. Accepts unsolicited manuscripts but prefers initial inquiry with outline. Guidelines available.

Notable 1995 title: *To Cast the Anchor*, Cyril Poole.

## Hartley & Marks Publishers

3661 West Broadway, Vancouver, B.C. V6R 2B8

Phone: (604) 739-1771  Fax: (604) 738-1913
Contact: Victor Marks, publisher

Established 1973. Publishes practical non-fiction. Subject areas include innovative health, meditation, personal self-help, architecture, building, country living, practical crafts and technical books, and practical Asian traditions. Produces about 10 titles each year.

## Herald Press

490 Dutton Drive, Waterloo, Ont. N2L 6H7
Phone: (519) 747-0161  Fax: (519) 747-5721
Contact: David Garber, senior editor

Established in 1908 in the U.S., and in 1974 in Canada. Owned by the Mennonite Church. Publishes religious and general books for a lay (non-scholarly) audience, written from an Anabaptist/Mennonite perspective. Publishes 30 titles a year on peace and justice, family, community, and Amish life. Accepts unsolicited manuscripts, but first send an outline and sample chapters. "Use a story approach when possible." Guidelines available.

Notable 1995 title: *No Longer Alone: Mental Health and the Church*, John Toews with Eleanor Loewen.

## Heritage House Publishing Co.

17921 – 55th Avenue, Suite 8, Surrey, B.C. V3S 6C4
Phone: (604) 574-7067  Fax: (604) 574-7067
Contact: Art Downs, editor

Established 1969. Specializes in original works on genealogy, history, travel, fishing, and general outdoors in British Columbia and Alberta. Averages 6 to 8 new books a year. Accepts unsolicited manuscripts.

Notable 1995 title: *Scarlet Tunic: On Patrol with the RCMP*.

## Highway Book Shop

R.R.1, Cobalt, Ont. P0J 1C0
Phone: (705) 679-8375  Fax: (705) 679-8511
Contact: Lois Pollard, assistant manager

Began its serious publishing program in 1970. Publishes adult trade – mainly by Canadian authors and with Northern themes. Priority given to local, northeastern Ontario history. Also interested in Native Canadian works. Adult and young adult fiction accepted on

Northern and Native themes. Averages 6 new titles each year. Accepts unsolicited manuscripts. First send inquiry with outline and/or sample chapters. Guidelines available.

Notable 1995 title: *Temiscaming Treasure Trails, Vol. 8*, Peter Fancy.

## Horsdal & Schubart Publishers
425 Simcoe Street, Suite 623, Victoria, B.C. v8v 4T3
Phone: (604) 360-2031  Fax: (604) 360-0829
Contact: Marlyn Horsdal, publisher/editor

Established 1985. Specializes in Canadian non-fiction, with an emphasis on the North, Western history and biography; also the occasional work of fiction. Published 10 titles in 1995. Accepts unsolicited manuscripts, but phone or send letter of inquiry first. "Made it through the first ten years, still enthusiastic, still growing."

Notable 1995 title: *The Spell of the Midnight Sun*, Maurice Cloughley.

## Hounslow Press
2181 Queen Street E., Suite 301, Toronto, Ont. M4E 1E5
Phone: (416) 698-0454  Fax: (416) 698-1102
Contact: Tony Hawke, publisher and general manager

Established 1972. Publishes popular non-fiction, illustrated books, and a distinguished line of Canadian fiction and poetry. Produced 8 new titles in 1995. "Our standards are high. Only top quality material will be accepted for publication, especially in the areas of fiction, poetry, and illustrated books." Send initial query letter with outline and sample.

Notable 1995 title: *Tokyo, My Everest: A Canadian Woman in Japan*, Gabrielle Bauer.

## House of Anansi Press
1800 Steeles Avenue W., Concord, Ont. L4K 2P3
Phone: (905) 660-0611  Fax: (905) 660-0676
Contact: Martha Sharpe, editor

A literary press publishing fiction, poetry, criticism and belles-lettres. Averages 10 to 12 new books a year – perhaps 3 poetry, 4 fiction, and 3 or 4 non-fiction titles. Does not accept unsolicited manuscripts. Send a letter of inquiry with an outline. Decisions on the year's list are usually made before July the previous year.

Notable 1995 title: *The Essential McLuhan*, ed. Eric McLuhan and Frank Zigrone.

## Hyperion Press

300 Wales Avenue, Winnipeg, Man. R2M 2S9
Phone: (204) 256-9204  Fax: (204) 255-7845
Contact: Dr. Marvis Tutiah, president

Established 1978. Specializes in craft and how-to books for all ages, and children's picture books (for under-12s). Averages 8 to 10 new titles a year. Accepts unsolicited manuscripts.

Notable 1995 title: *Best Ever Paper Airplanes*, Norman Schmidt.

## Irwin Publishing

1800 Steeles Avenue W., Concord, Ont. L4K 2P3
Phone: (905) 660-0611  Fax: (905) 660-0676
Contact: Norma Pettit, managing editor

Established 1945. Specializes in texts and teacher-support materials for elementary and high schools, some college, and professional books. Also, with sister company Stoddart Publishing, young adult novels. Released 17 titles in 1995. Accepts unsolicited manuscripts, but first query with outline.

Notable 1995 title: *Worldviews: The Challenge of Choice*, Ken Badley.

## James Lorimer & Co.

35 Britain Street, Toronto, Ont. M5A 1R7
Phone: (416) 362-4762  Fax: (416) 362-3939
Contact: publishing assistant

Established 1971. Specializes in books on Canadian politics, economics, and urban and social issues for the university and trade markets. Also children's/young adult (age 7 to 15) fiction addressing Canadian social issues. No picture books, fantasy, horror, or science fiction. Averages 15 new titles a year. Send for guidelines before submitting.

Notable 1995 title: *Canadian Women's Issues Vol. 2*, Ruth Roach Pierson and Marjorie Griffin Cohen.

## Jesperson Publishing

39 James Lane, St. John's, Nfld. A1E 3H3

Phone: (709) 753-0633  Fax: (709) 753-5507
Contact: Donna Snelgrove, publishing assistant

Established 1977. Publishes trade and educational books. Produces about 8 new titles a year. Accepts unsolicited manuscripts, but send a sample chapter first. Guidelines available.

Notable 1995 title: *Those in Peril*, Captain Joseph Prim and Mike McCarthy.

## Kalobon

2339 Dufferin Street, Suite 1405, Toronto, Ont. M6E 4Z5
Phone: (416) 789-2423
Contact: Ervin Bonkalo, director

Specializes in English and French scholarly works dealing with science, architecture, art, and literature of the medieval period. Query first.

## Key Porter Books

70 The Esplanade, 3rd Floor, Toronto, Ont. M5E 1R2
Phone: (416) 862-7777  Fax: (416) 862-2304
Contact: Susan Renouf, president and editor-in-chief

Established 1980. Specializes in high-profile non-fiction, business, biography, celebrity books, cookbooks, natural history, and the environment. Publishes 50 to 55 new titles a year. No unsolicited manuscripts. Guidelines available.

Notable 1995 title: *Don't Die Before You're Dead*, Yevgeny Yevtushenko.

## Kids Can Press

29 Birch Avenue, Toronto, Ont. M4V 1E2
Phone: (416) 925-5437  Fax: (416) 960-5437
Contact: Valerie Hussey, publisher

Established 1973. Publishes quality books for children of all ages, including picture books, fiction, and junior and senior level information books. Averages 25 new titles each year. "Please familiarize yourself with our list before sending a manuscript. Request a catalogue if you're having trouble getting a good sense of the entire publishing program." Note: At time of writing was not accepting unsolicited manuscripts. Send outline and sample chapters.

Notable 1995 title: *Pioneer Story*, Barbara Greenwood; illust. Heather Collins.

## Lancelot Press
P.O. Box 425, Hantsport, N.S. BOP IPO
Phone: (902) 684-9129  Fax: (902) 684-3685
Contact: William Pope, editor

Established 1966. Publishes mostly non-fiction of particular interest to Atlantic Canada, but also interested in work of high quality and general interest, though very few novels and poetry collections. Released 20 titles in 1995. Accepts unsolicited manuscripts, but first send outline and sample chapters.

Notable 1995 title: *Ordinary Magic: The Art of Alex Colville*, J.R.C. Perkin.

## Lester Publishing
56 The Esplanade, Suite 507A, Toronto, Ont. M5E IA7
Phone: (416) 362-1032  Fax: (416) 362-1647
Contact: Janice Weaver, managing editor

Established 1991. Publishes trade non-fiction and children's books. Adult list focuses on social issues and current affairs, with some literary fiction. Children's list includes high-quality picture books and young adult fiction. Averages 20 new titles a year. No unsolicited manuscripts. Send query letter with outline. Guidelines available.

Notable 1995 title: *Chrétien Volume 1: The Will to Win*, Lawrence Martin.

## Lone Pine Publishing
10426 – 81st Avenue, Suite 206, Edmonton, Alta. T6E IX5
Phone: (403) 433-9333  Fax: (403) 433-9646
Contact: Nancy J. Foulds, senior editor

Established 1980. Specializes in natural history, popular history, outdoor recreation, and travel. Most books have a regional focus. Now has offices in Vancouver, Edmonton, and Washington State. Publishes about 30 new titles each year. Accepts unsolicited manuscripts, but first send an inquiry.

Notable 1995 title: *Trail North: A Journey in Words and Pictures*, Robert Guest.

## Macfarlane, Walter & Ross

37A Hazelton Avenue, Toronto, Ont. M5R 2E3
Phone: (416) 924-7595  Fax: (416) 924-4254
Contact: Jan Walter, president

Established 1988. Publishes high-quality, popular non-fiction aimed at Canadian and international audiences, primarily in the fields of politics, business, history, biography, and popular culture. Produced 8 new titles in 1995. Accepts unsolicited manuscripts but send query first. Guidelines available.

Notable 1994 title: *On the Take: Crime, Corruption and Greed in the Mulroney Years*, Stevie Cameron.

## Macmillan Canada

29 Birch Avenue, Toronto, Ont. M4V 1E2
Phone: (416) 963-8830  Fax: (416) 923-4821
Contact: Karen O'Reilly, publisher

Publishes a variety of general trade non-fiction, primarily for and by Canadians. Specializes in cookbooks, sports, business, health, and nutrition. Averages 45 new books each year. No unsolicited manuscripts. Accepts inquiries with an outline and sample chapters.

Notable 1995 title: *Days of Victory*, Alex and Ted Barris.

## McClelland & Stewart

481 University Avenue, Suite 900, Toronto, Ont. M5G 2E9
Phone: (416) 598-1114  Fax: (416) 598-7764
Contact: editorial department

Established 1906. Publishes a wide selection of fiction, and non-fiction on biography, history, natural history, politics, religion, and sports. Also publishes poetry, reference books, and textbooks at the college level. Releases about 80 titles a year. "We are 'The Canadian Publisher' and take our role to publish the best in Canadian fiction, non-fiction, and poetry very seriously. With a stable of authors ranging from Margaret Atwood through Ken Dryden on to Leonard Cohen and then to Alice Munro and Pierre Trudeau, this house is not a good point of entry for the beginning author." No unsolicited manuscripts. Send an inquiry for fiction, an outline for non-fiction.

Notable 1995 title: *A Fine Balance*, Rohinton Mistry.

## McGill–Queen's University Press

McGill University, 3430 McTavish Street, Montreal, Que. H3A 1X9
Phone: (514) 398-3750  Fax: (514) 398-4333
Contact: Philip Cercone, editor
Queen's University office: Queen's University, Kingston,
   Ont. K7L 3N6
Phone: (613) 545-2155  Fax: (613) 545-6822
Contact: Professor Donald Akenson, editor
   Established 1969. Publishes scholarly books on Arctic and
Northern studies and history; political science with special empha-
sis on Canadian urban life; Commonwealth and Canadian litera-
ture; and books on architecture, philosophy and religion, North
American Native peoples, anthropology, and sociology. Averages 70
new titles a year, a third of which are destined for the trade market.
   Notable 1995 title: *A Biography of Conor Cruise O'Brien*, Donald
H. Akenson.

## McGraw-Hill Ryerson

300 Water Street, Whitby, Ont. L1N 9B6
Phone: (905) 430-5000  Fax: (905) 430-5020
Contact: Joan Homewood, publisher, consumer and trade division
   Established 1944. Publishes adult non-fiction consumer and ref-
erence books, notably in the areas of business and personal finance,
and to a lesser extent military history, hockey, and general interest.
Averages 20 trade titles a year. Accepts unsolicited manuscripts. No
fiction or children's manuscripts. Query letter and outline with
sample chapter must be submitted first.
   Notable 1995 title: *Infomedia Revolution*, Frank Koelsch.

## The Mercury Press

137 Birmingham Street, Stratford, Ont. N5A 2T1
Contact: Beverley Daurio, editor
   Established 1978. Publishes Canadian adult fiction, non-fiction,
poetry, and murder mysteries set in Canada. New short story writers
should pursue journal publication widely before submitting work.
Complete unsolicited manuscripts considered (with CV) but rarely
contracted. About 12 new titles each year. "Literary novels and well-
plotted mysteries are most in demand here currently. Editors love
writers more who provide clean, double-spaced copy, proper support

material, and always an adequately sized SASE for the manuscript's return." For an overview of list, send 9 in. × 12 in. SASE for catalogue.

Notable 1995 title: *Millicent: A Mystery*, Veronica Ross.

## Micromedia

20 Victoria Street, Toronto, Ont. M5C 2N8
Phone: (416) 362-5211  Fax: (416) 362-6161
Contact: Louise Fast, vice-president and general manager

Established 1972. Publishes microform, electronic, and print. Produces indexes, abstract databases, and printed directories for libraries, information centres, and research departments. Frequently offers employment to indexers and abstracters. No unsolicited manuscripts.

## Moonstone Press

175 Brock Street, Goderich, Ont. N7A 1R4
Phone: (519) 524-5645  Fax: (519) 524-6185
Contact: Peter Baltensperger, publisher

Established 1984. Publishes adult literary fiction, poetry, and creative non-fiction. Special areas of interest include mysticism, spirituality, symbolism, and surrealism. Averages 5 new titles a year. Accepts unsolicited manuscripts, but first send outline and sample chapters. No multiple submissions. "We look for literary excellence; no social issues or moralistic topics." Guidelines available.

Notable 1995 title: *Travels on the Private Zodiac*, Martin Samuel Cohen.

## NC Press

345 Adelaide Street W., Suite 400, Toronto, Ont. M5V 1R5
Phone: (416) 593-6284  Fax: (416) 593-6204
E-mail: ncpress@fox.nstn.ca
Contact: editorial department

Established 1970. Interested in books on art, economics, history, poetry, politics, women's issues, Native peoples, multiculturalism, the environment, agriculture, health, food, literary criticism, and theatre. Canadian non-fiction for the intelligent layperson. Averages 20 new titles a year. Send query first with outline and/or sample chapters.

Notable 1995 title: *Three Chinas*, Bill Purves.

## New Star Books

2504 York Avenue, Vancouver, B.C. V6K 1E3
Phone: (604) 738-9429  Fax: (604) 738-9332
Contact: Rolf Maurer, publisher

Publishes progressive books that challenge the status quo and fill a void left by the mainstream media. Subject areas include social issues, politics, and the environment. Averages 10 new titles a year. Accepts unsolicited manuscripts, but first send inquiry with outline. Guidelines available.

Notable 1995 title: *Grace Hartman: A Documentary Biography*, Susan Crean.

## NeWest Publishers

10359 – 82nd Avenue, Suite 310, Edmonton, Alta. T6E 1Z9
Phone: (403) 432-9427  Fax: (403) 432-9429
Contact: Eva Radford, editorial co-ordinator

Established 1977. Publishes literature and non-fiction from Western Canada, including books on the history and social concerns of western Canadians, play anthologies, first novels, and short story collections. Averages 8 new titles a year. No poetry. Accepts unsolicited manuscripts. Send outline and sample chapter. No editorial commentary given on rejected manuscripts. Guidelines available.

Notable 1995 title: *The Klein Revolution*, Mark Lisac.

## Nimbus Publishing

P.O. Box 9301, Station A, Halifax, N.S. B3K 5N5
Phone: (902) 455-4286  Fax: (902) 455-3652
Contact: Dorothy Blythe, managing editor

Established 1978. Publishes general trade books on all aspects of Atlantic Canada, including politics, social, cultural, and natural history, folklore and myth, biography, the environment, nautical books, cookbooks, children's, and photographic books. Most books are by first-time authors who have in-depth knowledge of their subject. Released 26 new titles in 1993. Accepts unsolicited manuscripts. Guidelines available.

Notable 1995 title: *Calculated Risk: Greed, Politics, and the Westray Tragedy*, Dean Jobb.

**NuAge Editions**
P.O. Box 8, Station E, Montreal, Que. H2T 3A5
Phone: (514) 272-5226  Fax: (514) 271-1218
Contact: the editor
  Established 1986 as a Concordia University project. Now run independently as a small press for English-language writers across Canada. Publishes fiction, drama, and non-fiction. Released 6 titles in 1995.

**Oberon Press**
350 Sparks Street, Suite 400, Ottawa, Ont. KIR 7S8
Phone: (613) 238-3275  Fax: (613) 238-3275
Contact: Nicholas Macklem, general manager
  Established 1966. Publishes Canadian literary fiction, poetry, and non-fiction such as history or memoirs. Produced 17 new books in 1995. Accepts unsolicited manuscripts, but first send outline and sample chapters. Multiple submissions not considered.
  Notable 1995 title: *Best Canadian Stories*, ed. David Helwig.

**Oolichan Books**
P.O. Box 10, Lantzville, B.C. VOR 2H0
Phone: (604) 390-4839  Fax: (604) 390-4839
Contact: Rhonda Bailey, publisher
  Established 1974. Publishes fiction, history, public policy, First Nations, health, children's, outdoors, biographies, special limited editions, and perhaps two books of poetry a year. Released 10 new titles in 1995. Considers unsolicited manuscripts, but send initial letter of inquiry and sample.
  Notable 1995 title: *Borrowed Time: Living with Cancer with Someone You Love*, Fred Edge.

**Orca Book Publishers**
P.O. Box 5626, Station B, Victoria, B.C. V8R 6S4
Phone: (604) 380-1229  Fax: (604) 380-1892
Contacts: Bob Tyrrell (adult and young adult); Ann Featherstone
  (children's and older juvenile)
  Established 1984. Adult titles comprise about half the list and include general non-fiction, guidebooks, outdoor adventure, and

history. A West Coast regional bias. Children's titles include picture books, older juvenile, and young adult novels emphasizing West Coast locations and universal themes. Historical stories and Oriental folktales considered. No poetry, sci-fi, or fantasy. Released 21 new titles in 1995. No adult unsolicited manuscripts. Send a query with outline and sample chapters. Unsolicited manuscripts accepted for children's picture books; for novels, send a query with first three chapters and outline. Guidelines available.

Notable 1995 title: *Tides of Change: Faces of the Northwest Coast*, Sheryl McFarlane, illust. Ken Campbell.

## Owl Books

179 John Street, 5th Floor, Toronto, Ont. M5T 3G5
Phone: (416) 971-5275  Fax: (416) 971-5294
Contact: submissions editor

Sister company to *OWL* and *Chickadee* magazines. Publishes high-quality, innovative information books, activity books, and picture books, with an emphasis on nature, science, and children's activities such as crafts. Averages 8 to 10 new titles a year. Accepts unsolicited manuscripts, but first send inquiry and outline, preferably with sample chapters. Before submitting, spend an hour or two familiarizing yourself with Owl books in the library. No response without SASE.

Notable 1995 title: *A Kid's Guide to the Brain*, Sylvia Funston and Jay Ingram.

## Oxford University Press

70 Wynford Drive, Don Mills, Ont. M3C 1J9
Phone: (416) 441-2941  Fax: (416) 441-0345
Contact: Susan Froud, managing director

Established in Canada in 1904. Publishes general trade, second and third year college texts, junior and senior high school textbooks, and children's books. Averages 40 new titles each year. Accepts unsolicited manuscripts, but first send a query with outline and sample chapters. Guidelines available.

Notable 1995 title: *Oxford Book of Canadian Short Stories* (2nd ed.), eds. Margaret Atwood and Robert Weaver.

## Pemmican Publications

1635 Burrows Avenue, Unit 2, Winnipeg, Man. R2X 0T1
Phone: (204) 589-6346  Fax: (204) 589-2063
Contact: Sue MacLean, managing editor

Established 1980. Specializes in children's picture books. Committed to publishing books that depict Métis and aboriginal cultures and lifestyles positively and accurately. Released 6 new titles in 1995. Accepts unsolicited manuscripts, but first send sample chapters. Guidelines available.

Notable 1995 title: *Nanabosho and the Woodpecker*, Joe McLellan, illust. Rhian Brynjolson.

## Penguin Books Canada

10 Alcorn Avenue, Suite 300, Toronto, Ont. M4V 3B2
Phone: (416) 925-2249  Fax: (416) 925-0068
Contact: editorial department

Established in Canada in 1974. Publishes a wide selection of trade fiction and non-fiction. Released 36 new hardcover titles and 88 books in 1995. No unsolicited manuscripts.

Notable 1995 title: *Shooting the Hippo: Death by Deficit and Other Canadian Myths*, Linda McQuaig.

## Playwrights Canada Press

54 Wolseley Street, 2nd Floor, Toronto, Ont. M5T 1A5
Phone: (416) 703-0201  Fax: (416) 703-0059
Contact: Tony Hamill, managing editor

Established 1972. Publishes Canadian plays in single editions, anthologies, and collections. All plays must have had professional theatre production. No unsolicited manuscripts, please. Query first.

## Polestar Press

1011 Commercial Drive, 2nd Floor, Vancouver, B.C. V5L 3X1
Phone: (604) 251-9718  Fax: (604) 251-9738
Contact: Michelle Benjamin, publisher

Established 1980. Publishes fiction and poetry, children's fiction and non-fiction, sports books, and general trade non-fiction. (No longer publishes illustrated children's books.) Released 12 new titles in 1995. Accepts unsolicited manuscripts, but prefers initial query with sample chapters. Guidelines available.

Notable 1995 title: *The Garden Letters*, Elspeth Bradbury and Judy Maddocks.

## The Porcupine's Quill
68 Main Street, Erin, Ont. NOB ITO
Phone: (519) 833-9158  Fax: (519) 833-9158
Contact: Tim Inkster, editor
Established 1974. Specializes in Canadian literary fiction. Publishes 10 titles a year. Does not often accept unsolicited manuscripts.

Notable 1995 title: *Popular Anatomy*, Keath Fraser.

## Pottersfield Press
R.R.2, Porters Lake, N.S. BOJ 2SO
Contact: Lesley Choyce, editor
Established 1979. Publishes general non-fiction, novels, and books of interest to Atlantic Canada. Particularly interested in biography proposals. Averages 5 new titles a year. Accepts proposals and/or full manuscripts. No phone calls, please.

## The Prairie Publishing Company
P.O. Box 2997, Winnipeg, Man. R3C 4B5
Phone: (204) 885-6496  Fax: (204) 775-3277
Contact: Ralph Watkins, editor/owner
Established 1969. A small publisher interested in manuscripts relating to Prairie history and development. Also publishes children's books and some biography. Accepts unsolicited manuscripts.

Notable 1995 title: *San-So-Blue*, Edna Emes.

## Prentice-Hall Canada
1870 Birchmount Road, Scarborough, Ont. MIP 2J7
Phone: (416) 293-3621  Fax: (416) 299-2540
Contact: Sara Borins, senior editor (trade)
Established 1960. Publishes trade non-fiction and education texts at all levels. Trade program specializes in business, personal finance, current affairs, and general reference. Published 20 titles

in 1995. Accepts unsolicited manuscripts, but first send outline and sample chapters.

Notable 1995 title: *Canadian Internet Handbook*, Jim Carroll and Rick Broadhead.

## Press Gang Publishers

225 East 17th Avenue, Vancouver, B.C. V5V 1A6
Phone: (604) 876-7787  Fax: (604) 876-7892
Contact: Barbara Kuhne, managing editor

Established 1974. "Press Gang Publishers Feminist Co-operative is committed to producing quality books with social and literary merit. We prioritize Canadian women's work and include writing by lesbians and by women from diverse cultural and class backgrounds. Our purpose is to represent the diversity of women's voices not represented by mainstream publishers. Our list features vital and provocative fiction and non-fiction." Published 8 new books in 1995. Send initial inquiry with sample chapter (fiction) or outline (non-fiction).

Notable 1995 title: *When Fox Is a Thousand*, Larissa Lai.

## Quarry Press

P.O. Box 1061, Kingston, Ont. K7L 4Y5
Phone: (613) 548-8429  Fax: (613) 548-1556
Contact: Bob Hilderley, president

Established 1965. Publishes literature, art history, popular culture, folklore, photography, local history. Averages 25 new titles a year. No unsolicited manuscripts. "Call or write for a catalogue of our books to determine the kind of work we publish. Don't inquire or submit blindly." Guidelines available.

## Ragweed Press Inc./gynergy books

P.O. Box 2023, Charlottetown, P.E.I. C1A 7N7
Phone: (902) 566-5750  Fax: (902) 566-4473
Contact: Sibyl Frei, managing editor

Established 1974. Publishes regional literature and history, children's books, and feminist and lesbian writing. Releases an average of 12 new titles a year. Accepts unsolicited manuscripts, but send an inquiry first.

Notable 1995 title: *Patient No More: The Politics of Breast Cancer*, Sharon Batt.

## Red Deer College Press
P.O. Box 5005, 56th Avenue and 32nd Street, Red Deer,
   Alta. T4N 5H5
Phone: (403) 342-3321  Fax: (403) 340-8940
Contacts: Dennis Johnson, managing editor; Tim Wynne-Jones,
   children's editor; Joyce Doolittle, drama editor
   Established 1975. Publishes poetry, fiction and non-fiction (including some gardening and cookbooks) for adults and children, illustrated children's books, young adult fiction, and drama. Produces 14 to 18 books a year. Query first with outline and sample chapters. Children's list is usually booked up 2 years in advance. Reports in 3 months. Manuscripts accepted for publication must be supplied on Mac disk in MS Word.
   Notable 1995 title: *The Third Suspect*, David Staples and Greg Owens.

## Reed Books Canada
204 Richmond Street W., Suite 300, Toronto, Ont. M5V 1V6
Phone: (416) 598-0045  Fax: (416) 598-0358
Contact: Susan Jasper, managing director
   Established in Canada in 1991. A division of Butterworths Canada, part of Reed International Books, and a major international book distributor. Publishes general trade fiction and non-fiction with a preference for adult non-fiction, and some children's illustrated books. Released 10 titles in 1995. No unsolicited manuscripts. Inquiries with outlines accepted.

## Reidmore Books
1200 Energy Square, 10109 – 106th Street, Edmonton,
   Alta. T5J 3L7
Phone: (403) 424-4420 or 1-800-661-2859  Fax: (403) 441-9919
Contact: Cathie Crooks, director, sales and marketing
   Established 1979. Produced 9 new titles in 1995. Publishes non-fiction, and specializes in educational titles developed to match a particular curriculum topic in social studies, elementary math, or

science. Some trade titles. No children's picture books. Accepts unsolicited manuscripts, but outline preferred first.

Notable 1995 title: *Canada: Its Land and People*, Don Massey and Patricia Shields.

## Rocky Mountain Books

4 Spruce Centre S.W., Calgary, Alta. T3C 3B3
Phone: (403) 249-9490  Fax: (403) 249-2968
Contact: Gillean Daffern, editor

Established 1976. Specializes in outdoor recreation (including skiing, hiking, climbing, biking, and whitewater), guidebooks, history pertaining to the Canadian Rockies, and the natural history of Alberta, British Columbia, and the Yukon. Averages 6 new titles a year. Accepts book proposals with outlines and writing samples. No complete unsolicited manuscripts.

Notable 1995 title: *Canmore and Kananaskis Country: Short Walks for Inquiring Minds*, Gillean Daffern.

## Ronsdale Press

3350 West 21st Avenue, Vancouver, B.C. V6S 1G7
Phone: (604) 738-1195  Fax: (604) 731-4548
Contact: R.B. Hatch, director

Established, as Cacanadadada Press, in 1988. Publishes trade books of literary value, specializing in fiction, poetry, and local history, with a good mix of first-time and established authors. Interested in quality and experimental literature. Averages 6 new titles a year. Accepts unsolicited manuscripts. "Ronsdale Press is not interested in pulp fiction or mass-market throwaways. Poets should already have published six poems in magazines. Please send the entire manuscript, or at least the first half – odd pages are of little value – and include a short bio." Guidelines available.

Notable 1995 title: *Blackouts to Bright Lights: Canadian War Bride Stories*, eds. B. Ledouceur and P. Spence.

## Royal British Columbia Museum

Publishing and Visual Services, 675 Belleville Street, Victoria,
   B.C. V8V 1X4
Phone: (604) 387-2478  Fax: (604) 387-5360

Contact: Gerry Truscott, editor-in-chief

Established 1912. Publishes scholarly and popular non-fiction concerning the human and natural history of British Columbia and the museum's activities. Interested in moving into children's books. All scientific work must be sponsored by an RBCM curator. Produced 4 new titles in 1995. No unsolicited manuscripts. Written inquiries should include outline.

Notable 1995 title: *Sunflowers of B.C., Vol. 2*, George Douglas, illust. Betty Stephen.

## Royal Ontario Museum

Publication and Print Services, 100 Queen's Park, Toronto,
    Ont. M5S 2C6
Phone: (416) 586-5581  Fax: (416) 586-5827
Contact: Glen Ellis, managing editor

Publishes manuscripts relating to the museum's collection, with some general-readership and children's books. Averages 10 new titles each year. No unsolicited manuscripts; inquiries only. Priority is given to (1) ROM authors, (2) research associates, (3) others.

Notable 1995 title: *The Bear-Walker and Other Stories*, Basil Johnston.

## Rubicon Publishing

116 Thomas Street, Oakville, Ont. L6J 3A8
Phone: (905) 849-8777  Fax: (905) 849-7579
Contact: Becky Flatt, editorial assistant

Established 1987. Publishes educational and children's litera-ture. Concerned to reflect the multicultural nature of Canadian society and avoid stereotyping people by sex, race, age, or physical or mental abilities. Released 8 titles in 1995. Accepts unsolicited manuscripts, but first send an outline. Guidelines available.

Notable 1995 title: *A Turtle Called Friendly*, Jean Sanguine.

## Scholastic Canada

123 Newkirk Road, Richmond Hill, Ont. L4C 3G5
Phone: (905) 883-5300  Fax: (905) 731-3482
Contact: Laura Peetoom, editor, children's books

Established in Canada in 1957. Specializes in children's books, both fiction and non-fiction, from preschool to young adult. Averages

50 titles a year. Also publishes professional materials for teachers. No unsolicited manuscripts; inquiries only.

Notable 1995 title: *The Gypsy Princess*, Phoebe Gilman.

## Script Publishing

839 – 5th Avenue S.W., Suite 200, Calgary, Alta. T2P 3C8
Phone: (403) 290-0800  Fax: (403) 241-8575
Contact: Doug McArthur, president

A small publisher specializing in non-fiction, reader-friendly health, parenting, and Good Question books for the Canadian and U.S. trade markets. Released 3 titles in 1995. Accepts unsolicited manuscripts, but first send inquiry with outline.

Notable 1995 title: *Parenting Today's Teenager Effectively: Hear Me, Hug Me, Trust Me*, Dr. G. Scott Wooding.

## Seal Books

105 Bond Street, Toronto, Ont. M5B 1Y3
Phone: (416) 340-0777  Fax: (416) 977-8488
Contact: Alison Maclean, editor

Established 1977. Publishes fiction and non-fiction paperbacks for the mass market, and commercial reprints. No unsolicited manuscripts.

Notable 1995 title: *On the Take: Crime, Corruption and Greed in the Mulroney Years* (pb), Stevie Cameron.

## Second Story Press

720 Bathurst Street, Suite 301, Toronto, Ont. M5S 2R4
Phone: (416) 537-7850  Fax: (416) 537-0588
Contact: Lois Pike or Margie Wolfe, editorial

A women's press specializing in quality fiction and non-fiction (women's health and social issues are of particular interest), children's picture books, and juvenile novels. Averages 12 titles a year. Accepts unsolicited manuscripts, but first send outline. Guidelines available.

Notable 1995 title: *Power Surge: Sex, Violence and Pornography*, Susan G. Cole.

## Self-Counsel Press

1481 Charlotte Road, North Vancouver, B.C. V7R 4B1

Phone: (604) 986-3366  Fax: (604) 986-3947
Contact: Ruth Wilson, managing editor

Established 1971. Specializes in self-help books on law and business by experts in their fields. Also publishes some reference and psychology books. Produces 15 to 20 new titles a year. Accepts unsolicited manuscripts, but prefers an initial inquiry, outline, and sample chapters. "Do your homework first! Ask for our catalogue, and be sure your idea fits into Self-Counsel's concept." Guidelines available.

Notable 1995 title: *Malaysia/Vietnam/Indonesia: A Kick Start Guide for Business Travellers* (3 books), Guy and Victoria Brooks.

## Somerville House Books

3080 Yonge Street, Suite 5000, Toronto, Ont. M4N 3N1
Phone: (416) 488-5938  Fax: (416) 488-5506
Contacts: Patrick Crean, editorial director; Jane Somerville,
    publisher

Established 1983. Publishes general trade books, focusing on children's non-fiction/educational and literature, with a small part of the program devoted to esoteric works of adult literary fiction and metaphysics. Published 8 new titles in 1993. Contact Anna Filippone by phone or letter for unsolicited manuscript inquiries (send outline and one sample chapter).

Notable 1995 title: *Mr. Sandman*, Barbara Gowdy.

## Sono Nis Press

1745 Blanshard Street, Victoria, B.C. V8W 2J8
Phone: (604) 382-1024  Fax: (604) 382-1575
Contact: Ann West, publisher, or Angela Addison, editor

Established 1968. Publishes history, historical biography, maritime history, transportation history, regional history, poetry, and some guidebooks. Produced 9 new titles in 1995. Accepts unsolicited manuscripts, but send inquiry first. Guidelines available.

Notable 1995 title: *Helicopters in the High Country: 40 Years of Mountain Flying*, Peter Corley-Smith.

## Stoddart Publishing Co.

34 Lesmill Road, Don Mills, Ont. M3B 2T6
Phone: (416) 445-3333  Fax: (416) 445-5967
Contact: Don Bastian, managing editor

Established 1964. Publishes timely, innovative, and original works across a broad range of non-fiction subjects, as well as fiction for adults, young adults, and children, and picture books. Produces 60 to 100 new titles each year. Accepts unsolicited manuscripts, but first send a synopsis and two sample chapters. Guidelines available.

Notable 1995 title: *Empire of the Soul: Some Journeys in India*, Paul William Roberts.

## Talon Books

1019 East Cordova Street, Suite 201, Vancouver, B.C. v6A 1M8
Phone: (604) 253-5261  Fax: (604) 255-5755
Contact: Karl Siegler, editor

Established 1967. Specializes in drama, serious fiction, poetry, popular non-fiction, women's literature, social issues, and ethnography. No unsolicited poetry or children's literature. For the rest, first send an inquiry with an outline.

Notable 1995 title: *The First Quarter of the Moon*, Michel Tremblay.

## Theytus Books

P.O. Box 20040, Penticton, B.C. v2A 8K3
Phone: (604) 493-7181  Fax: (604) 493-5302
Contact: Greg Young-Ing, manager

Established 1981. Publishes First Nations literature, fiction and non-fiction, art, music, and educational books by aboriginal authors. Released 8 new titles in 1993. Accepts unsolicited manuscripts, but first send an inquiry with outline. Guidelines available.

Notable 1995 title: *In Honour of Our Grandmothers*, Reisa Schneider and Gary Gottfriedson, artwork George Littlechild and Linda Spaner Dayan Frimer.

## Thistledown Press

633 Main Street, Saskatoon, Sask. s7H 0J8
Phone: (306) 244-1722  Fax: (306) 244-1762
Contact: Patrick O'Rourke, editor-in-chief

Established 1975. Specializes in Canadian poetry, short fiction, and young adult fiction. Published 14 new titles in 1995. The New Leaf Editions series is devoted to books of 64 pages by previously unpublished writers. No unsolicited manuscripts. Submit an inquiry with a sample and writing/publishing history. Guidelines available.

Notable 1995 title: *Dance of the Snow Dragon*, Eileen Kernaghan.

## Tundra Books

345 Victoria Avenue, Suite 604, Westmount, Que. H3Z 2N2
Phone: (514) 932-5434  Fax: (514) 484-2152
Contact: Arjun Basu, associate editor

Established 1967. Specializes in children's books as works of art. High quality children's books with lasting value. Averages 10 to 12 new titles a year. Does not accept unsolicited manuscripts, but welcomes letters of inquiry. "Take a look at our titles before submitting. With a few notable exceptions, such as Carrier, Tundra works with artists as authors." Guidelines available.

Notable 1995 title: *The White Stone in the Castle Wall*, Sheldon Oberman, illust. Les Tait.

## Turnstone Press

100 Arthur Street, Suite 607, Winnipeg, Man. R3B 1H3
Phone: (204) 947-1555  Fax: (204) 942-1555
Contact: James Hutchison, managing editor

Established 1976. A literary press publishing poetry, fiction, non-fiction, and literary criticism. Accepts unsolicited manuscripts.

Notable 1995 title: *One Room in a Castle*, Karen Connelly.

## UBC Press

6344 Memorial Road, Vancouver, B.C. V6T 1Z2
Phone: (604) 822-3259  Fax: (604) 822-6083
Contact: Jean Wilson, senior editor

Established 1971. Publishes non-fiction for scholarly, educational, and general audiences in the humanities, social sciences, and natural sciences. Subject areas include history, political science, law, anthropology, sociology, geography, art history, natural resources, the environment, and sustainable development. Releases about 30 new titles a year. No unsolicited manuscripts. Send an inquiry with outline and sample chapters. Guidelines available.

Notable 1995 title: *Canada and Quebec: One Country, Two Histories*, Robert Bothwell.

## United Church Publishing House

3250 Bloor Street W., 4th Floor, Etobicoke, Ont. M8X 2Y4
Phone: (416) 231-5931  Fax: (416) 232-6004
Contact: Ruth Bradley-St-Cyr, managing editor

Established in 1829 as Ryerson Press. Publishing program is not limited to "religious" matters, but rather reflects the broader interests of church members. Subjects include environmental and peace issues, social justice, and ethics. Averages 12 new titles a year. No unsolicited manuscripts. Send a letter of inquiry with a brief outline of material. Guidelines available.

Notable 1995 title: *The Man in the Scarlet Robe: Two Thousand Years of Searching for Jesus*, Michael McAteer and Michael Steinhauser.

## University of Alberta Press

141 Athabasca Hall, University of Alberta, Edmonton, Alta.
T6G 2E8
Phone: (403) 492-3662  Fax: (403) 492-0719
Contact: Glenn Rollans, director

Established 1969. Specializes in scholarly non-fiction and university-level textbooks, history, politics, natural sciences, Native studies, literary criticism, Slavic and Eastern European studies, Middle Eastern studies, anthropology, and archaeology. Mainly publishes original research with a strong Western Canadian interest. Averages 10 new titles a year. Accepts unsolicited manuscripts, but query first. Guidelines available.

Notable 1995 title: *Healing Waters: The Pilgrimage to Lac Ste. Anne*, Steve Simon.

## University of Calgary Press

2500 University Drive N.W., Calgary, Alta. T2N 1N4
Phone: (403) 220-7578  Fax: (403) 282-0085
Contact: Joan Barton, editorial secretary

Established 1981. Publishes scholarly and trade books in a wide variety of subject areas. Will consider any innovative scholarly manuscript. Released 9 new titles in 1995. A complete manuscript, with prospectus, will be considered if it satisfies scholarly criteria but also appeals to a larger audience. Guidelines available.

Notable 1995 title: *Doing Things the Right Way: Dene Traditional Justice in Lac La Martre, N.W.T.*, Joan Ryan.

## University of Manitoba Press

244 – 15 Gillson Street, University of Manitoba, Winnipeg,
   Man. R3T 5V6
Phone: (204) 474-9495  Fax: (204) 275-2270
Contact: C. Dahlstrom, managing editor

Established 1967. Publishes academic/scholarly books in the humanities and social sciences, including history, Native studies, Icelandic studies, and women's studies, and general interest books about the Prairie region. Averages 6 new titles each year. No unsolicited manuscripts. Inquiries only. Guidelines available.

Notable 1995 title: *Women of the First Nations*, ed. P. Chuchryk.

## University of Toronto Press

10 St. Mary Street, Suite 700, Toronto, Ont. M4Y 2W8
Phone: (416) 978-2239  Fax: (416) 978-4738
Contact: Bill Harnum, senior vice-president, scholarly publishing

Established 1901. A large university press publishing scholarly and general works, and academic journals. Editorial program includes classical, medieval, Renaissance, and Victorian studies, modern languages, English and Canadian literature, literary theory and criticism, women's studies, social sciences, Native studies, philosophy, law, religion, music, education, modern history, geography, and political science. Averages 125 to 130 new titles each year. Accepts unsolicited manuscripts, but first send inquiry with outline and sample chapter. Use *Chicago* or *MLA* for style, though internal consistency is the most important.

Notable 1995 title: *Selected Correspondence of Bernard Shaw*, ed. J. Percy Smith.

## Vanwell Publishing

1 Northrup Crescent, Box 2131, St. Catharines, Ont. L2M 6P5
Phone: (905) 937-3100  Fax: (905) 937-1760
Contact: Angela Dobler, general editor

Established 1983. Specializes in Canadian military history and biography. Publishes fiction and non-fiction, and children's non-fiction. Averages 9 titles a year. Reviews unsolicited manuscripts.

## Véhicule Press

P.O. Box 125, Place du Parc Station, Montreal, Que. H2W 2M9

Phone: (514) 844-6073  Fax: (514) 844-7543
Contact: Simon Dardick, general editor/publisher

Established 1973. Publishes fiction and poetry within the context of social history, and occasional titles on the history of science with a feminist orientation. Released 12 titles in 1995. Accepts unsolicited manuscripts. Poetry titles are booked until 1998.

Notable 1995 title: *Russia Between Yesterday and Tomorrow*, Marika Pruska-Carroll.

## Whitecap Books

351 Lynn Avenue, North Vancouver, B.C. v7J 2C4
Phone: (604) 980-9852  Fax: (604) 980-8197
Contact: Robin Rivers, editorial director

Established 1977. Specializes in natural history and regional guidebooks. Also interested in gardening, children's non-fiction, cooking, history, and giftbooks. Publishes 20 books a year. No fiction. Welcomes proposals and inquiries. Few unsolicited manuscripts are accepted, so check the list first.

Notable 1995 title: *Women of the Klondike*, Frances Backhouse.

## John Wiley & Sons Canada

22 Worcester Road, Rexdale, Ont. M9W 1L1
Phone: (416) 236-4433  Fax: (416) 236-4448
Contact: Elizabeth Fowler, assistant editor, trade

Established 1968. Publishes business, accounting, and finance books for Canadian professionals; also a growing number of trade books on current affairs and business. Averages 5 new titles a year. Written inquiries only.

Notable 1995 title: *Through the Money Labyrinth: A Canadian Broker Guides You to Stock Market Success*, Shirley Woods.

## Wilfrid Laurier University Press

Wilfrid Laurier University, Waterloo, Ont. N2L 3C5
Phone: (519) 884-0710, ext. 6123  Fax: (519) 725-1399
Contact: Sandra Woolfrey, director

Established 1974. Publishes scholarly books (and academic journals) in the humanities and social sciences, and general interest titles based on sound research. Subject areas include film, the environment, literary criticism, religious studies, Canadian studies, and history. Produced 12 new books in 1995. Accepts unsolicited manuscripts, but first send outline and sample chapter. Guidelines available.

Notable 1995 title: *Haven't Any News: Ruby's Letters from the Fifties*, ed. Edna Staebler.

## Wolsak and Wynn Publishers
P.O. Box 316, Don Mills P.O., Don Mills, Ont. M3C 2S7
Phone: (416) 222-4690  Fax: (416) 445-1816
Contact: Maria Jacobs, publisher/editor

Publishes poetry only – about 5 new books a year. Will consider unsolicited material after an initial written inquiry.

## Women's Press
517 College Street, Suite 233, Toronto, Ont. M6G 4A2
Phone: (416) 921-2425  Fax: (416) 921-4428
Contact: Martha Ayim or Ann Decter, co–managing editors

Established 1972. A feminist publishing collective committed to anti-racist/anti-classist publishing and to the development of feminism in Canada and internationally. Strongly interested in access to print for lesbians, disabled writers, and writers of colour. Publishes non-fiction, fiction, poetry, plays, and children's books. Averages 10 new titles a year. No longer accepts unsolicited manuscripts. Send a letter of inquiry and outline. Guidelines available.

Notable 1995 title: *Thinking Through: Essays on Feminism, Marxism and Anti-Racism*, Himani Bannerji.

## Wood Lake Books
10162 Newene Road, Winfield, B.C. V4V 1R2
Phone: (604) 766-2778  Fax: (604) 766-2736
Contact: David Cleary, publisher

Focuses on issues of values, justice, and family. Produced 10 new books in 1995. No unsolicited manuscripts. Send a letter of inquiry and outline.

Notable 1995 title: *There's Got to Be More*, Reginald Bibby.

## York Press
P.O. Box 1172, Fredericton, N.B. E3B 5C8
Fax: (506) 458-8748
Contact: Dr. Saad Elkhadem, editor

Established 1975. Publishes dictionaries, educational texts at the college level, scholarly publications, reference books, and manuscripts on literary criticism and comparative literature. Strong emphasis on high-quality creative writing and Arabic/Egyptian literature and scholarship. No unsolicited manuscripts or author guidelines. Query first.

Notable 1995 title: *García Márquez and Cuba*, Harley D. Oberhelman.

# 6

# LITERARY AGENTS

In the United States most writers, established or not, place their books through an agent; even magazine writers often sell their work this way. Literary agents have played a lesser role in Canadian publishing. The pool of agents has always been small here, and Canadian publishers have traditionally acted as agents for their authors when it comes to selling their works to foreign markets.

Like publishers, most agents are very circumspect about taking on unpublished writers, though publication in journals or high-quality magazines can help. Plenty of published writers don't use an agent. Some seek the advice of a lawyer when it comes to contract signing. Don't use the family solicitor for this, though, and bear in mind that very few lawyers in Canada specialize in publishing law. Far better to consult your regional branch of the Canadian Authors Association or the Writers' Union of Canada, who have access to all the necessary expertise and experience to help you pick through the minefield of the contract's small print.

There are, however, many advantages to securing a good agent. Most large publishers prefer to contract agented authors. A manuscript recommended by an agent will inevitably be taken more seriously than one submitted by an unknown writer. And it will probably be read and acted on sooner because the publisher can be confident that it has merit and is in a publishable condition. Indeed, books are occasionally contracted purely on the basis of a good proposal and a convincing pitch by the agent.

Established authors tend to use agents more, and may seek their counsel long before they actually begin writing a particular book. Because fiction is considerably harder to sell than non-fiction, fiction writers depend heavily on agents. Many literary agents, however, put a higher priority on maintaining a stable of proven non-fiction authors, because non-fiction sells in greater quantities than fiction, and since most agents work on commission, they will earn more from representing these clients.

Good agents deserve every penny they earn. Remember, they are not working for a salary; the efforts they expend hinge entirely on the promise of your future success. When you, the author, make money, the agent does too, so he or she will work hard to secure the best terms for you, the client. They develop long-term relationships with publishers and editors, with whom they can exchange ideas, learning their needs and interests, and they keep in close touch with what is sought after in the publishing marketplace. In so doing, they become expert at gauging the commercial possibilities of an author's proposal.

For new clients, it is on the strength of the agent's "first read" of the manuscript or proposal that he or she will agree to work with the writer. At contract-signing time, the agent can advise the writer on clauses that stipulate what rights the author should sell, or can negotiate every detail of a publisher's contract on the writer's behalf. The agent who fully understands the marketplace, publishing contracts, copyright law, and the broader sales possibilities of a book can negotiate a better publishing contract, often with a bigger advance against royalties.

Agents in Canada usually charge 15 or 20 per cent of the value of all rights sold. An agent today may evaluate a manuscript, suggest structural changes, sell the revised work to a publisher, negotiate the contract, secure an advance, and participate in designing a marketing program. He or she then often works closely with the author over the long term, helping the client to develop a career. Some agents are now, rather controversially, charging supplementary "handling" fees, which may cover the costs of everything from reading, evaluation, and editorial work to the agent's office expenses. But beware of agents who make more money from you, the author, than from the sale of your work. Insist on a strict accounting of fees and an upper limit to expenses.

This chapter lists most of the active literary agencies in Canada. Several others chose not to be included. Well-established agencies usually have a full slate of clients and consequently don't go out of their way to promote their services. As you will discover, agents tend to have very specific requirements and are becoming more and more selective. Below, you will find some advice on their subject interests and specialties; for further insights, ask the agent to send you a client list. Finding an agent, some claim, can be harder than finding a publisher! But every writer should consider the effort, since, in most cases, the relationship between agent and author is to great mutual advantage.

## Acacia House Publishing Services

51 Acacia Road, Toronto, Ont. M4S 2K6
Phone: (416) 484-8356  Fax: (416) 484-8356
Contact: Frances Hanna

Subject interests: Fiction with international potential. No horror, occult, science fiction, or adult fantasy. For non-fiction, no self-help, fitness, true crime, or business books.

Comments: Queries only, with writing sample (up to 50 pages). For evaluation, charges $1 per double-spaced page over 50 pages. Evaluates only complete manuscripts. All queries and submissions must be accompanied by SASE.

## Aurora Artists

3 Charles Street W., Suite 207, Toronto, Ont. M4Y 1R4
Phone: (416) 929-2042  Fax: (416) 922-3061
Contact: Janine Cheeseman

Subject interests: Reality-based stories.

Comments: Represents mostly film and television writers. No evaluation fee. No unsolicited manuscripts or unpublished writers. Query only. Include SASE to ensure response.

## Author Author Literary Agency

P.O. Box 34051, 1200 – 37th Street S.W., Calgary, Alta. T3C 3W2
Phone: (403) 242-0226  Fax: (403) 242-0226
Contact: Joan Rickard

Subject interests: Prefers adult fiction and non-fiction. Will also handle juvenile novels, adult and juvenile academic books, and New Age writing. No poetry or screenplays.

Comments: Welcomes unpublished writers. Accepts unsolicited queries and outlines. Studies and critiques unsolicited manuscripts if accompanied by reading fee. Reports within two weeks on queries, one month on manuscript outlines and up to three sample chapters, two months on complete manuscripts. Fees range from $75 for evaluating up to three sample chapters to $450 for full service (reading, editing, evaluating, and marketing) on an 85,000-word manuscript.

"We assist with and discuss methods to improve presentation and/or marketability. Study your chosen genre thoroughly to learn what publishers are buying. Ensure manuscripts are properly formatted. Always include SASE."

## Authors Marketing Services

200 Simpson Avenue, Toronto, Ont. M4K 1A6
Phone: (416) 463-7200  Fax: (416) 469-4444
E-mail: 102047.1111@compuserve.com
Contact: Larry Hoffman

Subject interests: Adult fiction and non-fiction.

Comments: No unsolicited manuscripts. Unpublished writers are charged evaluation/handling fees. Query only.

## The Bukowski Agency

125B Dupont Street, Toronto, Ont. M5R 1V4
Phone: (416) 928-6728  Fax: (416) 963-9978
Contact: Denise Bukowski

Subject interests: General adult trade books. Prefers literary fiction and non-fiction. No genre fiction (science fiction, romance, westerns); no children's or sports books; no scriptwriters or playwrights.

Comments: No unsolicited manuscripts or unpublished writers. Does not charge evaluation or other handling fees. Query first, by mail only, with writing samples and credentials. "What future projects do you have planned? Before making an investment in a little-known writer, I need to be convinced that you are not only talented but ambitious and driven as a writer, with an active career mapped out."

## Canadian Speakers' & Writers' Service

44 Douglas Crescent, Toronto, Ont. M4W 2E7
Phone: (416) 921-4443 Fax: (416) 922-9691
Contact: Matie Molinaro, Paul Molinaro, Julius Molinaro
Subject interests: Non-fiction, fiction, plays for the stage, television, and motion pictures. Also cartoons and subjects suited to animation adaptation.
Comments: Reads unpublished writers. Evaluation fees are charged based on medium and length. No unsolicited manuscripts.

## Great North Artists Management

350 Dupont Street, Toronto, Ont. M5R 1V9
Phone: (416) 925-2051 Fax: (416) 925-3904
Contact: Shain Jaffe
Subject interests: Plays and film and television properties.
Comments: No evaluation or other handling fees. No unpublished writers. No unsolicited manuscripts. Query only.

## The Helen Heller Agency

892 Avenue Road, Toronto, Ont. M5P 2K6
Phone: (416) 481-5430 Fax: (416) 486-1505
Contact: Helen Heller or Daphne Hart
Comments: No evaluation or other handling fees. No unpublished writers. No unsolicited manuscripts. Query by mail only.

## J. Kellock & Associates

11017 – 80th Avenue, Edmonton, Alta. T6G 0R2
Phone: (403) 433-0274
Contact: Joanne Kellock
Subject interests: Adult commercial and literary fiction; adult and children's non-fiction; all works for children, including picture books, first readers, middle readers, and young adult.
Comments: No unsolicited manuscripts. Written queries accepted. Reads unpublished writers. Evaluation and editorial fees charged. "There are two kinds of novels selling today: extraordinarily well-written commercial genre; and brilliantly written, stylistically innovative literature. Children's picture books are toughest to place, thus any first picture book must be unique, universal, and altogether wonderful. Do not supply illustrations with story unless

the illustrator has a Fine Arts degree or has previously illustrated a published book for children."

## Livingston Cooke

200 First Avenue, Toronto, Ont. M4M 1X1
Phone: (416) 406-3390  Fax: (416) 406-3389
Contact: Dean Cooke
  Subject interests: Non-fiction.
  Comments: Accepts inquiries, but no unsolicited manuscripts and no unpublished writers. At present, no evaluation or other handling fees are charged.

## Pamela Paul Agency

253A High Park Avenue, Toronto, Ont. M6P 2S5
Phone: (416) 769-0540  Fax: (416) 769-0540
Contact: Pamela Paul
  Subject interests: Film and television (writers and directors); literary fiction and non-fiction.
  Comments: No unsolicited manuscripts. Reads unpublished writers. No evaluation/handling fees. Written queries only. "A deliberately small agency with a quality list and special emphasis on selling literary properties for film and television."

## Beverley Slopen Agency

131 Bloor Street W., Suite 711, Toronto, Ont. M5S 1S3
Phone: (416) 964-9598
Contact: Beverley Slopen
  Subject interests: General fiction and non-fiction. No children's books, science fiction, or fantasy.
  Comments: No unsolicited manuscripts or unpublished writers. Does not charge evaluation/handling fees.

## Carolyn N. Swayze Literary Agency

W.R.P.S. Box 39588, White Rock, B.C. V4A 9P3
Phone: (604) 538-3478  Fax: (604) 531-3022
Contact: Carolyn N. Swayze
  Subject interests: Literary and genre adult fiction, non-fiction, young adult and children's. No romances, poetry, scripts, or screenplays.

Comments: Reads unpublished writers. No unsolicited manuscripts. Does not charge evaluation/handling fees. Will respond promptly to written inquiries that include a brief biography, synopsis of ms., three consecutive chapters, and SASE. Also provides legal services to authors.

**Westwood Vardey Literary Agents**
10 St. Mary Street, Suite 510, Toronto, Ont. M4Y 1P9
Phone: (416) 964-3302  Fax: (416) 975-9209
Contact: Jennifer Barclay
Subject interests: General and literary fiction and non-fiction. No poetry or short stories.
Comments: A busy agency that responds only to inquiries of current interest. No unsolicited manuscripts or unpublished writers.

# 7

# AWARDS, COMPETITIONS, & GRANTS

This greatly expanded chapter is divided into two sections: the first lists a broad range of the literary prizes and competitions open to Canadian writers; the second outlines the main sources of provincial and federal funding.

Most of the prizes and competitions may be applied for directly. Among several exceptions are premier awards such as the Harbourfront Festival Prize, conferred each year on a celebrated writer in mid-career, and McClelland & Stewart's prestigious Journey Prize, for the best short fiction from Canada's literary journals. In some cases, the judges prefer to receive submissions from publishers, but usually, so long as the application criteria are met, individual applications are also accepted.

Please note that application deadlines are subject to change, and that the following short entries do not include full eligibility criteria or entry conditions. Many contests, for instance, require a small entry fee, or the provision of several copies of the work so that they can be circulated among the nominating jury. Applicants should always write for full guidelines before making a submission.

Canadian writers are also eligible for a number of overseas-sourced awards, and you'll find these in standard international reference books such as *Literary Market Place*. New Canadian awards are usually advertised in such industry publications as *Books in Canada*, *Canadian Author*, and *Quill & Quire* – available in good bookstores and libraries – and in some literary journals.

Arts council and other government grants are designed to buy the writer time to devote to his or her work for a specified period in order to support a work-in-progress or the completion of a specific creative project through meeting a varying combination of living, research, travel, or professional development costs. Such financial support is most often targeted toward the successful published author, but gifted new writers are sometimes also eligible. Several provincial initiatives are open to new as well as established writers. As this book goes to press, the Canada Council's writer support programs, certainly the single most important source of assistance to writers across the country, remain "under review" while a major restructuring of Council programs and administration takes place, but there is cause to hope that a new, revamped scheme will have been launched by publication date. All these programs require applicants to develop detailed project proposals and budgets and to provide writing samples and other support materials.

## Awards & Competitions

### Alberta New Fiction Competition

Alberta Community Development, Arts & Cultural Industries
    Branch, 3rd Floor, Beaver House, 10158 – 103rd Street,
    Edmonton, Alta. T5J 0X6
Phone: (403) 427-6315
Deadline: December 1, 1997

A biennial competition open to all adult Alberta writers, from emerging to established authors. A cash prize of $4,500 goes to the best publishable full-length adult novel manuscript (minimum of 60,000 words).

### Alberta Playwriting Competition

Alberta Playwrights' Network, 1134 – 8th Avenue S.W., 2nd Floor,
    Calgary, Alta. T3E 4L6
Phone: (403) 269-8564 or 1-800-268-8564  Fax: (403) 269-8564
Deadline: October 15

A winning play script is selected in each of the following categories: an open category for a full-length play script on any subject (prize, $2,000 plus workshop); a "discovery" category for new writers (prize, $1,500 plus workshop); an open category for a one-act play (prize, $1,000 plus workshop). Alberta residents only. Also offers support for the development of new plays. Annual.

### Alberta Write for Radio Competition
Alberta Community Development, Arts & Cultural Industries
    Branch, 3rd Floor, Beaver House, 10158 – 103rd Street,
    Edmonton, Alta. T5J 0X6
Phone: (403) 427-6315
Deadline: November 1

For 15-minute radio drama scripts. A jury selects up to three winners, each of whom is awarded a $500 honorarium to offset the costs of the workshop as preparation for a possible contract with CBC Radio. Annual.

### Alberta Writing for Youth Competition
Alberta Community Development, Arts & Cultural Industries
    Branch, 3rd Floor, Beaver House, 10158 – 103rd Street,
    Edmonton, Alta. T5J 0X6
Phone: (403) 427-6315
Deadline: December 1996

A biennial competition offering Alberta writers a cash prize of $4,500. Manuscripts should be 40,000 words. Write for guidelines.

### The Alden Nowlan Award
Arts Branch, New Brunswick Department of Municipalities,
    Culture & Housing, P.O. Box 6000, Fredericton, N.B. E3B 5H1
Phone: (506) 453-2555   Fax: (506) 453-2416
Deadline: June 15, 1997

Designed to recognize excellence in English-language literary arts, this award offers a cash prize of $5,000 for the outstanding achievements and contribution to literature of a New Brunswick writer. A biennial award, it is next offered in 1997. Nominees must have been born in the province or have lived there for at least five years. No self-nominations considered.

### Ann Connor Brimer Award
Linda Hodgins, Dartmouth Regional Library, 60 Alderney Drive,
    Dartmouth, N.S. B2Y 4P8

Phone: (902) 464-2311  Fax: (902) 464-2284

Deadline: April 30

A $1,000 prize is awarded to the author of a fiction or non-fiction children's book published in the previous 12 months. Author must be resident of Atlantic Canada. Annual.

## Arthur Ellis Awards

Secretary/Treasurer, Crime Writers of Canada, P.O. Box 113, 3007
    Kingston Road, Scarborough, Ont. M1M 1P1

Deadline: December 31

Prizes are awarded in the following categories in the crime genre: the best novel, the best first novel, the best short story, and the best non-fiction. Cash prizes awarded depending on availability. Open to any writer resident in Canada or any Canadian living abroad. Setting and imprint immaterial. Annual.

## Authors' Awards

Janette Hatcher, Periodical Marketers of Canada, 175 Bloor Street
    E., Suite 1007, South Tower, Toronto, Ont. M4W 2R8

Phone: (416) 968-7218  Fax: (416) 968-6182

Deadline: July 31

Awarded to recognize outstanding Canadian writing in English-language mass market magazines and paperback books. Categories and prizes are as follows: Paperback non-fiction ($1,000), paperback fiction ($1,000), magazine–public affairs ($750). Special recognition is also given to the book of the year and to the author of the year. Annual.

## The B.C. Book Prizes

Alan Twigg, B.C. BookWorld, 3516 West 13th Avenue (rear),
    Vancouver, B.C. V6R 2S3

Phone: (604) 736-4011  Fax: (604) 736-4011

Deadline: December

A $2,000 prize is awarded in each category for the year's most outstanding achievement in fiction, non-fiction, children's literature, and poetry by a British Columbia writer. An equivalent prize is also conferred on the local book that "contributes most to an understanding of British Columbia." Governed by the West Coast Book Prize Society but now administered by *B.C. BookWorld*. Annual.

## B.C. Gas Lifetime Achievement Award

c/o B.C. BookWorld, 3516 West 13th Avenue (rear), Vancouver,
   B.C. V6R 2S3
Phone: (604) 736-4011

An annual $5,000 prize is awarded for an exemplary literary career by a British Columbia resident. Administered by *B.C. Book-World*.

## B.C. Historical Federation Writing Competition

c/o P. McGeachie, 7953 Rosewood Street, Burnaby, B.C. V5E 2H4
Phone: (604) 522-2062
Deadline: December 15

The Lieutenant-Governor's Medal for Historical Writing, together with a monetary prize ($100 to $300), is awarded annually to the author of the most significant book on any facet of British Columbia's history. Also, to encourage amateur historians and students, an annual monetary prize is awarded for the best article (maximum 3,000 words) published in the *B.C. Historical News* magazine (check for deadline).

## The bpNichol Chapbook Award

The Phoenix Community Works Foundation, 316 Dupont Street,
   Toronto, Ont. M5R 1V9
Phone: (416) 964-7919
Deadline: March 31

A prize of $1,000 is offered for the best poetry chapbook published in English in Canada. The chapbook should be between 10 and 48 pages long. Annual.

## The Bronwen Wallace Award

c/o The Writers' Development Trust, 24 Ryerson Avenue,
   Suite 201, Toronto, Ont. M5T 2P3
Phone: (416) 504-8222  Fax: (416) 504-9090
Deadline: January 31

An award of $1,000 is presented, in alternate years, to a Canadian poet or a Canadian short fiction writer under the age of 35 who is unpublished in book form but whose work has appeared in at least one independently edited magazine or anthology. Applicants should submit 10 pages of unpublished poetry in English

(1996) or up to 2,500 words of unpublished prose fiction in English (1997).

## Canadian Authors Association Awards

Jeffrey Holmes, 275 Slater Street, Suite 500, Ottawa, Ont. KIP 5H9
Phone: (613) 233-2846  Fax: (613) 235-8237

### Air Canada Award

Deadline: April

A prize comprising two return tickets to any destination served by Air Canada is awarded to the most promising young writer under 30. Contenders are nominated by the Canadian Authors Association (to whom recommendations should be sent) and other writers' associations. Annual.

### The Vicky Metcalf Body of Work Award

Deadline: December 31

A prize of $10,000 is awarded to the author of the best body of work by a Canadian, whether fiction, non-fiction, poetry, or picture books. Annual.

### The Vicky Metcalf Short Story Awards

Deadline: December 31

A prize of $3,000 is conferred on the writer of the best short story published in an English-language Canadian magazine or anthology during the previous year; the editor of this work receives a further $1,000. Annual.

### CAA Literary Awards

Deadline: December 15

A prize of $5,000 and a sterling-silver medal is awarded in recognition of the year's outstanding books in the categories of fiction, non-fiction, poetry, and drama by Canadian writers. Entries should manifest "literary excellence without sacrifice of popular appeal." Nominations from author, publisher, individual, or group eligible. Annual.

## Canadian Historical Association Awards

Joanne Mineault, 395 Wellington Street, Ottawa, Ont. KIA ON3
Phone: (613) 233-7885  Fax: (613) 567-3110

*John Bullen Prize*
Deadline: November 30
   A prize of $500 is awarded, in alternate years, for the best doctoral dissertation in Canadian history and the best doctoral dissertation in a field of history other than Canadian.

*The Wallace K. Ferguson Award*
Deadline: December 15
   A $1,000 prize is awarded for the best work of history by a Canadian writer on a non-Canadian subject. Annual.

*Sir John A. Macdonald Prize*
Deadline: December 15
   A prize of $1,000 is awarded in recognition of the non-fiction work of history "judged to have made the most significant contribution to an understanding of the Canadian past." Annual.

*The Hilda Neatby Prize in Women's History*
Deadline: February 1
   An annual non-cash prize is awarded for an academic article, published in a Canadian journal or book during the previous year, deemed to have made an original and scholarly contribution to the field of women's history.

**Canadian Library Association Book Awards**
CLA Membership Services, 200 Elgin Street, Suite 602, Ottawa,
   Ont. K2P IL5
Phone: (613) 232-9625  Fax: (613) 563-9895

*Book of the Year for Children Award*
   A commemorative medal is presented annually to the author of an outstanding children's book, suitable for children up to the age of 14, published in Canada during the previous calendar year. Any creative work (fiction, poetry, anthologies, etc.) will be deemed eligible. Author must be Canadian citizen or permanent resident. Nominations invited from CLA members and publishers.

*Young Adult Canadian Book Award*
   This award recognizes the author of an outstanding English-language book written in the preceding calendar year that appeals

to young adults between the ages of 13 and 18. The book must be a work of fiction published in Canada, and the author should be a Canadian citizen or landed immigrant. The winner receives a leather-bound book with the award embossed on the cover. Annual.

## The Chalmers Awards

Chalmers Awards Office, Ontario Arts Council, 151 Bloor Street
  W., Toronto, Ont. M5S 1T6
Phone: (416) 961-1660 or 1-800-387-0058  Fax: (416) 961-7796

*The Floyd S. Chalmers Canadian Play Awards*
  To honour the creation of original Canadian plays, four awards of $10,000 go to the writers of distinguished plays produced in Metro Toronto by any professional Canadian theatre group. Translations, adaptations, and collective creations are eligible. Each play is assessed in production and judged on the basis of the playwright's contribution rather than on its production values. Winners are chosen by a jury drawn from the Toronto theatre community. Administered by the Ontario Arts Council. Annual.

*The Chalmers Canadian Play Awards: Theatre for Young Audiences*
  Two annual awards of $10,000 honour Canadian playwrights of original plays for young audiences, defined as of school age from primary to Ontario Academic Credit levels. Plays must have been performed at least four times within a 50-km radius of Metro Toronto. Other conditions match those of the previous entry.

## City of Dartmouth Book Award

Charby Slernin, c/o Dartmouth Regional Library, 60 Alderney
  Drive, Dartmouth, N.S. B2Y 4P8
Phone: (902) 464-2312
Deadline: December
  Two prizes of $1,000 each are awarded to honour the fiction and non-fiction books that have contributed most to the enjoyment and understanding of Nova Scotia and its people. Open to any Canadian citizen or landed immigrant. Annual.

## City of Toronto Book Awards

Richard Frank, c/o City Clerk's Department, Communications

Division, 22nd Floor, East Tower, City Hall, Toronto,
Ont. M5H 2N2
Phone: (416) 392-0468  Fax: (416) 392-7999
Deadline: January 30

Prize money totalling $15,000 is apportioned in recognition of works of literary merit, in all genres, that are evocative of Toronto. Each shortlisted writer receives $1,000, the balance going to the winner. Annual.

### City of Vancouver Book Award

Russell Kelly, B.C. BookWorld, 3516 West 13th Avenue (rear),
    Vancouver, B.C. V6R 2S3
Phone: (604) 736-4011  Fax: (604) 736-4011
Deadline: June

A $2,000 cash prize is awarded in October at the opening of the Vancouver International Writers' Festival. Entered books must be primarily set in or about Vancouver, though the author's place of residence is not restricted, and the book may be written/published anywhere in the world. Books may be fiction, non-fiction, poetry, or drama, written for children or adults, and may deal with any aspects of the city, including its history, geography, current affairs, or the arts. Apply for guidelines. Annual.

### Dafoe Book Prize

J.E. Rea, Department of History, University of Manitoba,
    500 Dysart Road, Winnipeg, Man. R3T 2M8

A cash prize of $5,000 is awarded for a distinguished work of non-fiction by a Canadian, or an author resident in Canada, that "contributes to the understanding of Canada and/or its place in the world."

### David C. Saxon Humanitarian Essay Competition

c/o Secretary, Arts and Letters Competition, P.O. Box 1854,
    St. John's, Nfld. A1C 5P9
Deadline: March

Essays on a specified topic should be 2,000 to 4,000 words. First prize $1,000; second prize $750; third prize $500. An annual competition open only to residents of the province.

## Distance Writing Prize

*Geist*, 1062 Homer Street, Suite 100, Vancouver, B.C. v6B 2w9
Phone: (604) 681-9161  Fax: (604) 669-8250
Deadline: November 1

A $1,000 cash prize goes to the best unpublished fiction or non-fiction prose composition containing references to at least two Canadian towns separated by at least two time zones. Preferred length 2,500 words. Maximum length 4,000 words. Apply for full entry conditions. Annual.

## Edna Staebler Award for Creative Non-Fiction

Office of the President, Wilfrid Laurier University, 75 University
   Avenue W., Waterloo, Ont. N2L 3C5
Phone: (519) 884-0710
Deadline: May 19

A $3,000 prize is awarded for an outstanding work of creative non-fiction, which must be written by a Canadian and have a Canadian location and significance. A first and second prize may be awarded at the discretion of the jury. To be eligible, an entry must be the writer's first or second published book. Established to give recognition and encouragement to new writers. Administered by Wilfrid Laurier University. Annual.

## Federation of B.C. Writers Competitions

Federation of B.C. Writers, 4th Floor, 905 West Pender, Vancouver, B.C. v6c 1L6
Phone: (604) 683-2057

### Festival Writing Competition

Deadline: March 15

Open to B.C. emerging writers only. Send a sample of your work (up to 2,000 words) on any topic and in any genre. Thirty-six delegates will be chosen from all entries and will each receive partially subsidized accommodation and travel to the B.C. Festival of the Arts held in Kamloops in May, where they will have the opportunity to attend creative writing seminars and workshop their work. The top six entries will receive $100 and a book prize. Annual.

*Literary Writes Competition*
Deadline: September 8

Open to all Canadian citizens and residents. Topic/theme changes each year. Up to 2,000 words of unpublished work. The winner receives $500 and an opportunity to publish; second place-getter is awarded $350; honourable mentions collect $75. Annual.

## Gabrielle Roy Prize

Joe Pivato, Athabasca University, Learning Centre – Edmonton,
    2nd Floor, North Tower, 7th Street Plaza, 10030 – 107th Street,
    Edmonton, Alta. T5J 3E5
Phone: (403) 497-3418  Fax: (403) 497-3411

A medal and a $300 cash award are presented to the authors of the English- and French-language books deemed to be the best works of literary criticism published in the previous year. The competition is open to works published anywhere in the world, but the subject must be Canadian or Quebec writing, and submissions must be made by the publishers. Sponsored and administered by the Association for Canadian and Quebec Literatures. Annual.

## Geoffrey Bilson Award for Historical Fiction for Young People

Jeffrey Canton, Canadian Children's Book Centre, 35 Spadina
    Road, Toronto, Ont. M5R 2S9
Phone: (416) 975-0010  Fax: (416) 975-1839

The Canadian Children's Book Centre awards an annual prize of $1,000 to the author of an outstanding work of historical fiction for young people. The author must be Canadian, and the book must have been published in the previous calendar year. To be considered, a book must first have been selected for inclusion in the CCBC's Our Choice list. The winner is chosen by a jury appointed by the CCBC.

## The Giller Prize

Kelly Kelly, 21 Steepleview Crescent, Richmond Hill,
    Ont. L4C 9R1
Phone: (905) 508-5146  Fax: (905) 508-4469

Established in 1994, The Giller Prize awards $25,000 annually to the author of the best Canadian novel or short story collection in

English, according to a professional jury panel. The author must be a Canadian citizen or permanent resident of Canada, and the book must have been published by a professional publisher in Canada. Check for deadlines.

## The Gordon Montador Award

c/o The Writers' Development Trust, 24 Ryerson Avenue,
   Suite 201, Toronto, Ont. M5T 2P3
Phone: (416) 504-8222  Fax: (416) 504-9090

A $2,000 joint prize goes to the author and publisher of the year's best Canadian book of non-fiction on contemporary social issues. Annual.

## Government of Newfoundland & Labrador Arts & Letters Competition

Regina Best, Arts and Culture Centre, P.O. Box 1854, St. John's,
   Nfld. A1C 5P7
Phone: (709) 576-5253  Fax: (709) 729-5253
Deadline: March

Three prizes are normally awarded in each category in recognition of outstanding fiction, non-fiction, poetry, and drama by residents of Newfoundland. First prize $600; second prize $300; third prize $150. There is also a junior division (age 12 to 17) in the categories of prose and poetry. First prize $300; second prize $200; third prize $100. Annual.

## Governor General's Literary Awards

Josiane Polidori, Canada Council, P.O. Box 1047, 99 Metcalfe
   Street, Ottawa, Ont. K1P 5V8
Phone: (613) 566-4376  Fax: (613) 566-4410
Deadline: August 31

Seven awards of $10,000 are conferred in recognition of the best books of the year in English in the following categories: fiction, non-fiction, poetry, drama, children's books, translation, and illustration. Books must be submitted by publishers. Administered by the Canada Council. Annual.

## Harbourfront Festival Prize

Greg Gatenby, Harbourfront, 410 Queen's Quay W., Toronto,
Ont. M5V 2Z3
Phone: (416) 973-4760

This prestigious prize is awarded to a Canadian writer in mid-career who has made a substantial contribution to Canadian letters through his or her writing *and* his or her efforts on behalf of other Canadian writers or writing. A cash prize of $7,000 is supplemented by $4,000 in office equipment to enhance the writer's working environment. The winner is chosen by a jury of three. No submissions.

## The Hawthorne Poetry Award

Robin Skelton, Hawthorne Society of Arts and Letters,
1255 Victoria Avenue, Victoria, B.C. V8S 4P3
Phone: (604) 592-7032  Fax: (604) 592-7032
Deadline: March 31

A cash prize of $500, plus publication in the Hawthorne Chapbook Series, is awarded for the best submission of 12 to 20 poems by a Canadian resident.

## Hugh A. Smythe Science Writing Award

Robert Watts, Communications Co-ordinator, The Arthritis
Society, 250 Bloor Street E., Suite 901, Toronto, Ont. M4W 3P2
Phone: (416) 967-1414  Fax: (416) 967-7171
Deadline: October 31

A $1,000 cash prize and a commemorative medal is awarded to the writer of the best original published feature article about arthritis in each of two categories – newspapers and magazines. Articles must have been published between October 1 and September 30 of the past year. The winner is selected by a jury. Annual.

## International 3-Day Novel Contest

Anvil Press, 175 East Broadway, Suite 204A, Vancouver,
B.C. V5T 1W2
Phone: (604) 876-8710  Fax: (604) 879-2667
Brian Kaufman, sub-TERRAIN Magazine, P.O. Box 1575, Bentall
Centre, Vancouver, B.C. V6C 2P7
Phone: (604) 876-8710  Fax: (604) 879-2667

Research and outlines prior to the contest are permissible, but the actual writing must take place over the long weekend. Entries are judged by the editorial staff of Anvil Press and *sub-TERRAIN Magazine*. The winner receives a publishing offer from Anvil Press. "The world's most notorious literary marathon" is held during Labour Day weekend in September. Annual.

## IODE National Book Award

Marty Dalton, 40 Orchard View Boulevard, Suite 254, Toronto,
   Ont. M4R 1B9
Phone: (416) 487-4416  Fax: (416) 487-4417
Deadline: January 31

A $3,000 prize is awarded in recognition of the year's best children's book of at least 500 words. Must have been written by a Canadian, and have been published in the last year. Fairy tales, anthologies, and books adapted from other sources ineligible. Annual.

## IODE Toronto Book Award

Catherine Moore, 44 Strath Avenue, Etobicoke, Ont. M8X 1R3
Phone: (416) 231-5120
Deadline: December 1

A $1,000 prize is conferred on the author or illustrator of the best children's book of the year written by a Toronto area resident. Annual.

## Island Literary Awards

P.E.I. Council of the Arts, P.O. Box 2234, Charlottetown, P.E.I.
   C1A 8B9
Phone: (902) 368-4417  Fax: (902) 368-4418

The annual Island Literary Awards are sponsored by the P.E.I. Council of the Arts.

### *L.M. Montgomery P.E.I. Children's Literature Award*

Deadline: February 15

The L.M. Montgomery Prize ($500), Bookmark Prize ($200), and Friends of the Confederation Centre Prize ($100) are awarded to the authors of the three best manuscripts (maximum length 60 pages) written for children between ages 5 and 12. Must be original and unpublished. Authors must be Island residents.

### Carl Sentner Short Story Award
Deadline: February 15

Awards of $500 (first prize), $200 (second prize), and $100 (third prize) go to the authors of the best short stories. Authors must be Island residents. Not open to writers with one or more books published in the last five years.

### Milton Acorn Poetry Award
Deadline: February 15

Awarded to the author of a maximum of 10 pages of poetry. First prize: a trip for two between any two points in North America (excluding Boston). Open to residents of P.E.I. Authors of one or more books published in the last five years are not eligible.

### Cavendish Tourist Association Children's Literature Award
Deadline: February 15

Prizes of $75, $50, and $25 are awarded to P.E.I. students at elementary, junior, and senior high levels. Students may write five pages of poetry or a five-page short story on the topic of their choice.

### Feature Article Award
Deadline: February 15

The Guardian/Patriot Prize ($500), the Dunes Studio Gallery Second Prize ($200), and the Kindred Spirits Third Prize ($100) are awarded to the authors of the best feature articles that are unpublished or published within the last 12 months. Open to P.E.I. residents.

### New Voices Playwriting Competition Full Length Play
Deadline: February 15

For original plays (minimum playing time 1 hour 30 minutes) not previously produced. First prize is $1,000. Open to any professional or non-professional in P.E.I.

### New Voices Playwriting Competition One Act Play
Deadline: February 15

For original short plays (playing time 25 to 45 minutes) not previously produced. First prize $400, second prize $200, third prize $100. Open to any professional or non-professional in P.E.I.

*New Voices Playwriting Competition Radio Play*
Deadline: February 15

For original radio plays (playing time 30 to 60 minutes). First prize $300. Open to any professional or non-professional in P.E.I.

## Jewish Book Awards

Joan Tooke, Jewish Book Awards, Koffler Centre of the Arts, 4588
   Bathurst Street, North York, Ont. M2R 1W6
Phone: (416) 636-1880, ext. 299  Fax: (416) 636-5813
Deadline: February 1

For Canadian authors, published in Canada, writing on subjects of Jewish interest in the following categories: fiction, poetry, biblical/rabbinic scholarship, history, literature for young readers, scholarship on a Canadian Jewish subject, original translation from Yiddish or Hebrew, Yiddish writing, Holocaust history or literature. Awards vary with donor between $250 and $1,000. Annual.

## Jon Whyte Memorial Essay Prize

Writers Guild of Alberta, 11759 Groat Road, 3rd Floor,
   Edmonton, Alta. T5M 3K6
Deadline: September 15

Alberta writers are invited to submit essays of up to 3,500 words addressing the theme "The Changing Face of Alberta – A Personal Contemplation." The winning essay will earn a $2,000 prize from the Alberta Foundation for the Arts, will be published by the *Edmonton Journal* and the *Calgary Herald*, and will be produced for radio by CKUA (Access) Radio. Annual.

## The Journey Prize

Stacey Lukachko, McClelland & Stewart Inc., 481 University
   Avenue, Suite 900, Toronto, Ont. M5G 2E9
Phone: (416) 598-1114, ext. 341  Fax: (416) 598-7764
Deadline: January 15

The $10,000 Journey Prize is awarded to a new and developing writer of distinction. A selection of the best short fiction or novel excerpts published during the previous year in Canadian literary journals is collected in *The Journey Prize Anthology*, published by McClelland & Stewart. The prizewinner is drawn from this collection. McClelland & Stewart makes its own donation of $2,000 to the journal that first published the winning entry. Submissions accepted from journal editors only. Annual.

## The Keith Matthews Awards

Olaf Janzen, Department of History, Memorial University of
    Newfoundland, Sir Wilfred Grenfell College Campus, Corner
    Brook, Nfld. A2H 6P9
Phone: (709) 637-6282   Fax: (709) 639-8125
E-mail: olaf@kean.ucs.mun.ca

    Annual certificate awards are presented by the Canadian Nautical Research Society to the authors of the best scholarly book and the best article published during the previous calendar year either on a Canadian nautical or marine subject or by a Canadian on a foreign nautical or marine subject.

## The Kenneth Wilson Awards

Canadian Business Press, 40 Shields Court, Suite 201, Markham,
    Ont. L3R 0M5
Deadline: March

    Recognizing excellence in writing and graphic design in specialized business/professional publications, the competition is open to all Canadian business publications. Seven categories cover editorial, marketing, profiles, departments, features, and news stories. Editorial staff or freelance contributors may enter. Winners of gold and silver awards will receive a certificate and a cash prize. Annual.

## The Last Poems Poetry Contest

Brian Kaufman, *sub-TERRAIN Magazine*, P.O. Box 1575, Bentall
    Centre, Vancouver, B.C. V6C 2P7
Phone: (604) 876-8710   Fax: (604) 879-2667
Deadline: January 31

    Sponsored by *sub-TERRAIN Magazine* and Anvil Press. For "poetry that encapsulates North American experience at the close of the twentieth century." The winner receives a $200 cash prize plus publication in the spring issue of *sub-TERRAIN*. All entrants receive a four-issue subscription to *sub-TERRAIN*.

## League of Canadian Poets Awards

Sandra Drzewiecki, 54 Wolseley Street, 3rd Floor, Toronto,
   Ont. M5T 1A5
Phone: (416) 504-1657  Fax: (416) 703-0059

### Gerald Lampert Memorial Award

Deadline: January 31

A $1,000 cash award is given in recognition of the best first book
of poetry by a Canadian. Annual.

### National Poetry Contest

Deadline: January 31

Three prizes – of $1,000, $750, and $500 – are awarded for the
best unpublished poems not exceeding 75 written lines. Fifty of the
submitted poems, including the three winners, will be published in
an anthology. Annual.

### Pat Lowther Memorial Award

Deadline: January 31

A $1,000 prize recognizes the best book of poetry written by a
Canadian woman and published in Canada. Annual.

## The Lionel Gelber Prize

Marcia McClung, Applause Communications, 398 Adelaide Street
   W., Suite 1007, Toronto, Ont. M5V 1S7
Phone: (416) 504-7200
Deadline: July 1

Presented in October, an award of $50,000 goes to the year's best-
written book on international relations written in English or in
English translation appealing both to the scholarly and the general
reader. The winner is selected by a panel of six people knowledgeable in the field of international relations. Applicants may be of any
nationality, but the book must be available in Canada. Copyright
must be of the year of entry or after October of the previous year.
Bound manuscripts are also accepted. Annual.

## Maclean's In-Class Program Student Writing Awards

777 Bay Street, 8th Floor, Toronto, Ont. M5W 1A7
Phone: (416) 596-5514 or toll-free 1-800-668-1951

E-mail: inclass@hookup.net
Deadline: June

Students registered in a full- or part-time secondary program in Canada are invited to submit a 1,000-word paper on a topic chosen each year by the Maclean's In-Class Program. First prize is $1,000, second prize $500, third prize $200.

## The Macpherson Prize

The Canadian Political Science Association, 1 Stewart Street,
    Suite 206, University of Ottawa, Ottawa, Ont. KIN 6H7
Phone: (613) 564-4025  Fax: (613) 230-2746
Deadline: December

An award of $750 is made to the author of the best book published in English or French in the field of political theory. No textbooks, edited texts, collections of essays, or multiple-authored works will be considered. The award is conferred biennially; the deadline for the 1998 prize is December 1997 and applies to books published in 1996 and 1997. The author must be a Canadian citizen or permanent resident.

## The Malahat Review Long Poem Prize

Marlene Cookshaw, *The Malahat Review*, University of Victoria,
    P.O. Box 1700 MS 8524, Victoria, B.C. v8w 2y2
Phone: (604) 721-8524  Fax: (604) 721-7212
Deadline: March 1, 1997

Two prizes of $400, plus payment for publication, are awarded for the best original, unpublished long poems or cycle of poems of 5 to 15 pages. Entry fee covers one subscription to *Malahat*. Offered biennially.

## The Malahat Review Novella Prize

Marlene Cookshaw, *The Malahat Review*, University of Victoria,
    P.O. Box 1700 MS 8524, Victoria, B.C. v8w 2y2
Phone: (604) 721-8524  Fax: (604) 721-7212
Deadline: March 1, 1996, 1998

A prize of $400, plus payment for publication, is awarded for the best original, unpublished prose work no longer than 60,000 words. Entry fee covers one subscription to *Malahat*. Offered biennially.

## The Marian Engel Award

c/o The Writers' Development Trust, 24 Ryerson Avenue,
    Suite 201, Toronto, Ont. M5T 2P3
Phone: (416) 504-8222  Fax: (416) 504-9090

An award of $10,000 is conferred on a Canadian woman writer in mid-career, recognizing her collective works and the promise of her future contribution to Canadian literature. Canada's premier literary award for women. Annual.

## McNally Robinson Award for the Manitoba Book of the Year

Robyn Maharaj, Manitoba Writers' Guild, 100 Arthur Street,
    Suite 206, Winnipeg, Man. R3B 1H3
Phone: (204) 942-6134 or 942-5754
Deadline: December 31

Sponsored by McNally Robinson Booksellers, a $2,500 prize is awarded for an outstanding book in any genre written by a Manitoba resident. Annual.

## Morguard Literary Awards

Franca Vettese, REIC, 2200 Lakeshore Boulevard W., Suite 305,
    Toronto, Ont. M8V 1A4
Phone: (416) 253-0803  Fax: (416) 253-0884

Recognizes outstanding articles relevant to the Canadian real estate industry. Sponsored by the Real Estate Institute of Canada and Morguard Investments Ltd., a $2,000 prize goes to the winner in each of two categories: practising industry writers and academic writers. Submissions must be original, unpublished articles, or speeches given in the past 12 months, 3,000 to 6,000 words long. Annual.

## Mr. Christie's Book Awards

Marlene Yustin, c/o Christie Brown and Co., 2150 Lakeshore
    Boulevard W., Toronto, Ont. M8V 1A3
Phone: (416) 503-6050  Fax: (416) 503-6010
Deadline: January 31

Awards of $7,500 each are presented in three categories, in English and in French: the best children's book (7 years and under), the best children's book (8 to 11 years), and the best children's book (12 to 16 years). The winners are chosen by an expert panel, which judges entries on their ability to inspire the imagination of the reader, to recognize the importance of play, to bring delight and edification, and to help children understand the world, both intellectually and emotionally. Open to Canadian citizens or landed immigrants at the time of the book's publication. Annual.

## The Nathan Cohen Award

Jeniva Berger, Award Chair, 181 University Avenue, Suite 2100,
   Toronto, Ont. M5H 3M7
Phone: (416) 367-8896  Fax: (416) 367-8896
Deadline: March 4

The only annual English-language award in North America honouring excellence in theatre criticism of live theatre productions. An award of $500 is presented in each of two categories: Long Review (reviews, profiles, and other theatrical features of 1,000 to 4,000 words) and Short Review (reviews of up to 1,000 words). Up to three items may be submitted in either or both categories. Entries must have been published between November 30 and December 1 of the previous year.

## National Business Book Awards

Arianna Venditti, Coopers & Lybrand, 5160 Yonge Street, North
   York, Ont. M2N 6L3
Phone: (416) 224-2140
Deadline: mid-December

An annual award of $10,000 recognizes excellence in business writing. When another entry also excels, a second prize of $5,000 is sometimes conferred. At the time of writing, Coopers & Lybrand were still looking for a co-sponsor. Annual.

## National Magazine Awards

Sandra Eikins, National Magazine Awards Foundation, 109
   Vanderhoof Avenue, Suite 207, Toronto, Ont. M4G 2H7
Phone: (416) 422-1358  Fax: (416) 422-3762
Deadline: January 9

The 17 written categories are as follows: one-of-a-kind articles (any hard-to-classify non-fiction article); humour; business; science, health, and medicine; public issues; fiction (commissioned by the magazine); poetry (commissioned by the magazine); arts and entertainment; sports and recreation; columns (3 columns by the same writer in the same magazine); travel; service (presenting practical, useful information); essays; personal journalism; profiles; editorial package (a theme issue reflecting collaboration between editors and writers); words and pictures (an article relying for its impact on text and visuals). Canadian staff or freelance contributors are eligible. Magazine publishers or editors or freelancers may submit. Gold awards are $1,500, silver awards $500. As well, the President's Medal, worth $3,000, is awarded to an article considered the "Best of Show." Annual.

### Nepean Public Library Short Story Contest

Marlene McCausland, Nepean Public Library, 101 Centrepointe Drive, Nepean, Ont. K2G 5K7
Phone: (613) 727-6646  Fax: (613) 727-6677
Deadline: March 31

For an original, unpublished, English-language story written by an adult (18 years and over) Ontario resident in the National Capital Region. First prize $500; second prize $250; third prize $100.

### Ottawa-Carleton Book Award

Arts Office, Regional Municipality of Ottawa-Carleton, Ottawa-Carleton Centre, 111 Lisgar Street, Ottawa, Ont. K2P 2L7
Phone: (613) 560-1239  Fax: (613) 560-1380
Deadline: January 20

A $2,000 award is presented each year to both an English and a French author of a book of literary merit published within the previous two calendar years. Alternating annually between the categories of fiction and non-fiction, the 1997 award will be for fiction. The authors must reside in the Regional Municipality of Ottawa-Carleton and be Canadian citizens or landed immigrants. Entries are reviewed by professional juries. Awards are presented at the Ottawa Valley Book Festival in May.

### Ottawa Little Theatre Annual Canadian One-Act Playwriting Competition

George Stonyk, Ottawa Little Theatre, 400 King Edward Avenue, Ottawa, Ont. KIN 7M7
Phone: (613) 233-8948  Fax: (613) 233-8027

Deadline: May 31

With the object of encouraging literary and dramatic talent in Canada, the competition, for an unproduced original one-act play in English (playing time 25 to 49 minutes) is open to professional and non-professional Canadian playwrights resident in Canada including landed immigrants. First prize, the Solange Karsh Award, consists of $1,000 and a gold medal; second prize, the Dorothy White Award, is $700; third prize, the Gladys Cameron Watt Award, is $500.

**The Penny Dreadful Short Story Contest**
Brian Kaufman, *sub-TERRAIN Magazine*, P.O. Box 1575, Bentall
    Centre, Vancouver, B.C. v6c 2p7
Phone: (604) 876-8710  Fax: (604) 879-2667
Deadline: May 15

Sponsored by *sub-TERRAIN Magazine* and Anvil Press. The winner receives a $200 cash prize plus publication in the summer issue of *sub-TERRAIN*. All entrants receive a four-issue subscription. Any unpublished fiction of 2,000 words or less is eligible. One-time, one-story entry fee; additional stories may be submitted with a supplementary fee.

**PRISM international Short Fiction Contest**
*PRISM international*, Department of Creative Writing, University
    of British Columbia, Buch E-462, 1866 Main Mall, Vancouver,
    B.C. v6t 1z1
Phone: (604) 822-2514  Fax: (604) 822-3616
E-mail: prism@unixg.ubc.ca
Deadline: December 1

A $2,000 prize is awarded for the best original, unpublished short story (up to 25 double-spaced pages). Five runner-up prizes of $200 are also conferred. There is no limit on the number of stories that may be entered. Works of translation are eligible. All entrants receive a one-year subscription to *PRISM international*, who buy First North American serial rights for all works accepted for publication. Annual.

**QSPELL Book Awards**
Jeanne Randle, 1200 Atwater Ave., Montreal, Que. h3z 1x4

Phone: (514) 933-0878  Fax: (514) 933-0878
Deadline: May 31

Prizes, each worth $2,000, are awarded for the finest work of fiction, non-fiction, and poetry written in English by a writer who has lived in Quebec for at least three of the past five years. Annual.

### The Ruth Schwartz Children's Book Award

The Literature Office, Ontario Arts Council, 151 Bloor Street W.,
 Toronto, Ont. M5S 1T6
Phone: (416) 969-7437  Fax: (416) 961-7796

A panel of children's booksellers selects two shortlists of five young adult and five picture books in February; two juries of children then select a winner in each category. There is no application process; all Canadian children's trade books published in the previous year are eligible. The awards ($3,000 for the picture book category, shared between author and illustrator; $2,000 for the YA category) are presented by the OAC at the annual CBA convention in June or July.

### Saskatchewan Writers' Guild Awards

Paul Wilson, P.O. Box 3986, Regina, Sask. S4P 3R9
Phone: (306) 757-6310  Fax: (306) 565-8554
E-mail: swg@unibase.unibase.com
Deadline: June

*SWG Annual Literary Awards*

Prizes of over $5,000 are conferred to recognize excellent unpublished manuscripts by both new and developing Saskatchewan writers. Awards rotate between fiction, non-fiction, poetry, and children's literature. Each year there is also a competition for a book-length manuscript, with the genre rotating between fiction, poetry, non-fiction, and drama. Annual.

*City of Regina Writing Award*

Provides $4,000 to enable a Regina writer to work on a specific project.

### Short Grain Writing Contest

Business Manager, P.O. Box 1154, Regina, Sask. E4P 3B4

Phone: (306) 244-2828
Deadline: January 31

Offers $3,000 in prizes for original, unpublished works in three categories: prose poem (a lyric poem written in prose in 500 words or less), postcard story (a work of narrative fiction written in 500 words or less), and dramatic monologue (500 words or less). In each case, first prize is $500, second prize $300, third prize $200. Annual.

## The Smiley Prize

The Canadian Political Science Association, 1 Stewart Street,
    Suite 206, University of Ottawa, Ottawa, Ont. KIN 6H7
Phone: (613) 564-4025  Fax: (613) 230-2746
Deadline: December

An award of $750 is made to the author or authors of the best book published in English or French in a field relating to the study of government and politics in Canada. No textbooks, edited texts, or collections of essays will be considered. The award is conferred biennially; the deadline for the 1998 prize is December 1997 and applies to books published in 1996 and 1997.

## Smithbooks/Books in Canada First Novel Award

Adrian Stein, Publisher, *Books in Canada*, 130 Spadina Avenue,
    Suite 603, Toronto, Ont. M5V 2L4
Phone: (416) 703-9880
Deadline: December 31

A $5,000 prize is awarded for the best first novel published in English by a Canadian. Annual.

## Stephen Leacock Humorous Short Story Competition

Leacock Heritage Festival, P.O. Box 2305, Orillia, Ont. L3V 6S3
Phone: (705) 325-3261
Deadline: July 14

For original unpublished Canadian humorous stories in English of 1,000 words or less. First prize $500; second prize $200. No restrictions on theme, content, or number of entries. Annual.

## Stephen Leacock Memorial Medal for Humour

Jean Bradley Dickson, P.O. Box 854, Orillia, Ont. L3V 6K8
Phone: (705) 325-6546

Deadline: December 31

A sterling-silver medal together with the Laurentian Bank of Canada Cash Award of $5,000 is awarded for the year's best humorous book written by a Canadian in prose, verse, or as drama. Send 10 copies of book, $25 entry fee, plus author bio and photo. Annual.

### Stephen Leacock Poetry & Limerick Awards

The Orillia International Poetry Festival, P.O. Box 2307, Orillia, Ont. L3V 6S2

Deadline: November 30

Cash prizes of $5,000 (first place), $1,000 (second), and $500 (third) are awarded for the best unpublished English-language poetry of any description, not exceeding 50 lines. Prizes of $1,000 (first), $500 (second), and $200 (third) go to the best unpublished English-language limerick of any subject, theme, or content. Multiple entries welcome. Annual.

### Student Writing Awards

Adrian Stein, Publisher, *Books in Canada*, 130 Spadina Avenue, Suite 603, Toronto, Ont. M5V 2L4

Phone: (416) 703-9880

Deadline: July 15

Three prizes are awarded in each of two categories: poetry (up to 2 poems with a total maximum of 2,500 words) and short fiction (maximum 2,500 words). First prize is $1,000, second prize $500, third prize $250. Entrants must be full-time undergraduate students. Co-sponsored by Book City and *Books in Canada*. Annual.

### Theatre B.C.'s Annual Canadian National Playwriting Competition

Jim Harding, c/o 1005 Broad Street, Suite 307, Victoria, B.C. V8W 2A1

Phone: (604) 381-2443  Fax: (604) 381-4419

Deadline: June 17

For original, unproduced full-length and one-act stage plays submitted by resident Canadian professional and non-professional playwrights. Cash awards are $1,500 (full-length), $1,000 (one-act), and $750 (special merit), plus one week's professional dramaturgy at Theatre B.C.'s New Play Workshops in November. Submissions should be made under a pseudonym. Send for guidelines.

## Tilden/CBC Radio/Saturday Night Literary Awards

Robert Weaver, CBC Radio Performance, P.O. Box 500, Station A, Toronto, Ont. M5W 1E6

Phone: (416) 205-6001

Deadline: January 9

One prize of $10,000 is awarded in each category to the writers of the year's most outstanding short stories, poetry, and personal essays (which may be memoirs, autobiographical sketches, or travel sketches). Required length: 2,000 to 3,500 words. No faxes please. Annual.

## Trillium Book Award

Gartly Wagner, Ministry of Culture, Tourism and Recreation, Libraries and Community Information Branch, 77 Bloor Street W., 3rd Floor, Toronto, Ont. M7A 2R9

Phone: (416) 314-7629  Fax: (416) 314-7635

Deadline: November 15/December 17

To honour outstanding achievement in writing by Ontario authors, a $12,000 prize is presented to the author of the winning English-language and the winning French-language books. A further $2,500 goes to the publishers. The works may be in any genre – fiction, non-fiction, children's, poetry, drama. Annual.

## VanCity Book Prize

c/o B.C. BookWorld, 3516 West 13th Avenue (rear), Vancouver, B.C. V6R 2S3

Phone: (604) 736-4011

Deadline: May 15

A $4,000 prize is awarded for the best British Columbia book of fiction or non-fiction pertaining to women's issues. Author should be B.C. resident. Publishers are invited to submit eligible titles. Administered by *B.C. BookWorld*. Annual.

## Western Magazine Awards

Tina Baird, 3898 Hillcrest Avenue, North Vancouver, B.C. V7R 4B6

Phone: (604) 984-7525  Fax: (604) 985-6262
Deadline: last Friday of January

Awards of $500 are conferred in nine categories: business; science, technology, and medicine; arts, culture, and entertainment (inc. spectator sports); travel and leisure (inc. lifestyle and participatory sports); profile; regular column or department; fiction; human experience; public issues. Open to magazines whose main editorial offices are in the four western provinces, the Yukon, or Northwest Territories, and Canadian writers or full-time residents whose work appeared during the previous calendar year. Magazine publishers or editors and individual writers may submit.

### Winners' Circle Short Story Contest

Bill Belfontaine, Canadian Authors Association, Metropolitan
   Toronto Branch, 33 Springbank Ave., Scarborough,
   Ont. MIN IG2
Phone: (416) 698-8687  Fax: (416) 698-8687
Deadline: November 30

A cash prize of $500 and four others of $100 are awarded for the best new short stories (2,500 to 3,500 words) by Canadian authors. Ten more entrants receive honourable mentions. All 15 stories are published in the *Winners' Circle Anthology*. Opens July 1 each year. Multiple submissions encouraged. Send SASE for guidelines.

### Writers' Federation of New Brunswick Literary Competition

Anna Mae Snider, Writers' Federation of New Brunswick,
   103 Church Street, P.O. Box 37, Station A, Fredericton,
   N.B. E3B 4Y2
Phone: (506) 459-7228
Deadline: February 14

Annual cash prizes (1st – $200, 2nd – $100, 3rd – $30) are awarded in the following categories: poetry, fiction, non-fiction, children's literature (poetry and prose). Manuscripts can be on any subject and should not exceed 15 pages (4,000 words) for prose, 100 lines or 5 poems; minimum submission of 10 poems in children's category. All awards are open to New Brunswick residents only.

*The Richards Prize*

An award of $400 goes to the author of a collection of short stories, a short novel, or a substantial portion (up to 30,000 words) of a longer novel. Work must be unpublished although some individual stories may have been.

*The Alfred G. Bailey Prize*

A cash prize of $400 is awarded for an outstanding unpublished poetry manuscript of at least 48 pages. Some individual poems may have been previously published or accepted for publication.

## Writers' Federation of Nova Scotia Awards

Jane Buss, 1809 Barrington Street, Suite 901, Halifax,
  N.S. B3J 3K8
Phone: (902) 423-8116  Fax: (416) 422-0881

*Atlantic Writing Competition*
Deadline: August 27

Six categories for unpublished manuscripts – novel, non-fiction book, short story, poetry, writing for children, and play – receive small cash prizes of between $50 to $200 for first, second, and third placegetters. Atlantic residents only.

*Thomas Raddall Atlantic Fiction Award*
Deadline: April 15

A $3,000 prize is awarded for an outstanding novel or collection of short stories, in English or French, by a native or resident of Atlantic Canada. Co-sponsored by the Writers' Development Trust. Annual.

*Evelyn Richardson Memorial Literary Trust Award*
Deadline: April 15

A $1,000 prize is awarded for an outstanding work of non-fiction by a native or resident of Nova Scotia. Annual.

## Writers Guild of Alberta Annual Awards

c/o Writers Guild of Alberta, 11759 Groat Road, 3rd Floor,
  Edmonton, Alta. T5M 3K6

Phone: (403) 422-8174  Fax: (403) 422-2663
Deadline: December 31

A $500 prize is awarded for excellent achievement by an Alberta writer in each of the following categories: children's literature, drama, non-fiction, novel, poetry, short fiction, and best first book. Annual.

## The Writers' Union of Canada Short Prose Competition for Developing Writers

Competition, The Writers' Union of Canada, 24 Ryerson Avenue, Toronto, Ont. M5T 2P3
Deadline: November 3

An award to discover developing writers of fiction and non-fiction. A $2,500 first prize and $1,000 second prize are awarded for the best pieces of unpublished prose of between 2,000 and 2,500 words by a Canadian citizen or landed immigrant who has not previously been published in book format. The first-placed author agrees to permit publication of the winning entry in *Books in Canada*. Apply for full entry conditions. Annual.

# Grants

## Alberta Foundation for the Arts

Scot Morison, Alberta Community Development, Arts Branch, 3rd Floor, Beaver House, 10158 – 103rd Street, Edmonton, Alta. T5J 0X6
Phone: (403) 427-6315  Fax: (403) 422-9132

Four categories of writing grants are available to the professional, published writer: The Senior Writer Grant, to a maximum of $25,000, is available to veterans with at least four published books (or equivalent) behind them. The Intermediate Writer Grant, worth a maximum of $11,000, is designed for the professional who has published at least one book (or equivalent). The Junior Writer Grant, of up to $4,000, is open to unpublished writers. In addition, the Special Project Grant of up to $5,000 may be applied for. Competition deadlines are May 1 for the senior category, May 1 and October 1 for the others.

## British Columbia Ministry of Small Business, Tourism & Culture

Cultural Services Branch, 800 Johnson Street, 5th Floor, Victoria, B.C. v8v 1x4

Phone: (604) 356-1728  Fax: (604) 387-4099

Contact: Walter K. Quan, Co-ordinator, Arts Awards Programs

Assistance to a maximum of $5,000 for specific creative projects is available for professional writers of B.C. with at least two published books behind them. One juried competition is held annually.

## The Canada Council

350 Albert Street, P.O. Box 1047, Ottawa, Ont. KIP 5V8

Phone: 1-800-263-5588, (613) 566-4376 locally or a.h.

Fax: (613) 566-4410

The federal Canada Council has hitherto offered Canadian writers substantial financial support through its Grants to Artists Program. Also, the Explorations Program was one of the few sources of significant support to emerging writers. At the time of writing, all Canada Council support programs were under review, although it is promised that, following a period of restructuring, new programs will be introduced that will offer comparable support. Write for eligibility conditions and guidelines.

## Conseil des arts et des lettres du Québec

79, boulevard René-Lévesque Est, 3e étage, Québec, P.Q. GIR 5N5

Phone: (418) 643-1707 or 1-800-897-1707  Fax: (418) 643-4558

500, Place d'Armes, 15e étage, Montréal, P.Q. H2Y 2W2

Phone: (514) 864-3350 or 1-800-608-3350  Fax: (514) 864-4160

Created in 1993 as a corporation under the jurisdiction of the Minister of Culture and Communications. The Grant Program for Professional Artists offers several types of grants to creative writers who have published at least one book with a professional publisher or four texts in cultural periodicals, or have broadcast radio scripts. Applicants must be Canadian citizens or landed immigrants, and have lived in Quebec for at least 12 months. The program is open to French and English writers.

## Manitoba Arts Council

525 – 93 Lombard Avenue, Winnipeg, Man. R3B 3B1

Phone: (204) 945-0422  Fax: (204) 945-5925
Contact: Pat Sanders, Writing and Publishing Officer

Several potential sources of funding for writers: The Writers A Grant, worth up to $10,000, is designed to support concentrated work on a major writing project by professional Manitoba writers who have published two books and who show a high standard of work and exceptional promise. The Writers B Grant, for Manitoba writers with one published book, is worth up to $5,000. The Writers C Grant, worth up to $2,000, for emerging writers with a modest publication background, is available to support a variety of developmental writing projects. The Major Arts Grant supports personal creative projects of 6 to 10 months' duration by writers of exceptional accomplishment. Covering living and travel expenses, and project costs, this grant is worth up to $25,000. Finally, published Manitoba writers can apply for a Short-Term Project Grant, to a maximum of $1,000, to support significant career opportunities. Write for guidelines, eligibility criteria, and application procedures.

### New Brunswick Department of Municipalities, Culture & Housing

Arts Branch, P.O. Box 6000, Fredericton, N.B. E3B 5H1
Phone: (506) 453-2555  Fax: (506) 453-2416

Several potential sources of funding support exist for the professional writer in New Brunswick. Funds up to a maximum $6,000 in any two-year period may be applied for in the form of a Creation Grant to support the research, development, and execution of an approved original project. The Arts Awards Program offers study grants worth $1,000 to $2,500 to student and professional writers.

### Newfoundland & Labrador Arts Council

P.O. Box 98, Station C, St John's, Nfld. A1C 5H5
Phone: (709) 726-2212  Fax: (709) 726-0619

Newfoundland writers can apply to the NLAC for funding support under the Project Grant Program. Project grants are intended to help individuals carry out work in their field and may be used for living expenses and materials, study, and travel costs. Grants generally range from $500 to $2,000 or slightly higher. The amount of grant money available is based on the number of applications.

**Northwest Territories Arts Council**
Department of Education, Culture and Employment,
    Government of the N.W.T., P.O. Box 1320, Yellowknife,
    N.W.T. X1A 2L9
Phone: (403) 920-3103  Fax: (403) 873-0107
Contact: Tom Hudson, Arts Liaison Co-ordinator
    The mandate of the N.W.T. Arts Council is to nurture and
promote the visual, literary, and performing arts in the territories.
Contributions of up to $21,400 (10 per cent of the total funding
budget) may be applied for. Deadlines are January 31 and April 30.
For applications and guidelines, call or write to the Arts Liaison Co-
ordinator.

**Nova Scotia Department of Education & Culture**
Cultural Affairs Division, P.O. Box 578, Halifax, N.S. B3J 2S9
Phone: (902) 424-6389  Fax: (902) 424-0710
    The professional writer may apply for a project grant to a
maximum of $2,000 to assist with the cost of completing research
or manuscript preparation for a project in which a trade publisher
has expressed serious interest. Writers must have been resident in
Nova Scotia for at least 12 months prior to application.

**Ontario Arts Council**
The Literature Office, 151 Bloor Street W., Toronto, Ont. M5S 1T6
Phone: (416) 969-7437  Fax: (416) 961-7796
    The Ontario Arts Council offers three main grant programs for
Ontario-based writers. The Writers' Reserve program assists talented new, emerging, and established writers in the creation of new
work in fiction, poetry, writing for children, literary criticism, arts
commentary, history, biography, or politics/social issues. Writers'
Reserve grants are awarded through designated book and periodical publishers, who recommend authors for funding support up
to a maximum of $5,000. The Works-in-Progress program offers
support (up to a maximum of $20,000) in the completion of major
book-length works of literary merit in poetry or prose by published
writers. Finally, the Arts Writing program supports (up to $5,000
per project) the creation by published Ontario writers of new
works of criticism, commentary, and essays on literature, the arts,

and the media intended for periodical publication or inclusion in an anthology or catalogue, or documentary scripts for radio broadcast. Write to the Literature Office, Ontario Arts Council, for detailed guidelines and application forms for all these programs.

## Prince Edward Island Council of the Arts
P.O. Box 2234, Charlottetown, P.E.I. CIA 8B9
Phone: (902) 368-4410  Fax: (902) 368-4417
   Arts assistance grants to the value of $3,000 are available to support Island writers.

## Saskatchewan Arts Board
3475 Albert Street, T.C. Douglas Building, 3rd Floor, Regina,
   Sask. S4S 6x6
Phone: (306) 787-4056 or 1-800-667-7526 (Sask.)
   Fax: (306) 787-4199
   Under the Individual Assistance Program: A Grants, for professional, provincially or nationally recognized artists/writers, offer up to $20,000 for creative work, up to $10,000 for professional development, or $5,000 for research. B Grants, for professionals who have completed basic training or education in their discipline, offer up to $12,000 for creative work, $7,500 for professional development, or $3,500 for research. C Grants, for emerging professionals, offer up to $4,000 for creative work, $4,000 for professional development, or $1,500 for research. Deadlines: March 1 and October 1 each year.

   Travel grants of up to $1,000 cover travel and living expenses incurred by artists/writers who wish to enhance their career by participating in significant artistic events.

   The Literary Arts Program supports writers as well as book and periodical publishers and literary organizations. Literary Arts Project Grants aim to meet the needs of professional or emerging Saskatchewan writers. The Literary Playscript Commissioning Program supports the creation, performance, and appreciation of new literary works by Saskatchewan playwrights. The Literary Script Reading Program provides, at a subsidized rate, professional evaluation of manuscripts by other Saskatchewan writers, who receive a fee for their services.

**Yukon Department of Tourism**
Arts Branch, P.O. Box 2703, Whitehorse, Yukon YIA 2C6
Phone: (403) 667-8592  Fax: (403) 667-4656

Yukon writers may be eligible for an Advanced Artist Award of up to $5,000 for a specific project. Funding for the program is obtained from lotteries revenues and administered by the Arts Branch.

# 8

# PROFESSIONAL DEVELOPMENT

Writers at every level of experience can extend their skills and find fresh ideas through all manner of writing courses and workshops. Some believe creative writing is best fostered in the university or college environment, by working with a good teacher who understands literary devices and structures and the power of language. Many skills peculiar to non-fiction writing, generally considered more a craft than an art, can be learned through courses or workshops led by experienced writers who have discovered not only how to refine ideas, but how to research them, transform them into workable structures, and, finally, market them. Some creative writers swear by the hothouse atmosphere, creative exchange of ideas, and collective reinforcement to be derived from workshops led by expert facilitators.

Local branches of the Canadian Authors Association, libraries, and the adult education classes offered by boards of education are some sources of writing courses and workshops. Regional writers' associations sometimes organize them, too, and are always a good source of information about what's currently available in your area.

This chapter is divided into two parts: first, a review of some of the country's most interesting writing schools, workshops, and retreats; second, a sample of the kind of opportunities for the development of writing skills currently offered by Canadian colleges and universities.

This larger section includes most significant writing and journalism programs – in the mainstream and in extension departments – as well as a number of university-based workshops. The list is far from exhaustive. Many universities, colleges of applied arts, and community colleges offer writing courses at some level, depending on staff availability and demand. Not all courses are taught every year, and programs can change at short notice. Continuing education courses are open to all, but entry to credit courses is generally limited to those with specific academic prerequisites – though experienced writers can sometimes win special permission from the course convenor. Find out where you stand before developing your plans.

The summer courses, generally about a week long and built around daily small-group workshop sessions, offer participants the chance to increase their technical skills, to submit their work to group scrutiny and critical feedback, and to enjoy, and learn from, the company of fellow writers as well as editors, agents, and other publishing people. Courses are sometimes streamed in order to cater to different levels of experience. Workshop facilitators are often nationally or internationally acclaimed authors, and some course participants enrol simply for the chance to work with them, but the best facilitators aren't necessarily the top literary names.

The workshop experience can be intense and demanding, and the rewards illusive. To get most from them, bring at least one well-developed piece of writing with you, be prepared to work hard during and outside the main sessions, but also use the opportunity to rub shoulders with other seekers, to network, and to bask in that all-too-rare sense of a community of writers.

Finally, for those writers harried by family and job obligations, frustrated by the distractions of city living, and with a manuscript they simply must finish, writers' retreats and colonies offer peaceful seclusion, a beautiful rural setting, and a "room of one's own" in which to work without interruption, with meals and accommodation taken care of. Note that these are not teaching situations.

The writer's opportunities for professional development are extraordinarily diverse in Canada. Before you commit yourself, define your needs and carefully evaluate each program to see how it might meet these needs.

## Creative Writing Schools, Workshops, & Retreats

**The Banff Centre for the Arts**
P.O. Box 1020, Station 28, 107 Tunnel Mountain Drive, Banff,
    Alta. TOL 0C0
Phone: (403) 762-6180  Fax: (403) 762-6345
E-mail: arts_info@banffcentre.ab.ca
Contact: Office of the Registrar

Offers a wide range of non-credit journalism and creative writing courses. One of Canada's foremost writing schools, founded in 1933, Banff offers promising writers a five-week summer course on full scholarship (10 fiction writers and 10 poets are chosen each year, having submitted a full-length, unedited manuscript or work-in-progress). Participants in these writing studios work independently, with a resource available for consultation and editorial assistance. The school also offers programs in radio drama and dramatic writing for TV, a film and theatre workshop, and a playwright's colony. The arts journalism program provides established journalists with an opportunity to develop a major essay or article on a subject in the arts.

The Leighton Studios provide a year-round working retreat for professional artists. Established writers with a new project are encouraged to apply at least six months in advance of their preferred starting date. Applicants should seek government or agency funding to help support their stay; the Banff Centre provides discounts according to need. Studio fees are $43/day.

**Crowsnest Pass Writers' Workshop & Retreat**
c/o absinthe, P.O. Box 61113, Kensington P.O., Calgary,
    Alta. T2N 4S6
Phone: (403) 283-6802  Fax: (403) 283-6802

No workshops or retreats will be held in 1996. Contact for information on 1997.

**En'owkin International School of Writing**
En'owkin Centre, 257 Brunswick Street, Penticton, B.C. V2A 5P9
Phone: (604) 493-7181  Fax: (604) 493-5302
Contact: Office of the Registrar

Offers Native students a two-year credit program leading to a certificate in First Nations Creative Writing awarded jointly with the University of Victoria. Established First Nations writers, dramatists, and visual artists work directly with students to assist them to find their voice as writers through an appreciation of First Nations cultural and literary traditions. Graduates receive a two-year credit toward a Bachelor of Fine Arts degree at University of Victoria.

### The Humber School for Writers

Humber College, 205 Humber College Boulevard, Toronto,
  Ont. M9W 5L7
Phone: (416) 675-5094
Contact: Nancy Abell

One of Canada's best although youngest schools for writers offers a week-long, immersion, summer writing workshop in fiction and poetry in August. A residency option is offered. Workshop fee about $775, plus $230 for full board. Each year the school also offers a unique 30-week certificate program in creative writing, beginning in January. This extraordinary program offers promising writers the opportunity to send their work-in-progress (novel, short stories, or poetry) directly to their instructor, who provides editorial feedback by mail on a continuing basis throughout the academic year. Current instructors include the distinguished writers Bonnie Burnard, Catherine Bush, Timothy Findley, Joe Kertes, Paul Quarrington, D.M. Thomas, and Eric Wright. Admission is decided on the basis of a 15-page writing sample along with a detailed proposal of the work to be completed during the course. Enrolment, which must be made by mid-November, is limited. At the time of writing, the fee for Canadians and permanent residents is $954.

### Kootenay School of Writing

112 West Hastings Street, Suite 401, Vancouver, B.C. V6B 1G8
Phone: (604) 688-6001

Developed on the model of the artist-run centre, this is the only writer-run centre in Canada. Offers writing workshops, run by practising writers, in poetry, fiction, and theoretical concerns (e.g., modernism and gender, Foucauldian theory) in the fall and spring. Hosts regular readings and talks by visiting writers. All events are open to the public, most for a small charge.

## Maritime Writers' Workshop

Department of Extension and Summer Session, University of
  New Brunswick, P.O. Box 4400, Fredericton, N.B. E3B 5A3
Phone: (506) 454-9153
Contact: Glenda Turner, co-ordinator

An annual, week-long, limited-enrolment summer program
designed to help writers at all levels of experience. Offers instruction in fiction, non-fiction, poetry, and writing for children. As well
as workshops and individual tuition, the program includes
lecture/discussions, public readings by instructors (all successful
published writers), and other special events. All participants are
required to submit manuscript samples of their work by May.
Tuition fees are $300 (room and meal charges extra). Scholarships
up to the full cost of tuition and board are awarded on the basis of
need and talent.

## Sage Hill Writing Experience

P.O. Box 1731, Saskatoon, Sask. S7K 3S1
Phone: (306) 652-7395

Sage Hill's 10-day summer writing workshops are held every
August at the Sage Hill Conference Centre in rural Saskatchewan,
75 kilometres northeast of Saskatoon, or at St. Michael's Retreat
Centre in Lumsden, in the beautiful Qu'Appelle Valley, north of
Regina. Both centres have private rooms with writing areas, meeting
rooms, recreational facilities, and home-style cooking. The program
offers workshops at introductory, intermediate, and advanced levels
in fiction, poetry, and playwriting (though not all these courses are
available each year). The low instructor-to-writer ratio (usually 6 to
1) and high-quality faculty (all established writers) help make these
workshops among the most highly valued in Canada. Substantial
individual tuition time is also considered important. Fees per course
of $475 include accommodation and meals. Scholarships are avail-
able. Enrolment is limited. Applicants should send for guidelines.
Registration deadline is May 1.

Two annual Youth Writing Camps, for Saskatchewan writers aged
13 to 18, are held in August. For these free, five-day creative writing
day camps, held in Saskatoon and Regina, out-of-towners need
to arrange their own accommodation and travel. Application deadline is June 1. Also, a Fall Poetry Colloquium, held in October, an

intensive, three-week workshop/retreat, which is also open to writers from outside Saskatchewan. Tuition fee is $300; board fees to be announced (application deadline August 11).

## Saskatchewan Writers/Artists Colonies & Retreats

c/o P.O. Box 3986, Regina, Sask. S4P 3R9
Phone: (306) 757-6310  Fax: (306) 565-8554

The Saskatchewan Colonies were established in 1979 to provide an environment where writers and artists (especially but not exclusively from Saskatchewan) could work free from distractions in serene and beautiful locations. They are not teaching situations but retreats, offering uninterrupted work time and opportunities for a stimulating exchange of ideas with fellow writers and artists after hours. Costs are subsidized by the Saskatchewan Lotteries Trust. St. Peter's Abbey is a Benedictine Abbey near the town of Humboldt. Emma Lake is in forest country north of Prince Albert.

A six-week summer colony (July–August) and a two-week winter colony (February) are held at St. Peter's Abbey. Applicants may request as much time as they need, but accommodation, in private rooms, is limited to eight people per week. Emma Lake hosts a two-week summer colony in August. Participants are housed in cabins or single rooms. Individual retreats of up to a month are offered year round at St. Peter's, with no more than three individuals being accommodated at a time. Fees, including meals, are $100 per week. Applicants are required to submit a 10-page writing sample, a résumé, description of work to be done at the colony, and two references. It's best to book two to three months ahead in each case.

## Sechelt Writer-in-Residence Programs

Festival of the Written Arts, P.O. Box 2299, Sechelt, B.C. VON 3AO
Phone: (604) 885-9631  Fax: (604) 885-3967

Five-day writer-in-residence workshops are held three times a year – in spring, summer, and fall. Past workshops, all led by celebrated established writers, have focused on the writing of fiction in many genres, and of poetry, history, travel, cookbooks, as well as scriptwriting and writing for magazines. Participants range from beginners to published authors. Classes are limited to 10 to 12 students to allow adequate time for individual tuition. Fees, inclusive of tuition, accommodation, and meals, in 1994, the last year the workshops were offered, were $265 to $295 (building renovations meant none were offered in 1995). Write or phone for further information.

## University of Toronto Writers' Workshop

Chris Rosati, 158 St. George Street, Toronto, Ont. M5S 2V8
Phone: (416) 978-0765  Fax: (416) 978-6666

A week-long summer course (held in July) pivoting around daily intensive three-hour workshops, with up to 12 participants per instructor. The course also includes individual consultations, skill-building sessions, visiting writers, editors, and other experts, and readings. Admission is based on writing samples: a 20-page (maximum) work-in-progress is worked on during the week; each workshop requires a sample of 3 to 10 pages. Tuition fee is about $450, less residence accommodation. Limited financial assistance may be available.

## West Coast Women & Word

1675 West 8th Street, Unit 219, Vancouver, B.C. V6J 1V2
Phone: (604) 730-1034

Since 1982, the West Coast Women and Word Society has been supporting women writers and writing through workshops, Canada Council readings, and other literary events. Workshops draw experienced facilitators and established authors as well as new and emerging writers. All events are open to the public; in some cases, a small charge is made. Produces a monthly newsletter. Write for information.

# Creative Writing & Journalism at Colleges & Universities

## University of British Columbia

204 – 2075 Wesbrook Mall, Vancouver, B.C. V6T 1Z1
Phone: (604) 822-2712  Fax: (604) 822-3599
Contact: Department of Creative Writing

The Creative Writing Department offers programs of study leading to BFA and MFA degrees. A wide range of creative writing courses are available, including writing for screen and television, the novel and novella, short fiction, stage plays, radio plays and features, non-fiction, applied creative non-fiction, writing for children, translation, and poetry. A joint MFA with the theatre or film department is also possible. Students may choose to take a double major in creative writing and another subject. A diploma in applied creative non-fiction is open to graduates and those with professional experience.

The literary journal *PRISM international* (see Chapter 2) is edited by department graduate students.

## Cambrian College of Applied Arts & Technology

1400 Barrydowne Road, Sudbury, Ont. P3A 3V8
Phone: (705) 566-8101 or 1-800-461-7145  Fax: (705) 524-7334
Contact: Office of the Registrar

Offers diploma courses leading to a journalism major.
Continuing Education holds evening creative writing classes.
Publishes *The Shield*, a biweekly journalism lab paper.

## Camosun College

3100 Foul Bay Road, Victoria, B.C. V8P 5J2
Contact: Cathy Carson, articulation/education liaison officer

The English Department offers creative writing courses in prose fiction, drama, and poetry as well as professional writing. Courses in writing for the print and electronic media are offered as components of the two-year Applied Communications program. Students write and produce *Camas,* a college news magazine, and some radio and cable television programs.

Continuing Education offers various journalism courses.

Students are encouraged to submit material to *Camas* and two other campus journals, *The Camosun Review* and *The Bound With Glue Review*, and the student newspaper *Nexus*.

## Canadore College of Applied Arts & Technology

P.O. Box 5001, 100 College Drive, North Bay, Ont. P1B 8K9
Phone: (705) 474-7600, ext. 5123  Fax: (705) 474-2384
Contact: Mark Sherry, Director of Admissions & Liaison

The two-year print journalism diploma program includes courses in research and interviewing, newswriting, feature writing, keyboard skills, photojournalism, communications, and Canadian politics and economics. Journalism students produce a weekly newspaper, *The Quest*.

Continuing Education offers a course in creative writing and courses in business writing. Canadore's Summer School of the Arts holds week-long creative writing workshops.

## Carleton University

Student Liaison and Publication Services, 315 Administration
  Building, 1125 Colonel By Drive, Ottawa, Ont. KIS 5B6
Phone: (613) 788-3663 or 1-800-267-7366 (Ontario and Quebec)
  Fax: (613) 788-3517
Contact: Jean Mullan, Assistant Director of Admissions (Liaison)

The School of Journalism offers a four-year program leading to an honours Bachelor of Journalism for students who have completed a first degree. A one-year master's degree program is available for students with a BJ and journalists with substantial working experience. Students may be eligible for the two-year master's program. Some creative writing courses are also given through the Department of English Language and Literature, including restricted-entry seminars in poetry and fiction.

The Carleton Professional Development Centre offers an introductory course in creative writing and several courses in technical and business writing.

Publishes the student newspaper *The Charlatan*.

## Centennial College of Applied Arts & Technology

P.O. Box 631, Station A, Scarborough, Ont. MIK 5E9
Phone: (416) 462-8800  Fax: (416) 462-8801
Contact: Gary Schlee, department co-ordinator

The Communication Arts Department offers a three-year (or a two-year "fast track") diploma program in print journalism, broadcasting, and creative advertising. Also a two-year diploma program in corporate communication. Programs include courses in reporting, editing, scriptwriting, broadcast journalism, production for radio and television, documentary film writing, cinematography, magazine writing, public relations, newspaper feature writing, computer graphics, and more. Various courses are also offered in the extension program. All programs emphasize practical skills.

## Concordia University (Loyola Campus)
7141 Sherbrooke Street W., Montreal, Que. H4B 1R6
Phone: (514) 848-2624
Contact: Bruce Smart, Registrar

The English Department's Creative Writing program offers workshops in playwriting, poetry, and fiction, and gives courses in advanced composition and non-fiction, leading to bachelor's and master's degrees. The Department of Fine Arts offers courses in playwriting through its theatre program. The Journalism Department has degree programs offering courses in writing and reporting, feature and magazine writing, editing, and writing for radio and television news and public affairs. Undergraduate and graduate programs have quotas, so students are screened for admission.

## Conestoga College of Applied Arts & Technology
299 Doon Valley Drive, Kitchener, Ont. N2G 4M4
Phone: (519) 748-3516  Fax: (519) 895-1097
Contact: Betty Martin, Registrar

An 80-week journalism diploma program prepares graduates to work as reporter–photographers in newspapers or magazines, or as story editors and reporters for radio or television stations. Graduates are equipped with such editing skills as headline writing, design, and layout. Each student spends a minimum of two months working on a local newspaper or magazine. Courses in public relations and research and computer skills are also offered. Selected students from the University of Waterloo can study journalism at Conestoga for one year, and eventually earn a combined college diploma and university degree.

Courses available through the Centre for Continuing Education include How to Say What You Mean – in Writing, Writing for Children, Writing for Fun and Profit, and Creative Writing Workshop.

## Douglas College
P.O. Box 2503, New Westminster, B.C. V3L 5B2
Phone: (604) 527-5400  Fax: (604) 527-5095
Contact: Maurice Hodgson, convenor, creative writing

College credit and university transfer courses in creative writing and communication are available. Courses include Introductory

Fiction, Drama, Poetry; second-year courses in short fiction; a multi-genre course; screen writing; and personal narrative.

The Print Futures professional writing program is a two-year diploma program preparing students for a professional writing career. Includes courses in writing, research, editorial, and design skills, public relations writing, and writing for magazines and trade publications. For more information, contact the English and Communications Department (ph. [604] 527-5465).

Publishes the literary journal *Event* (see Chapter 2).

## Durham College of Applied Arts & Technology

2000 Simcoe Street N., P.O. Box 385, Oshawa, Ont. L1H 7L7
Phone: (905) 721-2000  Fax: (905) 721-3195
Contact: Applied Arts Division for CA program; Ann-Marie
Bambino, program officer, Continuous Learning Division

Offers a Communication Arts program leading to a two-year diploma in journalism or advertising, or a three-year public relations diploma. Graduates of other colleges and universities may qualify for direct entry into a special one-year program concentrating on practical subjects.

Continuous Learning offers non-credit courses Creative Writing and Getting Published.

Publishes *The Chronicle*, a college newspaper that provides students with experience in writing, editing, design, layout, art, photography, and production.

## George Brown College of Applied Arts & Technology

P.O. Box 1015, Station B, Toronto, Ont. M5T 2T9
Phone: (416) 867-2092  Fax: (416) 867-2302
Contact: Peggy Needham, Co-ordinator, English Department

Offers a wide range of creative writing courses and seminars, with the option of qualifying for a certificate in creative writing. Included are Writing for Magazines 1 and 2, Writing a Novel, Creating Short Stories 1 and 2, Poetry and Fiction Workshops, Writing TV Scripts That Sell, Writing for Children, Writing Science Fiction and Fantasy, Romance Writing 1 and 2, Writing Mysteries, and Journalism: Springboard to a Career, among others. Classes are held three times a year, one night a week. Courses in technical and business writing are also offered.

George Brown's biennial Storymakers writing conference (next one 1997), held over a weekend in August, offers a choice of workshops, guest speakers, and readings. Registration fee in 1995 was $180, including some meals.

## Georgian College of Applied Arts & Technology
1 Georgian Drive, Barrie, Ont. L4M 3X9
Phone: (705) 728-1951  Fax: (705) 722-5123
Contact: School of Continuing Education, instructors Tom
   Arnett, Paul Lima, and Heather Kirk
The School of Continuing Education offers a very broad range of useful part-time courses on demand, including Writing the Novel, Scriptwriting, Write Better, Creative Writing, Getting Your Writing Published, Writing for Business, Short Story Writing, Fiction Writing, Planning Your Novel, and Writing for Children.

## Holland College
140 Weymouth Street, Charlottetown, P.E.I. CIA 4Z1
Phone: (902) 566-9591  Fax: (902) 566-9505
Contact: Martin Dorrell, Journalism Instructor
The Creative Arts Department offers a two-year diploma program in journalism.
Publishes *The Surveyor*.

## Humber College of Applied Arts & Technology
205 Humber College Boulevard, Etobicoke, Ont. M9W 5L7
Phone: (416) 675-3111  Fax: (416) 675-2427
Contact: Inquiry Centre
Offers a three-year diploma course in print and broadcast journalism.
See separate listing early in this chapter for the Humber School for Writers.

## University of King's College, School of Journalism
6350 Coburg Road, Halifax, N.S. B3H 2A1
Phone: (902) 422-1271  Fax: (902) 425-8183
Contact: Patricia Robertson, registrar
Two journalism programs are offered: the first, a four-year program, leads to an honours BJ degree, for students entering directly

from high school; the second, an intensive one-year program, leads to a BJ, for students who already have a bachelor's degree. Students in the four-year honours program take courses in arts or science at Dalhousie University. All students take courses in broadcast and print journalism, research techniques, interviewing, history of journalism, media law, and journalism ethics, and select from a wide variety of optional courses. Both programs teach journalism from a practical point of view.

## Langara College
100 West 49th Avenue, Vancouver, B.C. v6s 1j8
Phone: (604) 323-5415  Fax: (604) 323-5555
Contact: Journalism Department Secretary
    The Journalism Department offers the following credit courses: Fundamentals of Reporting, Editing and Design, Photojournalism, Broadcasting, Advanced Reporting, Specialty Writing, Deadline Writing, Magazine Writing, Electronic Publishing, Media Law, Media and Society.
    The Continuing Education program includes: Fundamentals of Reporting, Editing and Publication Design, Broadcasting, and Electronic Publishing.
Phone: (604) 323-5236  Fax: (604) 323-5555
Contact: Roger Holdstock, English Department instructor
    The English Department offers three creative writing credit courses: Fiction, Poetry/Stageplay, and Poetry/Screenplay.

## Loyalist College of Applied Arts & Technology
P.O. Box 4200, Belleville, Ont. k8n 5b9
Phone: (613) 969-1913 (Post Secondary Admissions Office)
Contact: Phone the Post Secondary Admissions Office or write to the Registrar
    Two-year full-time journalism program includes courses in newspaper production, feature writing, and scriptwriting. There is also the option of a two-year agricultural journalism program.

## Mohawk College
P.O. Box 2034, Hamilton, Ont. l8n 3t2
Phone: (905) 575-1212  Fax: (905) 575-2378

Contact: Terry Mote, Manager, Student Liaison, Employment, and Awards

Creative Writing, Writing for Radio, Script Writing, Grammar and Composition for Media are courses within the Media Studies program.

Continuing Education offers Creative Writing as a 13-week credit course. The two-year full-time Broadcast Journalism diploma program includes a range of broadcasting and media courses. Continuing Education has two 13-week credit courses: Report Writing – Business; and Report Writing – Technical.

Publishes the college newspaper *The Satellite*.

## Mount Royal College

4825 Richard Road S.W., Calgary, Alta. T3E 6K6
Phone: (403) 240-0148
Contact: Admissions Advising Centre

Offers a Journalism Diploma program, a Professional Writing Certificate program, and a variety of non-credit creative writing courses.

The two-year Journalism Diploma focuses on newswriting, editing, photojournalism, and related subjects taught in a classroom/newsroom setting. Students produce a regular newspaper, and a one-month practicum with an off-campus newspaper is included in the fourth semester. (Contact Communications Department at [403] 240-6909.)

The two-semester full-time Professional Writing certificate begins every fall and is designed to develop skills in creative, nonfiction, and technical/business writing. (Contact English Department at [403] 240-6451.)

The Creative Writing program offered through the college's extension faculty offers a wide variety of courses for fiction and nonfiction writers, including Writing for Film and Television, Writing Historical Fiction, and Journal Writing for Men and Women. (Contact the Faculty of Continuing Education and Extension at [403] 240-6012.)

## University of New Brunswick

P.O. Box 4400, Fredericton, N.B. E3B 5A3

Phone: (506) 453-4666  Fax: (506) 453-4599
Contact: Office of the Registrar

Two creative writing courses with a BA credit are offered. Also an MA degree with a creative writing option (i.e., one-third of course work, plus thesis).

Continuing Education provides a non-credit fundamentals of writing course.

The university has a writer-in-residence and sponsors the Maritime Writers' Workshop. Also publishes *The Brunswickan*.

## University of Ottawa
550 Cumberland, P.O. Box 450, Station A, Ottawa, Ont.
KIN 6N5
Phone: (613) 562-5700  Fax: (613) 562-5104
Contact: George H. von Schoenberg, Registrar

The Department of English offers both introductory and advanced workshops in fiction and poetry writing. The department annually sponsors a prominent Canadian writer as writer-in-residence, and draws in many other distinguished writers to meet formally and informally with students and staff.

Journalism, technical, and business writing courses are available through the Service for Continuing Education.

Continuing Education offers creative writing courses, such as Poetry Workshop, Creative Writing (beginners), Popular Fiction Writing, Advanced Fiction Workshop, and Writing for Results, depending on staff availability and demand.

The Department of English sponsors the monthly journals *Bywords*, *Graffito*, and *Host Box*; the Canadian Short Story Series; and *Reappraisals of Canadian Literature*. It also publishes a series of critical volumes including the Friday Circle Broadside and the Chap Book Series. Other campus publications include *Fulcrum*, the student newspaper, and *Alumni News*, a quarterly journal. All accept freelance contributions.

## Parkland Regional College
72 Melrose Avenue, Yorkton, Sask. S3N 1Z2
Phone: (306) 783-6566  Fax: (306) 786-7866
Contact: University Co-ordinator

The University of Saskatchewan runs a two-year pre-journalism off-campus course and junior and senior degree credit English courses in Yorkton.

Non-credit courses are offered as requested by community groups in the region.

## University of Regina

Regina, Sask. S4S 0A2
Phone: (306) 585-4137  Fax: (306) 585-4815
Contact: Faculty of Arts, General Office

A four-year Bachelor of Arts in Journalism and Communication (BAJC) is offered, as well as a Bachelor of Journalism. Admission to these programs is limited. Many creative writing courses are available, and although a student cannot major in creative writing, three or four courses may be applied to an English major.

Continuing Education offers journalism and creative writing courses and sponsors writers' conferences (ph. [306] 779-4806).

The English Department usually offers credit courses in creative writing, and produces the literary journal *The Wascana Review* biannually.

## Ryerson Polytechnical Institute

350 Victoria Street, Toronto, Ont. M5B 2K3
Phone: (416) 979-5000
Contact: Faculty of Applied Arts (979-5319); Continuing Education (979-5035)

A highly respected school of journalism. The Faculty of Applied Arts offers a four-year degree program, which also includes courses in English literature and the humanities. Students may choose to specialize in newspaper, magazine, or broadcast streams after second year. Also a two-year program for postgraduate students. Students produce *The Ryersonian*, a weekly newspaper, and the biannual *Ryerson Review of Journalism*, as well as news and public affairs programs for radio and television.

Continuing Education offers part-time certificate programs in magazine journalism and publishing, and a wide range of creative writing courses and workshops. Also courses in screen writing, media writing and technical writing. Journalism courses include

Feature Writing for the Freelance Market, Freelancing: The Future, and Writing for Print Media.

*The Eyeopener* is another student-run publication on campus.

## Seneca College of Applied Arts & Technology

1750 Finch Avenue E., North York, Ont. M2J 2X5
Phone: (416) 491-5050  Fax: (416) 491-9187
Contact: Office of the Registrar

Options in television and radio scripting, playwriting, and journalism are available to day students in the Broadcasting/Radio & Television program at the School of Communication Arts. A one-year post-diploma program in Corporate Communications offers day students the opportunity to engage in an intensive learning experience designed to graduate mature, flexible communicators with good writing, technical, managerial, and human skills who can quickly become productive in a corporate communications position.

Continuing Education offers courses in various creative writing subjects. These change each semester according to demand and the availability of suitable instructors.

## Université de Sherbrooke

Sherbrooke, Que. J1K 2R1
Phone: (819) 821-7681  Fax: (819) 821-7966
Contact: Office of the Registrar

Offers a BA co-operative program in Professional Writing in English. Includes courses in journalism, translation, technical writing, and writing for advertising and public relations. Designed for anglophones, students must also have a working knowledge of French. Co-op students experience paid work terms and gain a full year's professional experience by the time they graduate.

## Sheridan College

1430 Trafalgar Road, Oakville, Ont. L6H 2L1
Phone: (905) 845-9430, ext. 2349  Fax: (905) 815-4051
Contact: Joyce Wayne, co-ordinator

The Journalism Department offers a two-year diploma in print journalism; also a one-year postgraduate program. Students produce a weekly newspaper, *The Sheridan Sun* (5,000 copies, 28 times a year) and two issues of *Light Waves*, the campus magazine.

Courses include newswriting, magazine writing, coaching/editing, desktop publishing, page design, electronic imaging, Internet, Pagemaker, Quark Express, and corporate communications.

Continuing Education also offers various writing courses.

## Simon Fraser University at Harbour Centre

515 West Hastings Street, Vancouver, B.C. V6B 5K3
Phone: (604) 291-5077  Fax: (604) 291-5098
Contact: Kristine Búffel, program assistant

The Writing and Publishing program of the School of Continuing Studies offers 20 to 25 non-credit creative writing courses each fall and winter/spring semester, encompassing a very broad range of professional development courses for writers, editors, and others working in publishing. Includes non-credit certificates in business and technical writing.

## University of Toronto

Toronto, Ont. M5S 1A1
Phone: (416) 978-3190  Fax: (416) 978-2836 (Dept. of English)
Phone: (416) 978-2400  Fax: (416) 978-6666 (School of Continuing Studies)
Contact: Alvan Bregman, Assistant Vice-Provost, Arts and Science

Each year the English Department offers credit courses in creative writing. The School of Continuing Studies offers non-credit courses in business and creative writing on campus and via distance education. A writer-in-residence gives a non-credit course in creative writing through the English Department.

The University of Toronto Press publishes *U of T Quarterly* and many academic journals. There are two campus newspapers, *The Varsity* and *the newspaper*; individual colleges also publish their own student newspapers. Student literary magazines include *Acta Victoriana* (Victoria College), *Salterra* (Trinity College), and *The Gargoyle* (University College). Hart House publishes a literary annual.

## University of Toronto School of Continuing Studies

158 St. George Street, Toronto, Ont. M5S 2V8
Phone: (416) 978-0765  Fax: (416) 978-6666
Contact: Chris Rosati, program co-ordinator

Liberal Studies offers a broad range of non-credit creative and practical writing courses and workshops. Fields covered include scriptwriting for film and television, the novel, short fiction, story-building, writing for business, and English usage.

See separate entry earlier in this chapter for Continuing Studies' annual Writers' Workshop.

## Trinity Western University

7600 Glover Road, Langley, B.C. V2Y IYI
Phone: (604) 888-7511  Fax: (604) 888-7548
Contact: Cam Lee, Director of Admissions

The English Department offers two courses in creative writing. The Communications Department offers an Introduction to Journalism course.

## University of Victoria

P.O. Box 1700, Victoria, B.C. V8W 2Y2
Phone: (604) 721-7306  Fax: (604) 721-8653
Contact: Department of Writing

Through the Department of Writing, students can major in creative writing, choosing courses (lectures and workshops) in fiction, non-fiction, poetry, drama, aspects of journalism, publishing, and multimedia. The Writing Co-operative Education program is open to students working toward a career in writing, publishing, or communications; work terms are designed to combine practical work experience with course study. The department also offers a new one-year post-program diploma in writing and editing.

## Wilfred Laurier University

English Department, Wilfred Laurier University, Waterloo,
    Ont. N2L 3C5
Phone: (519) 576-6068  Fax: (519) 884-8854
Contact: Chair of English

The English Department offers credit courses in creative writing and writing for the media.

## University of Windsor

Windsor, Ont. N9B 3P4
Phone: (519) 253-4232/2289  Fax: (519) 973-7050

Contact: Dr. W.H. Herendeen, Chair, Department of English

Writing courses are available at both the general and honours level. Students may take a BA honours or an MA degree in creative writing. The BA requires completion of eight creative writing courses. There is also a BA, general and honours, degree and an MA in communication studies, with courses available in news writing, scriptwriting, broadcasting, and press studies. An honours co-op MA in English is also offered.

Creative writing classes will be available during the summer of 1996 through the Summer Writing Institute.

Publishes *The University of Windsor Review, University of Windsor Magazine,* and *The Lance.*

## York University

4700 Keele Street, North York, Ont. M3J 1P3

Phone: (416) 736-5910  Fax: (416) 736-5460

Contact: Professor R. Teleky, co-ordinator, or Sue Parsram, administrative secretary

Offers students the chance to major in creative writing, with workshop courses in poetry, prose, fiction, screenwriting, playwriting, and other related subjects.

# 9

# WRITERS' ORGANIZATIONS & SUPPORT AGENCIES

**Alberta Department of Community Development**
Arts & Cultural Industries Branch, 3rd Floor, Beaver House,
    10158 – 103rd Street, Edmonton, Alta. T5J 0X6
Phone: (403) 427-6315

**Alberta Foundation for the Arts**
5th Floor, Beaver House, 10158 – 103rd Street, Edmonton,
    Alta. T5J 0X6
Phone: (403) 427-9968  Fax: (403) 422-1162

**Association of Canadian Publishers**
2 Gloucester Street, Suite 301, Toronto, Ont. M4Y 1L5
Phone: (416) 413-4929  Fax: (416) 413-4920
2 Daly Avenue, Ottawa, Ont. K1N 6E2
Phone: (613) 567-5276  Fax: (613) 567-1159

**Association of English-language Publishers of Quebec**
    **(AEAQ)**
1200 Atwater Avenue, Suite 3, Montreal, Que. H3Z 1X4
Phone: (514) 932-5633  Fax: (514) 932-5456

**Book & Periodical Council**
35 Spadina Road, Toronto, Ont. M5R 2S9
Phone: (416) 975-9366  Fax: (416) 975-1839

**British Columbia Ministry of Small Business, Tourism & Culture**
Cultural Services Branch, 800 Johnson Street, 5th Floor, Victoria, B.C. v8v 1x4
Phone: (604) 356-1718  Fax: (604) 387-4099

**The Canada Council**
350 Albert Street, P.O. Box 1047, Ottawa, Ont. k1p 5v8
Phone: 1-800-263-5588; (613) 566-4334 local or a.h.
  Fax: (613) 598-4390

**Canadian Authors Association**
275 Slater Street, Suite 500, Ottawa, Ont. k1p 5h9
Phone: (613) 233-2846  Fax: (613) 235-8237

**Canadian Book Marketing Centre**
2 Gloucester Street, Suite 301, Toronto, Ont. m4y 1l5
Phone: (416) 413-4930  Fax: (416) 413-4920

**Canadian Children's Book Centre**
35 Spadina Road, Toronto, Ont. m5r 2s9
Phone: (416) 975-0010  Fax: (416) 975-1839

**Canadian Copyright Licensing Agency (formerly Canadian Reprography Collective, cancopy)**
6 Adelaide Street E., Suite 900, Toronto, Ont. m5c 1h6
Phone: (416) 868-1620  Fax: (416) 868-1621

**Canadian Magazine Publishers Association**
130 Spadina Avenue, Suite 202, Toronto, Ont. m5v 2l4
Phone: (416) 504-0274

**Canadian Poetry Association**
P.O. Box 340, Station B, London, Ont. n6a 4w1
Phone: (519) 660-8976

**Canadian Society of Children's Authors, Illustrators & Performers (canscaip)**
542 Mount Pleasant Road, Suite 103, Toronto, Ont. m4s 2m7
Phone: (416) 322-9666

## Crime Writers of Canada
P.O. Box 113, 3007 Kingston Road, Scarborough, Ont. MIM IPI
Phone: (416) 266-0277

## Editors' Association of Canada (EAC)
35 Spadina Road, Toronto, Ont. M5R 2S9
Phone: (416) 975-1379  Fax: (416) 975-1839
P.O. Box 1688, Bentall Centre P.O., Vancouver, B.C. V6C 2P7
Phone: (604) 681-7184

## Federation of British Columbia Writers
P.O. Box 2206, Main Post Office, Vancouver, B.C. V6B 3W2
Phone: (604) 683-2057  Fax: (604) 683-8269

## Federation of English Writers of Quebec
c/o Scott Lawrence, 478 Red Cross, Lasalle, Que. H8R 2X9

## Island Writers Association (P.E.I.)
P.O. Box 1204, Charlottetown, P.E.I. CIA 7M8
Phone: (902) 566-9748

## League of Canadian Poets
54 Wolseley Street, 3rd Floor, Toronto, Ont. M5T 1A5
Phone: (416) 504-1657  Fax: (416) 703-0059

## Literary Press Group
2 Gloucester Street, Suite 301, Toronto, Ont. M4Y 1L5
Phone: (416) 413-4929  Fax: (416) 413-4920

## Literary Translators Association of Canada
1030, rue Cherrier, Suite 510, Montreal, Que. H2L 1H9
Phone: (514) 526-6653  Fax: (514) 526-0826

## Magazines Canada
50 Holly Street, Toronto, Ont. M4S 3B3
Phone: (416) 482-7307  Fax: (416) 482-9633

**Manitoba Arts Council**
525 – 93 Lombard Avenue, Winnipeg, Man. R3B 3B1
Phone: (204) 945-2237  Fax: (204) 945-5925

**Manitoba Writers' Guild**
100 Arthur Street, Suite 206, Winnipeg, Man. R3B 1H3
Phone: (204) 942-6134  Fax: (204) 942-5754

**New Brunswick Department of Municipalities, Culture & Housing**
Arts Branch, P.O. Box 6000, Fredericton, N.B. E3B 5H1
Phone: (506) 453-2555  Fax: (506) 453-2416

**Newfoundland & Labrador Department of Tourism & Culture**
Cultural Affairs Division, P.O. Box 1854, St. John's, Nfld. A1C 5P9
Phone: (709) 729-3650  Fax: (709) 729-5952

**Northwest Territories Arts Council**
Department of Education, Culture and Employment, Government of the N.W.T., P.O. Box 1320, Yellowknife, N.W.T. X1A 2L9
Phone: (403) 920-3103  Fax: (403) 873-0107

**Nova Scotia Department of Tourism, Culture & Recreation**
Cultural Affairs Division, P.O. Box 456, Halifax, N.S. B3J 2R5
Phone: (902) 424-6389  Fax: (902) 424-2668

**Ontario Arts Council**
151 Bloor Street, Suite 500, Toronto, Ont. M5S 1T6
Phone: (416) 961-1660  Fax: (416) 961-7796

**Prince Edward Island Council of the Arts**
P.O. Box 2234, Charlottetown, P.E.I. C1A 8B9
Phone: (902) 368-4410  Fax: (902) 368-4417

**PEN (Poets, Playwrights, Essayists, Editors, & Novelists)**
The Writers' Centre, 24 Ryerson Avenue, Toronto, Ont. M5T 2P3
Phone: (416) 860-1448  Fax: (416) 860-0826

**Periodical Writers Association of Canada**
The Writers' Centre, 24 Ryerson Avenue, Toronto, Ont. M5T 2P3
Phone: (416) 868-6913  Fax: (416) 860-0826

**Playwrights Union of Canada**
54 Wolseley Street, 2nd Floor, Toronto, Ont. M5T 1A5
Phone: (416) 947-0201  Fax: (416) 947-0519

**QSPELL (Quebec Society for the Promotion of English
   Language Literature)**
c/o Fraser Hickson Library, 4855 Kensington Avenue, Montreal,
   Que. H3X 3S6
Phone: (514) 845-5811/489-5301  Fax: (514) 845-6917

**Saskatchewan Arts Board**
3475 Albert Street, T.C. Douglas Building, 3rd Floor, Regina,
   Sask. S4S 6X6
Phone: (306) 787-4056 or 1-800-667-7526 (Sask.)
   Fax: (306) 787-4199

**Saskatchewan Writers' Guild**
P.O. Box 3986, Regina, Sask. S4P 3R9
Phone: (306) 757-6310  Fax: (306) 565-8554

**Speculative Writers Association of Canada**
10523 – 100th Avenue, Edmonton, Alta. T5J 0A8
Phone: (403) 424-7943  Fax: (403) 424-7943

**Writers' Alliance of Newfoundland & Labrador**
P.O. Box 2681, St. John's, Nfld. A1C 5M5
Phone: (709) 739-5215  Fax: (709) 739-0630

**Writers' Federation of Nova Scotia**
1809 Barrington Street, Suite 901, Halifax, N.S. B3J 3K8
Phone: (902) 423-8116  Fax: (902) 422-0881

**Writers Guild of Alberta**
10523 – 100th Avenue, Edmonton, Alta. T5J 0A8 (main office)
Phone: (403) 426-5892  Fax: (403) 424-7943

223 – 12th Avenue S.W., Suite 104, Calgary, Alta. T2R 0G9
   (regional office)
Phone: (403) 265-2226

## Writers Guild of Canada

35 McCaul Street, Suite 300, Toronto, Ont. M5T 1V7
Phone: (416) 979-7907  Fax: (416) 979-9273

## Writers' Union of Canada

The Writers' Centre, 24 Ryerson Avenue, Toronto, Ont. M5T 2P3
Phone: (416) 868-6914  Fax: (416) 860-0826
3102 Main Street, 3rd Floor, Vancouver, B.C. V5T 3G7
Phone: (604) 874-1611

## Yukon Department of Tourism

Arts Branch, P.O. Box 2703, Whitehorse, Yukon Y1A 2C6
Phone: (403) 667-8592  Fax: (403) 667-4656

# 10

# BOOK RESOURCES

For those seeking practical advice and inspiration from books about their craft, there is a cornucopia of writer's resource books on the market – style guides and practical handbooks, personal meditations, teach yourself marketing primers as well as more advanced "workshops" on the narrative and descriptive arts. With more published every year, only a short selection is offered here.

## Stylebooks, Handbooks, & Guides

*The Canadian Style: A Guide to Writing and Editing*, Department of the Secretary of State of Canada, Dundurn Press, Toronto, 1985.

*The Canadian Writer's Guide: Official Handbook of the Canadian Authors' Association* (11th ed.), Fitzhenry & Whiteside, Toronto, 1992.

*The Chicago Manual of Style* (14th ed. rev.), University of Chicago Press, Chicago, 1993.

*Editing Canadian English*, Freelance Editors' Association of Canada, Douglas & McIntyre, Vancouver, 1988.

*The Globe and Mail Style Book 1995*, Penguin, Toronto, 1994.

Appelbaum, Judith. *How to Get Happily Published*, HarperPerennial, New York, 1992.

Ballon, Rachel Friedman. *Blueprint for Writing: A Writer's Guide to Creativity, Craft and Career*, Lowell House, Los Angeles, 1995.

Barker-Sandbrook, Judith. *Thinking Through Your Writing Process*, McGraw-Hill Ryerson, Toronto, 1989.

Bernstein, Theodore M. *Watch Your Language*, Atheneum, New York, 1976.

——. *Miss Thistlebottom's Hobgoblins: The Careful Writer's Guide to the Taboos, Bugbears and Outmoded Rules of English Usage*, Simon & Schuster, New York, 1971.

Birkett, Julian. *Word Power: A Guide to Creative Writing*, A. & C. Black, London, 1993.

Blackburn, Bob. *Words Fail Us: Good English and Other Lost Causes*, McClelland & Stewart, Toronto, 1993.

Block, Lawrence. *Telling Lies for Fun and Profit: A Manual for Fiction Writers*, William Morrow, New York, 1994.

Blundell, William E. *The Art and Craft of Feature Writing*, Plume, New York, 1988.

Braine, John. *Writing a Novel*, Methuen, London, 1974.

Burgett, Gordon. *The Travel Writer's Guide* (2nd ed.), Prima, Rocklin, CA, 1992.

——. *How to Sell More Than 75 % of Your Freelance Writing*, Prima, Rocklin, CA, 1995.

Cheney, Theodore A. Rees. *Getting the Words Right: How to Rewrite, Edit & Revise*, Writer's Digest Books, Cincinnati, 1983.

Clayton, Joan. *Journalism for Beginners: How to Get into Print and Get Paid for It*, Piatkus, London, 1992.

Cumming, Carman, and McKercher, Catherine. *The Canadian Reporter: News Writing and Reporting*, Harcourt Brace Canada, Toronto, 1994.

Drobot, Eve, and Tennant, Hal. *Words for Sale* (3rd ed.), Periodical Writers Association of Canada, 1991.

Frank, Thaisa, and Wall, Dorothy. *Finding Your Writer's Voice: A Guide to Creative Fiction*, St. Martin's Press, New York, 1994.

Franklin, Jon. *Writing for Story*, Atheneum, New York, 1986.

Gage, Diane, and Coppess, Marcia. *Get Published: Editors from the Nation's Top Magazines Tell You What They Want*, Henry Holt, New York, 1994.

Gardner, John. *The Art of Fiction: Notes on Craft for Young Writers*, Vintage, New York, 1983.

Gibaldi, Joseph, and Achtert, Walter S. *The MLA Handbook for*

*Writers of Research Papers*, Modern Language Association of America, New York, 1988.

Giltrow, Janet. *Academic Writing* (2nd ed.), Broadview, Peterborough, 1994.

Goldberg, Natalie. *Writing Down the Bones: Freeing the Writer Within*, Shambhala, Boston and London, 1986.

———. *Wild Mind: Living the Writer's Life*, Bantam, New York, 1990.

Hemley, Robin. *Turning Life into Fiction*, Story Press, Cincinnati, OH, 1994.

Hodgins, Jack. *A Passion for Narrative: A Guide for Writing Fiction*, McClelland & Stewart, Toronto, 1993.

Kane, Thomas S., and Ogden, Karen C. *The Canadian Oxford Guide to Writing*, Oxford University Press, Toronto, 1993.

Konner, Linda. *How to Be Successfully Published in Magazines*, St. Martin's Press, New York, 1990.

Kozak, Ellen M. *From Pen to Print: The Secrets of Getting Published Successfully*, Henry Holt, 1990.

Legat, Michael. *An Author's Guide to Publishing*, Robert Hale, London, 1987.

———. *The Nuts and Bolts of Writing*, Robert Hale, London, 1989.

———. *Writing for Pleasure and Profit*, Robert Hale, London, 1987.

Mandell, Judy. *Book Editors Talk to Writers*, John Wiley and Sons, New York, 1995.

McCormick, Mona. *The Fiction Writer's Research Handbook*, Plume, New York, 1988.

McKeown, Thomas W., and Cram, Carol M. *Better Business Writing*, Clear Communications Press, Vancouver, 1990.

Mencher, Melvin. *News Reporting and Writing* (3rd ed.), W.C. Brown, Dubuque, Iowa, 1984.

Messenger, William E., and de Bruyn, Jan. *The Canadian Writer's Handbook* (2nd ed.), Prentice-Hall Canada, Toronto, 1986.

Miller, Casey, and Swift, Kate. *The Handbook of Nonsexist Writing* (2nd ed.). Harper & Row, New York, 1988.

Novakovich, Josip. *Fiction Writer's Workshop*, Story Press, Cincinnati, 1995.

Peterson, Franklynn, and Kesselman-Turkel, Judi. *The Magazine Writer's Handbook*, Prentice-Hall, Englewood Cliffs, NJ, 1982.

Potter, Clarkson N. *Writing for Publication*, Plume/Penguin, New York, 1991.

Rubens, Philip, ed. *Science and Technical Writing: A Manual of Style*, Henry Holt, New York, 1992.

Seidman, Michael. *From Printout to Published*, Carroll & Graf, New York, 1988.

Smith, Nancy. *The Fiction Writers' Handbook*, Piatkus, London, 1991.

Strunk, William, Jr., and White, E.B. *The Elements of Style* (3rd ed.), Macmillan, New York, 1979.

Taylor, Bob, ed. *The Canadian Press Stylebook* (rev.), The Canadian Press, Toronto, 1989.

Waller, Adrian. *Writing! An Informal, Anecdotal Guide to the Secrets of Crafting and Selling Non-Fiction*, McClelland & Stewart, Toronto, 1987.

Williams, Joseph M. *Style: Toward Clarity and Grace*, University of Chicago, Chicago, 1990.

Wilson, John M. *The Complete Guide to Magazine Article Writing*, Writer's Digest Books, Cincinnati, 1993.

Zinsser, William. *On Writing Well: An Informal Guide to Writing Nonfiction* (4th ed.), HarperCollins, New York, 1991.

## Dictionaries & Thesauruses

*The Collins Dictionary & Thesaurus*, Collins, London and Glasgow, 1990.

*The Concise Oxford Dictionary*, Clarendon Press, Oxford, 1995.

*Fowler's Modern English Usage* (2nd ed.), rev. Sir Ernest Gowers, Oxford University Press, Oxford, 1965.

*Funk & Wagnalls Modern Guide to Synonyms*, ed. S.I. Hayakawa, Funk & Wagnalls, New York, 1986.

*Gage Canadian Dictionary*, Gage Educational Publishers, Toronto, 1983.

*New Webster's Dictionary & Thesaurus of the English Language*, Lexicon, New York, 1991.

*The Oxford Thesaurus*, Clarendon Press, Oxford, 1991.

*The Oxford Writers' Dictionary*, R.E. Allen, Oxford University Press, Oxford, 1990.

*The Penguin Canadian Dictionary*, Penguin Canada/Copp Clark Pitman, Toronto, 1990.

*The Penguin Dictionary of Writers & Editors*, Bill Bryson, Penguin, London, 1991.

*Roget's II*, Houghton Mifflin, Boston, 1988.

*Webster's Ninth New Collegiate Dictionary*, Thomas Allen, Toronto, 1991.

## Yearbooks & Other Regularly Published Reference Sources

*The Book Trade in Canada*, compiled and edited by Eunice Thorne and Ed Matheson, Ampersand, Ottawa. (annual)

*CARD* (*Canadian Advertising Rates & Data*), Maclean-Hunter, Toronto. (monthly)

*Canadian Publishers Directory*, published biannually as a supplement to *Quill & Quire* magazine.

*Literary Agents of North America* (4th ed.), Arthur Ormont and Léonie Rosenstiel, eds., Author Aid/Research Associates International, New York. (annual)

*Literary Market Place: The Directory of American Publishing*, R.R. Bowker, New York. (annual)

*Matthews Media Directory*, published 3 times a year by Canadian Corporate News.

*Novel & Short Story Writer's Market*, Robin Gee, ed., Writer's Digest Books, Cincinnati. (annual)

*Poetry Markets for Canadians* (6th ed.), League of Canadian Poets and Mercury Press, Toronto, 1996.

*Sources: The Directory of Contacts for Editors, Reporters & Researchers*, published biannually as a supplement to *Content* magazine.

*Writers' & Artists' Yearbook*, A. & C. Black, London. (annual)

*Writer's Market*, Mark Kissling, ed., Writer's Digest Books, Cincinnati. (annual)

## Major Canadian Magazine Publishers

*Bowes Publishers Ltd.*, P.O. Box 7400, Station E, London, Ont. N5Y 4X3. Phone (519) 473-0010. Fax (519) 473-2256. (farm)

*Canada Wide Magazines Ltd.*, 4180 Lougheed Highway, Suite 401, Burnaby, B.C. V5C 6A7. Phone (604) 299-7311. Fax (604) 299-9188. (consumer and business magazines)

*Key Publishers Ltd.*, 59 Front Street E., 3rd Floor, Toronto, Ont. M5B 1B3. Phone (416) 364-3333. (consumer and business)

*Maclean Hunter Ltd.*, 777 Bay Street, Toronto, Ont. M5W 1A7. Phone (416) 596-5000.

1001 de Maisonneuve ouest, Suite 1000, Montreal, Que. H3A 3E1. Phone (514) 845-5141. (consumer and business)

*Naylor Communications Ltd.*, 124 West 8th Street, North Vancouver, B.C. V7M 3H2. Phone (604) 985-8711.

100 Sutherland Avenue, Winnipeg, Man. R2W 3C7. Phone (204) 947-0222.

920 Yonge Street, 6th Floor, Toronto, Ont. M4W 3C7. Phone (416) 961-1028. Fax (416) 924-4408.

210 – 10139 117th Street, Edmonton, Alta. T5K 2L3. Phone (403) 428-6164. (business)

*Southam Inc.*, 1450 Don Mills Road, Don Mills, Ont. M3B 2X7. Phone (416) 445-6641.

3300 Côte Vertu, St.-Laurent, Que. H4R 2B7. Phone (514) 339-1399. Fax (514) 339-1396. (business)

*Telemedia Publishing*, 25 Sheppard Avenue W., Suite 100, North York, Ont. M2N 6S7. Phone (416) 733-7600. Fax (416) 733-8272.

2001 University Street, Suite 900, Montreal, Que. H3A 2A6. Phone (514) 499-0561. (consumer)

# INDEX OF CONSUMER, LITERARY, & SCHOLARLY MAGAZINES

The 1996
# Canadian
## ENCYCLOPEDIA *Plus*

## Puts facts about Canada and the world at your fingertips

"A must-have for Canadians." – *Toronto Star*

"An incredible resource ... there are other encyclopedias, but this one is Canadian – it's much more relevant – *Calgary Herald*

"It's all the encyclopedia you need ... far more material than *Encarta*." – *Vancouver Sun*

### *The 1996 Canadian Encyclopedia Plus* contains:

The Canadian Encyclopedia
The Gage Canadian Dictionary
The Columbia Encyclopedia
Electronic Thesaurus

In a total of 50,000 articles, *The 1996 Canadian Encyclopedia Plus* provides accurate Canadian information from the original and unsurpassed *Canadian Encyclopedia*, and world facts from *The Columbia Encyclopedia,* which has been described as "exceptional" with a "scope ... as wide as the universe" by the *Times Literary Supplement.*

With over 17 million words, thousands of illustrations, animations, movies, audio clips, and a wealth of other features, *The 1996 Canadian Encyclopedia Plus* is the most complete reference work on Canada and the world – all on one inexpensive, easy-to-use multimedia CD-ROM.

**Macintosh and Windows versions on same disc**